BEYOND THE WALL

Migrants, Migration, and the Border

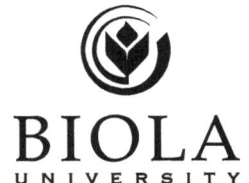

BIOLA
UNIVERSITY

© 2017 by Biola University
Department of Media, Journalism, and Public Relations

Published by Biola Avenue Press
Imprint of the Department of Media, Journalism, and Public Relations
13800 Biola University Drive, La Mirada, CA 90639

Printed in the United States of America

ISBN 978-0-9839572-5-6

Requests for information should be addressed to:
Dr. Tamara J. Welter
Chair
Department of Media, Journalism, and Public Relations
Biola University
13800 Biola University Drive, La Mirada, CA 90639

Project Advisor
Michael Longinow

Visual Advisor
Tamara Welter

**Book Design Director
and Cover Design**
Janelle Mejia

Cover photo
Alyssa Yee

Book Design Consultant
Rafael Polendo

Contributors
Dayna Bayne
Alex Bell
Aili Acone-Chavez
Dempsey Floria
Jessica Goddard
Molli Kaptein
Jenna Kubiak
Rebecca Mitchell
Jenny Oetzell
David Oh
Jubilee Pham
Sarah Pineda
Ana Waltschew
Anna Warner
Alyssa Yee

Table of Contents

Previous titles from
Biola Avenue Press

Mission of Hope (2009)

Skid Row: You Don't Come Down Here Without Change (2010)

Dominican Dream: A Passion for Baseball, A Love of Family, and a Hope for the Future (2011)

Growing Up in East L.A. (2014)

Haitian Eyes, Haitian Hands (2015)

Biola Avenue Press is an imprint of the Department of Media, Journalism and Public Relations at Biola University. The books it produces are part of an upper level course aimed at giving students practical experience with in-depth reporting, writing, photojournalism and graphics design aimed at guiding students in cross-cultural topics in the U.S. and in other countries.

Introduction

We started out in a little classroom in one of Biola University's oldest buildings with windows to the South. We put the desks in a circle and got to know each other: name, background, interest in migration and immigrants. It was a 3-unit class on Tuesdays.

When we began it was just a class—assignments, deadlines, attendance. It was an upper division course called Media Narrative Project, one of several capstone experiences available to journalism students. This book project was the latest in a series created by students over the last eight years, released under the Biola Avenue Press imprint (the one we created under our department to launch the first project).

But as we proceeded, week by week, the class became a team—mostly women, two men. There were reporter/writers, photojournalists, designers.

I had begun selling this project to the students over Christmas break. I assigned them topics based on what I knew about their interests. I began building the passion. A few responded with notes about how they were ready, excited, a little nervous.

We divided the work. Everyone was assigned at least one chapter. There were written chapters and photo chapters, but all chapters contained visuals; this was a book that would use the language of visual meaning and design as a gateway into stories not everyone sees or understands.

Our topic was not new. The border at Tijuana has been the stuff of movies, books, music and legend for generations. Immigration is not new. We are a nation of immigrants. And the struggle of people to be free is a motto emblazoned on a statue in New York Harbor: part of the ethos of what it means to be a person of these United States.

But interpretation of the journey, the struggle toward freedom is a changing reality. And this book was conceived as a place for hard questions about who suffers under the winds of political and economic fortune blowing across our southern separation.

Part of our work was individual, some of it two-by- two, some done as whole-team inquiry. As a team—in our classroom—we heard from experts in the worlds of the injured and broken-hearted: people who know immigrants and immigration, and who help with it.

Norberto Santana, an Orange County journalist and editor came with fire in his eyes, a tight laugh, and a quick, deft way of putting things. He told stories of investigative reporting about migrant policy, about exposing government corruption, about the majority culture's lethargy and stagnation. And he modeled relentlessness. His message to the students was bravery, skepticism and the asking of hard questions—lots of them.

Amber Amaya, a Biola journalism grad, came from the Coachella Valley on her birthday. In the valley, her work is with young women and men, teens who learn they can: "se puede." She uses media skills to craft critical thinking, leadership and community development in a part of California few understand. It is a region of Mexican migration. Amber gripped the podium and warned us not to discount people in their teens who know so much about the pain of immigration that they, ironically, struggle with their own vernacular of passion, their eyes ablaze with what they've seen and experienced.

David Benavides leaned on the front table in class and told our team of his family's journey across the border, of his upbringing in Los Angeles and of his alienation as a young Latino man on a mostly-white Biola University campus in the 1990s. Yet he spoke of his university experience as formative: shaping him into a healer, a compassionate manager, a gentle activist, a more insightful listener to the stories of those from his background. And his theology spoke as much through his stories as through his fingers, his motorcycle helmet and his gaze around that room, listening to the students' vision for journalistic inquiry.

And like the best journalists, we got out a lot. We went to East Coachella where Amber met us and guided us step by step: schools, downtown sidewalks, a front porch, a backyard. We went to San Diego's side of the border wall (guided patiently, through mud, by Shaun and Maria Sheehan of The Global Immersion Project). We heard about Border Angels and water in the desert from Craig Pinney in a tiny but picturesque office in a community center. And we toured parts of Tijuana, led by Samuel Perez, an authority on what the border wall means. He introduced us to deported U.S. military personnel, men left behind. He translated for us as mothers of DREAM students sat before us with eyes that had become dry from too many tears. Their anguish gripped our souls.

Individual students and groups of two or three took to the freeways: to Los Angeles, to Santa Ana, to San Diego, to the Coachella Valley.

We returned to campus not merely weary. We came back broken. The pain we'd seen, heard, smelled, touched was in our minds and hearts. And now we had to tell it, say it, convey it. We clicked through our chapters: again and again. How would we put this? How would we tell the stories? How to begin? How to end?

We decided, as a class that to write a book was not enough. A Web presence—blogs, photos, video, audio—speaking of our inquiry and reporting was also not enough.

We would need to make the story known. Some, too many, had marginal awareness—or disagreed that the pain surrounding migrants and migration even exists. Some would disagree with the very premise of our inquiry. These, of anyone, needed to hear the whole story.

So dialogue and promotion was part of our task. The conversation was one we had begun and would need to continue.

I am the product of immigration. My father came to Chicago from the Ukraine in the 1940s as a teen and his family suffered much in the transition to life in this country. My mother was born in Chicago but her parents are Mexican, arriving from north central Mexico in the 1920s. Gun violence was part of what she became too familiar with growing up on the South Side. So this book project, for me, had personal meaning. But to see these students delving into the depths of a complex topic was, once again, a reminder that the work of journalism education is not merely about facts, concepts or skills with technology. It is about life-to- life conveyance of meaning. And at Biola, it bears a layer of spiritual formation, of God-breathed, shared understanding, that I even now feel humbled to have been part of.

Michael A. Longinow, Ph.D
Professor of Media and Journalism

MICHAEL LONGINOW is an award-winning former news reporter for daily newspapers in northern Illinois (the greater Chicago area) and west central Georgia (outside Atlanta). He began teaching journalism in 1989 at Asbury University where he helped students launch a bilingual newspaper serving migrant Hispanic workers and their families living in central Kentucky. He came to Biola in 2005, helping build the journalism program and crafting a cross-cultural approach to journalism that now reaches into all four concentrations within that program. He chaired the department until 2014, when he stepped away from that role to turn his full attention to teaching, curriculum development and writing. He serves as faculty adviser to Biola's print and online student-run weekly newspaper, The Chimes.

Foreword

For those of us living in Southern California, immigration is truly a local story.

Yet it's much more than just walls and protests.

Here, immigrants teach us every day about the vibrancy of the human spirit.

They teach us about hard work, family, dedication and enterprise.

And while the face of immigration here often speaks languages other than English, they all understand on a deep level the most American of concepts.

Freedom and liberty...

They know what's it's like to lose freedom. They can taste the beauty of individual liberty. And they know with hard work in America, they can get ahead.

They are the ultimate optimists.

This is why they come here.

Yet over the past few decades, it seems America has become stuck on how to process these new arrivals and our immigration visa and enforcement system hasn't kept up, swelling the ranks of undocumented people.

This past election, our nation also seemed to turn away from viewing immigration as an intensely American act.

Indeed, with new talk of ICE raids, detention centers, sanctuary cities and building border walls, our current president seems to be doubling down on his campaign rhetoric to spike immigration enforcement.

While the rule of law is important in any democracy, so is the concept of justice.

I grew up in an immigrant neighborhood in Southeast Los Angeles and those experiences fueled my own path into journalism and public policy.

As a reporter for the Orange County Register, I spent nearly a year looking into our failed immigration enforcement system, both in Orange County and the Mexican border, and found a complex, expensive behemoth with little direction, compassion or effectiveness.

Today, as publisher for Voice of OC—a non profit newsroom covering public policy in Orange County—we continue to track immigrant communities and immigration debates in places like Santa Ana and Anaheim as well as the county government.

I continue to be stunned that so much of that discussion is fueled by misperceptions, often times spurred both by mainstream media and politicians anxious to find a good issue.

Both treat immigration like an entertainment story.

Yet it's much more.

Biola students have gone the other way, spending time to really look at this issue from a human perspective. They've dived deeply into a complete look at the issue and asked themselves some tough questions as writers.

We should all follow their suit and strive to truly understand the stranger in our land.

Often times, we find they aren't that strange.

In fact, many times when we look hard enough, we find our own reflection.

Norberto Santana

NORBERTO SANTANA is an award-winning investigative reporter with 20 years of experience at major daily newspapers. Before founding Voice of OC in 2009, Santana was a lead investigative reporter for the Orange County Register and spent a decade covering local governments across Southern California. His work has included exposes on Orange County public safety spending, deportation policies, and misuse of funds at the San Diego Red Cross. In addition to his experience as a journalist, the Southern California native has a master's in Latin American Studies and has worked as an elections analyst with the National Endowment for Democracy.

MIGRATION *in* NUMBERS

people

families

migrants

52% Hispanic   **48%** other ethnicities

K-12 Students

20% Hispanics without health insurance

31% poverty rate for Hispanics 17 and younger

27%

$22,000

14,991,000

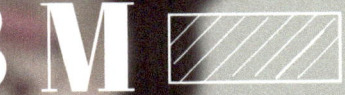

6.5% U.S. population   1980

17.3% U.S. population   2017

28 Median Age of Hispanics

$22,000 Median Annual Personal Earnings of Hispanics, Age 16+

55.3 M

Hispanics in California; over 1/5 of these are undocumented
84% are of Mexican origin

1769   1781   1821   1841-2   1846-8   1924   1943   1986

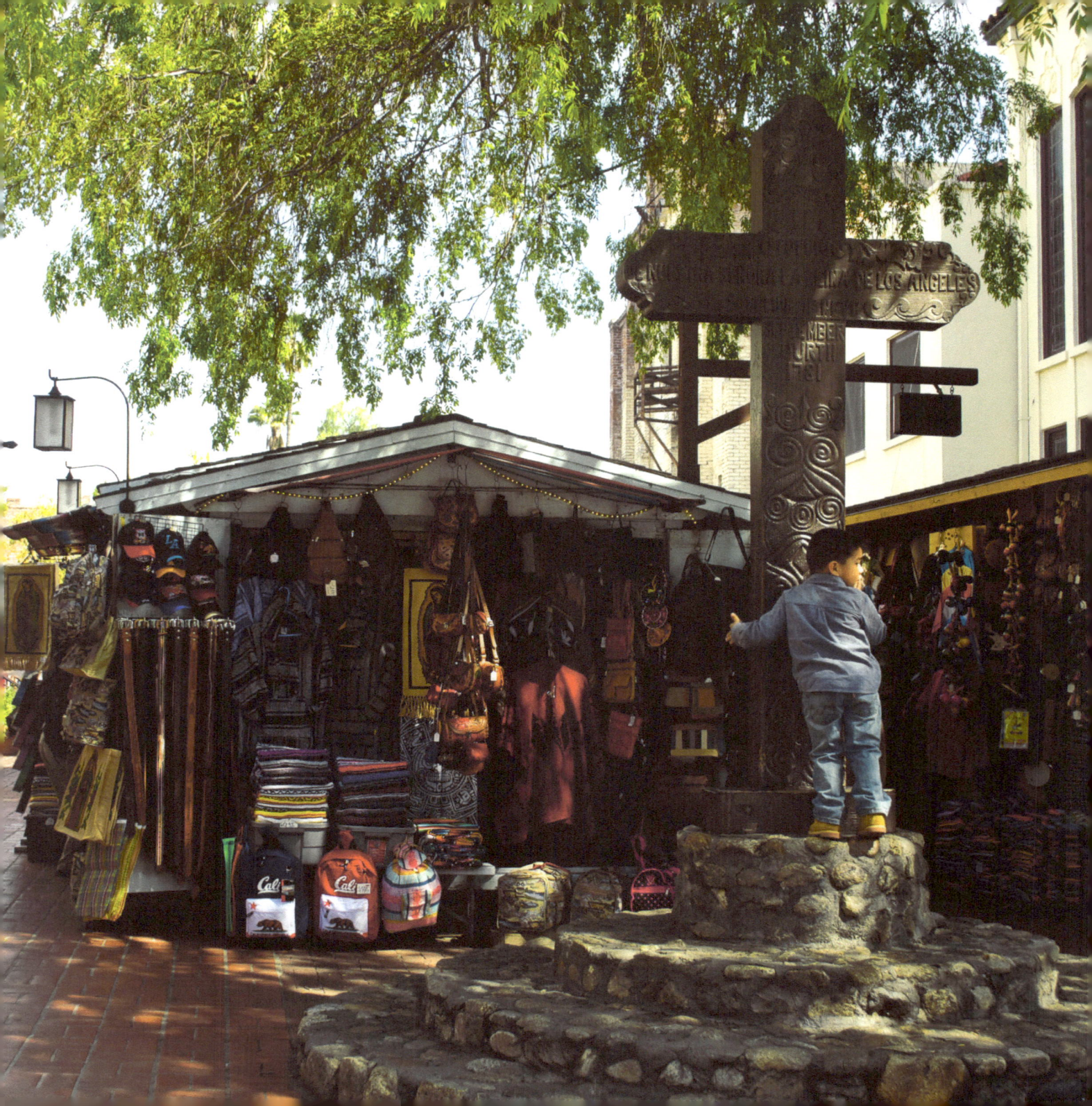

1 The History and Background of Migrants in Orange County and Los Angeles

By Jehn Kubiak

Photos by Aili Acone-Chavez

> " It's unfortunate really—how everyone can live on the same soil yet not even know the first thing about their neighbors. "

Ciore Taylor, *The Conversation Starts Here: A Perspective of Self, Culture, and the American Society*

One woman and her daughters started a long-lasting family legacy from a small closet with a few wooden tables and benches, a charcoal burning bracero, a supply shack, and water drawn from a gas station. A seven-year-old girl fled wartime woes, endured a dangerous boat ride, and learned a completely new language for freedom in America. These are only two of the countless stories about people who started new lives in Los Angeles and Orange County and shaped the community around them. A record 45.5 million tourists visited Los Angeles in 2015, according to tourism officials, but many remain unaware of the city's identity as a cultural mecca. A whole different world shares the same space that Los Angeles skyscrapers and business buildings occupy. Anyone can drive to the heart of Downtown Los Angeles and encounter several different ethnic groups all within a mile radius of each other as they sample little bites from other cultures, gaze upon exhibits in museums, and browse local vendors' shops. Several Hispanics call East Los Angeles and Santa Ana home today. In addition, the Asian population in both Orange County and Los Angeles has transformed into several cultural enclaves. According to the 2016 United States Census Bureau data, Hispanics and Latinos make up 47 percent of Los Angeles and 33 percent of Orange County residents, respectively. In addition, Asian-Americans make up 13 percent of Los Angeles and 17 percent of Orange County. People from these two ethnicities have greatly shaped both regions and contributed rich historical legacies.

El Pueblo de Los Angeles

Downtown Los Angeles received its first settlers after Felipe de Neve first founded El Pueblo De Los Ángeles in 1781 along with 44 families from New Spain. These Pobladores constructed adobe houses, the town's first streets, and the central plaza. The Spanish Empire originally controlled Los Angeles from 1781-1821 during this period, but the Pueblo eventually became part of the Republic of Mexico between 1821-1848. Growth in the agricultural, transportation, and light industries as well as problems that resulted from the Mexican Revolution drew a new crop of immigrants to Los Angeles in the 1900's. In the heart of El Pueblo, Christine Sterling revived the Plaza area and created Calle Olvera, also known as Olvera Street, as a center of tourism and romance amid dismal war conditions. She wanted to form a Mexican-style market and allowed merchants to do activities like leatherwork, glass blowing, food vending, or playing musical instruments.

Chinatown and Little Tokyo

The first large scale immigration of Asians to the United States occurred in 1848 during the California Gold Rush. The first Japanese-American settlers arrived in El Dorado County in 1869 and included a group of 22 samurai colonists from the Wakamatsu Tea and Silk Farm Colony. Other Japanese immigrants who arrived during this period fled racial tensions in San Francisco. A quick drive over the 101 Freeway leads to Little Tokyo, one of the largest Japanese communities today, which arose after sailor Charles Kame opened a Japanese restaurant on East First Street. Los Angeles County currently contains about 250,000 Japanese, more than any other region in the United States.

The start of an Olvera Street family legacy

About two million people still venture to Olvera Street's marketplace each year to buy goods from street vendors, eat authentic cuisine at Mexican restaurants, listen to live musicians, and walk through seven historic museums. Susanna Macmanus currently manages the El Cielito Lindo puesto and Las Anitas restaurant at Olvera Street's entrance. Her grandmother, Aurora Guerrero, started the puesto after Sterling first established Olvera Street. Macmanus' mother, Ana Natalia Guerrero, originally established the restaurant in 1947. A small plaque on the puesto's exterior tells the Guerrero family story. Aurora Guerrero gathered all her belongings, along with her three children, and left the small rural village of Huánuco, Zacatecas in 1927. She traveled to the U.S. searching for her husband, who came to the United States to work and send money back to the family through the Bracero program, which employed many Mexican men in the California agricultural industry. She settled in Chinatown, cleaned houses, and worked in a foundry. Her other daughter, Belen, found employment on Olvera Street. The entire family soon worked for various shopkeepers and eventually rented a small closet from the El Paseo Inn owners and moved to Cesar Chavez Avenue, where the stand sits today. Aurora Guerrero made food in a little kitchen, bundled it in cloth manteles, and carried trays as she rode the trolley. The community liked her food, which was simple and made without preservatives. After the Inn owners left for Mexico, the family asked Sterling if they could start a new business. She approved their request with one condition— the stand had to sell something different because vendors usually sold popular food items like enchiladas and tacos. Aurora Guerrero did not see any taquitos and created her famous taquitos with avocado sauce.

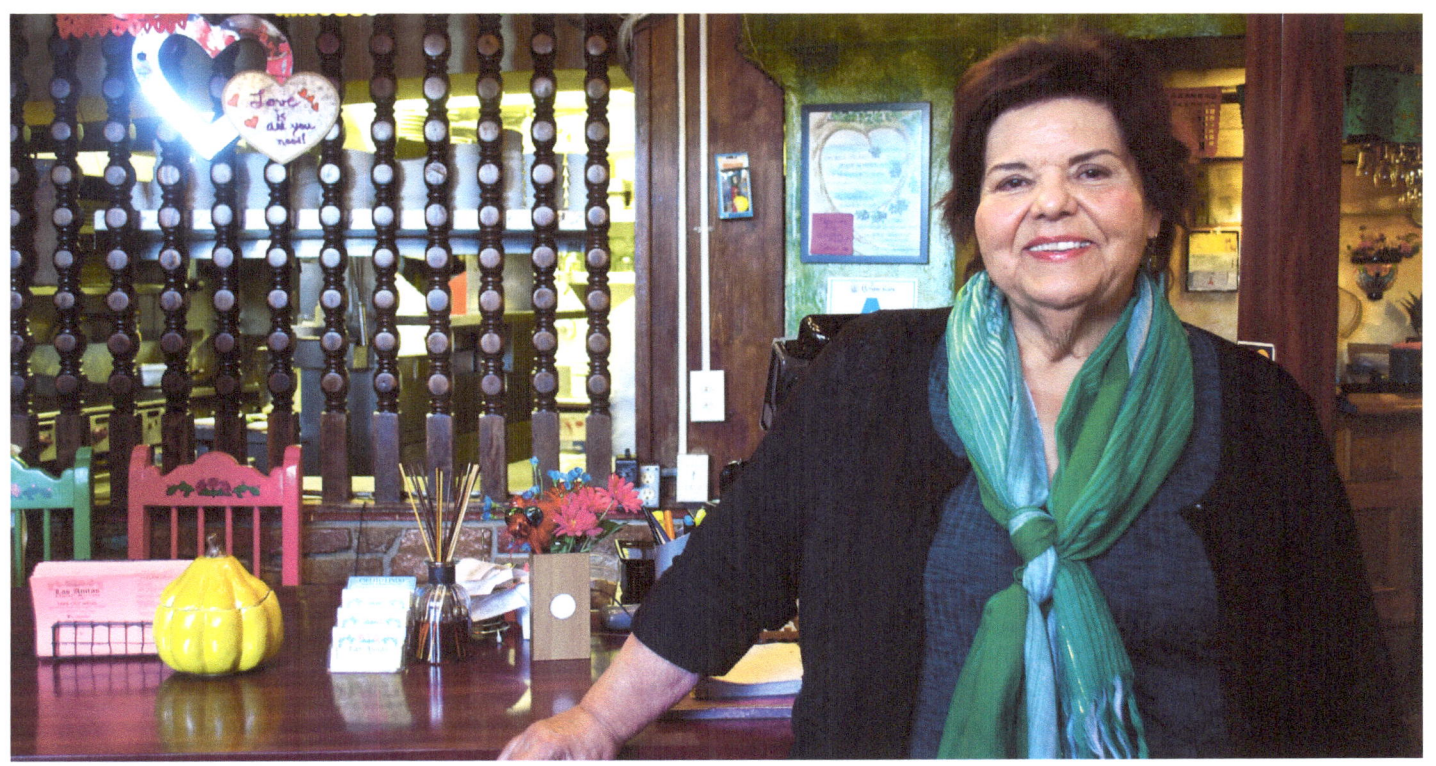

Susanna Macmanus, current manager of the El Cielito Lindo puesto and Las Anitas restaurant on Olvera Street, welcomes locals with family-values, warm stories, and massive plates of delcious food. Macmanus stands at the receiving counter near the entrance of Las Anitas restaurant.

The recipe became a hit, especially with local celebrities. Orson Wells catered the taquitos to his parties and visited the shop often. He came in one day and wrote "Orson Wells ate 43 taquitos in 1981" on a plyboard. Later on, the whole family started their own restaurants. Ana Natalia Guerrero originally created Las Anitas on North Broadway next to the Mason Theater, but she lost the original building after the State of California purchased it for the State Building in 1951. However, Sterling helped Ana Natalia Guerrero and allowed her to move into the Italian Hall's basement. Both businesses have continued strong since then and have become favorite Olvera Street destinations. Macmanus continues the Guerrero family legacy by cooking food with the same recipes and fresh ingredients her mother and grandmother used. The vivid colors, papel picado, rainbows of chairs with painted embellishments, painted walls, flowers and tile floor make customers that dine in the restaurant instantly feel as if they walked into a home kitchen. Macmanus believes many people came back for more of her mother and grandmother's cooking because they carefully crafted delicious food for her customers. "You could tell it was wholesome and you could tell there was love in it. That's always a seller," Macmanus said. Some tourists loved the food so much that they brought cold packs with them

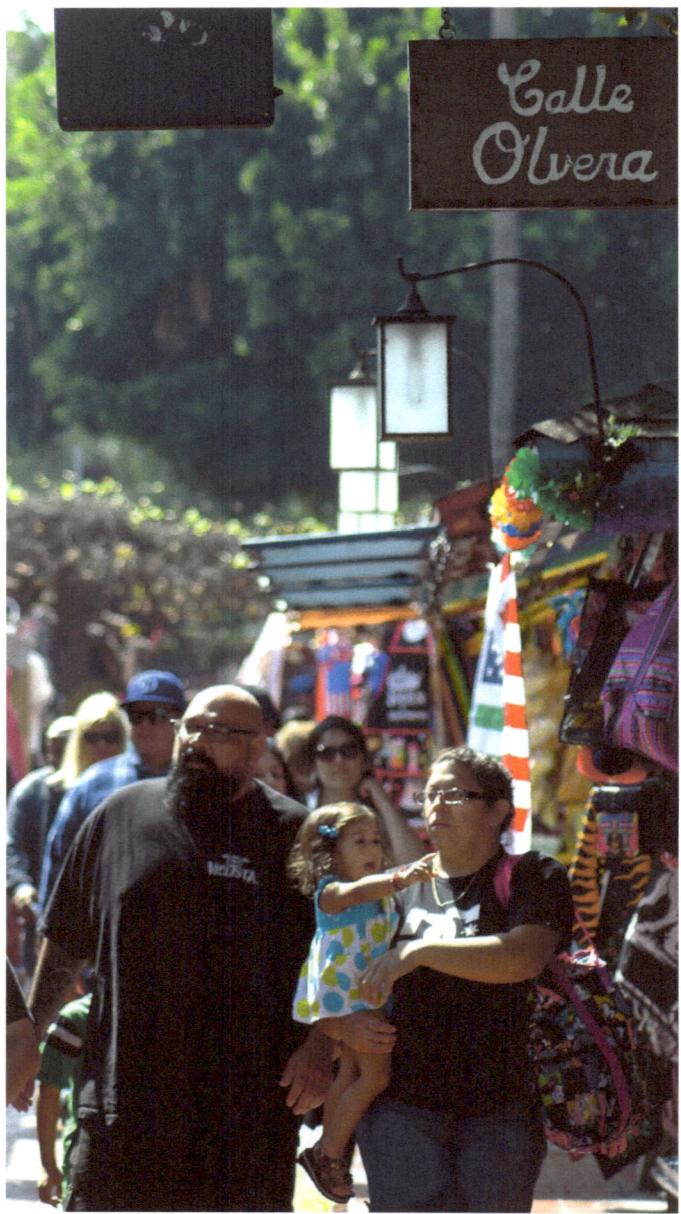

Calle Olvera, also known as Olvera Street, is packed with locals on a Friday morning. Seen in the background, a combination of the American and Mexican flag flows freely in the cool Spring breeze.

and took the food back to other countries, such as Norway. Macmanus said the City of Los Angeles diligently preserves Olvera Street's historical roots and family legacies. "The idea is to preserve something—the past," Macmanus said.

IMPACT OF ETHNIC TENSIONS, WWII
AND SUBURBANIZATION

Many American natives did not readily receive the foreigners who occupied their country, leading to various ethnic tensions that started in the late 1800's and continued throughout the next century.

CHINATOWN'S MASSACRE

Several Chinese ventured to Los Angeles for jobs, but Americans who also sought employment developed anti-Semitic feelings that culminated in the Chinese Massacre of 1871, one of the most violent events in Los Angeles history. Congress passed the Chinese Exclusion Act in 1882, which suspended Chinese immigration for 10 years and prohibited Chinese naturalization, according to the U.S. Customs Service. This exclusion measure decreased Chinese immigration into the United States, made it difficult for them to obtain citizenship, and forced many to relocate to other areas. The Chinese first experienced relief from the exclusion policies through the 1892 Geary Act, which allowed Chinese laborers to travel to China and reenter the United States. The construction of Union Station occurred in the middle of Old Chinatown in 1931 and forced the community to move. Sterling, who already sought to restore romanticism to a war-torn Los

Angeles, redeveloped another new area for the Chinese and called it "China City." She believed the city could preserve Chinese racial and cultural integrity if she helped consolidate the different communities into one district, but some Chinatown residents did not support her vision. Peter SooHong felt that Chinese-Americans should only control Chinatown, so he developed his own project called New Chinatown and founded the Los Angeles Chinatown Association in 1937, which financed the project's construction. A couple other leaders, Erle Webster and Adrian Wilson, designed a new Central Plaza that fostered community and became a tourist attraction. The current Old Chinatown Plaza lies south of the Dodger Stadium. Sterling and Soohoo both finished their projects in 1938 and Chinatown eventually became a tourist destination with merchants that sold curios and exotic souvenirs. Despite all these renovations, a fire destroyed the area in 1948.

COMMUNITY SUPPORT

The Great Depression during World War II economically devastated Americans across the nation, including the immigrants in Downtown Los Angeles, who could not easily find work or receive the assistance they needed. Macmanus recalls a story her family often repeated about the ways the community supported each other during the war. Aurora Guerrero lacked food and money necessary to support five children, so she sent one of her daughters next door to ask the neighbor

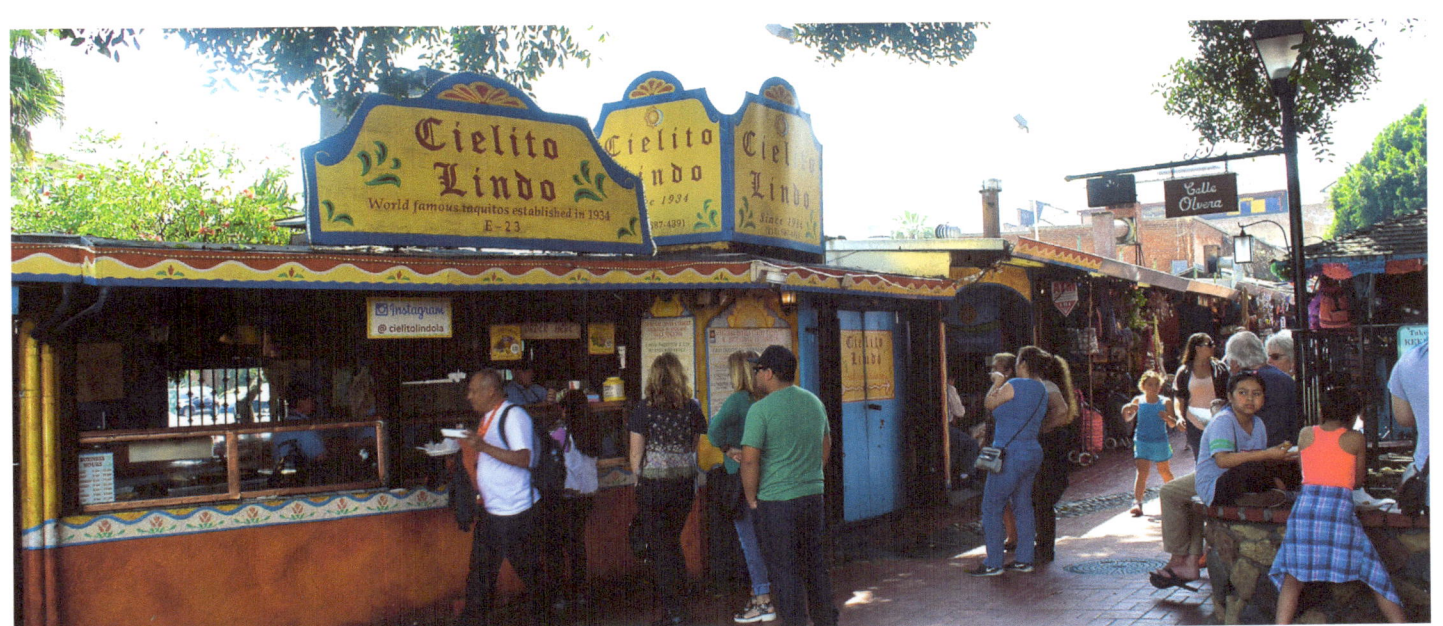

Locals gather at beloved El Cielito Lindo on Olvera Street to grab a bite for lunch.

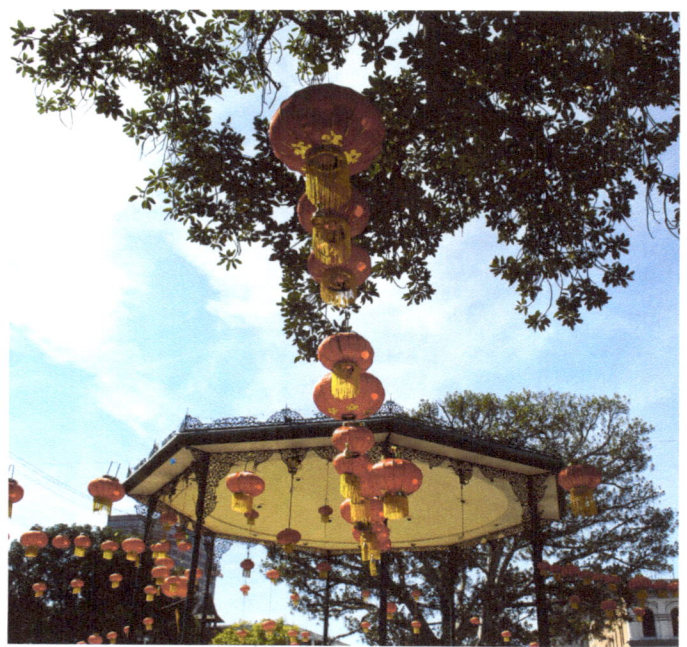

In preparation for the Lantern Festival in Chinatown, red and gold lanterns delicately adorn the skies around the gazebo at the main plaza, representing diversity.

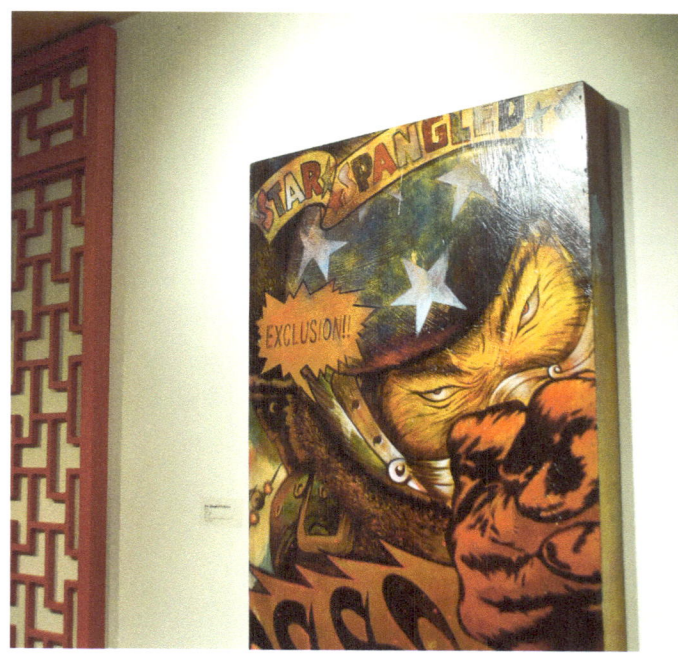

Located in the Chinese American Museum hangs a painting near the entrance of the musuem. "Star Spangled Exclusion" is painted in bold letters.

for a baked potato. Everyone in the community relied on each other for assistance. She explained how her family and a few other women supported each other and distributed boxes of cornmeal, potatoes, and sacks of flour around the neighborhood. She also learned about cultural differences during this time. For example, her grandmother originally did not make Americanized recipes like tamale pies or flour tortillas because these foods did not include indigenous products like corn. However, she and other women in the community adjusted their recipes for others in the community. The war also increased ethnic tensions because many white Americans believed immigrants stole their jobs. Although many Mexican-Americans were born in the United States, fought in the war, or served on the domestic front, others did not welcome them. Ethnic tensions between white Americans and Mexican-Americans sparked a few different conflicts, including the La Placita immigrant raid in Olvera Street. Uniformed and plainclothed Los Angeles police blocked exits, apprehended them in the Plaza, ordered them to show proof of residency, and deported several back to their home country by railroad. Approximately 60 percent of these deportees were legal U.S. citizens. During these riots, servicemen and civilians also attacked neighborhoods in the East Los Angeles barrios. In addition, President Franklin D. Roosevelt signed Executive Order 9066 after the attack on Pearl

Harbor and forced more than 120,000 Japanese-Americans from Los Angeles into internment camps, which caused them to lose much of their personal property. Unlike the other groups, hope for future generations of Chinese immigrants came near the end of the war after President Franklin Roosevelt signed the Magnuson Immigration Act in 1943, which repealed the Exclusion Act and lifted restrictions on naturalization. Despite the original decreased Chinese immigration, the Immigration and Nationality Act of 1965 increased the number of Chinese immigrants from 105 to 20,000 each year and caused overcrowding in Monterey Park in the 1980's.

THE LOST COMMUNITY OF CHAVEZ RAVINE

Suburbanization also contributed to ethnic enmity in Los Angeles when a post-war population created a need for more housing and city developments. Although the Pueblo finally received justice when the State of California recognized the area as an official State Park, other Mexican-Americans lost their land due to eminent domain for construction projects like the Hollywood Freeway and Dodgers Stadium. Chavez Ravine was a small community of Mexican-American families that settled in present-day Anaheim and lived in poor conditions. Los Angeles residents shuddered at this sight of wooden shacks, roaming animals and

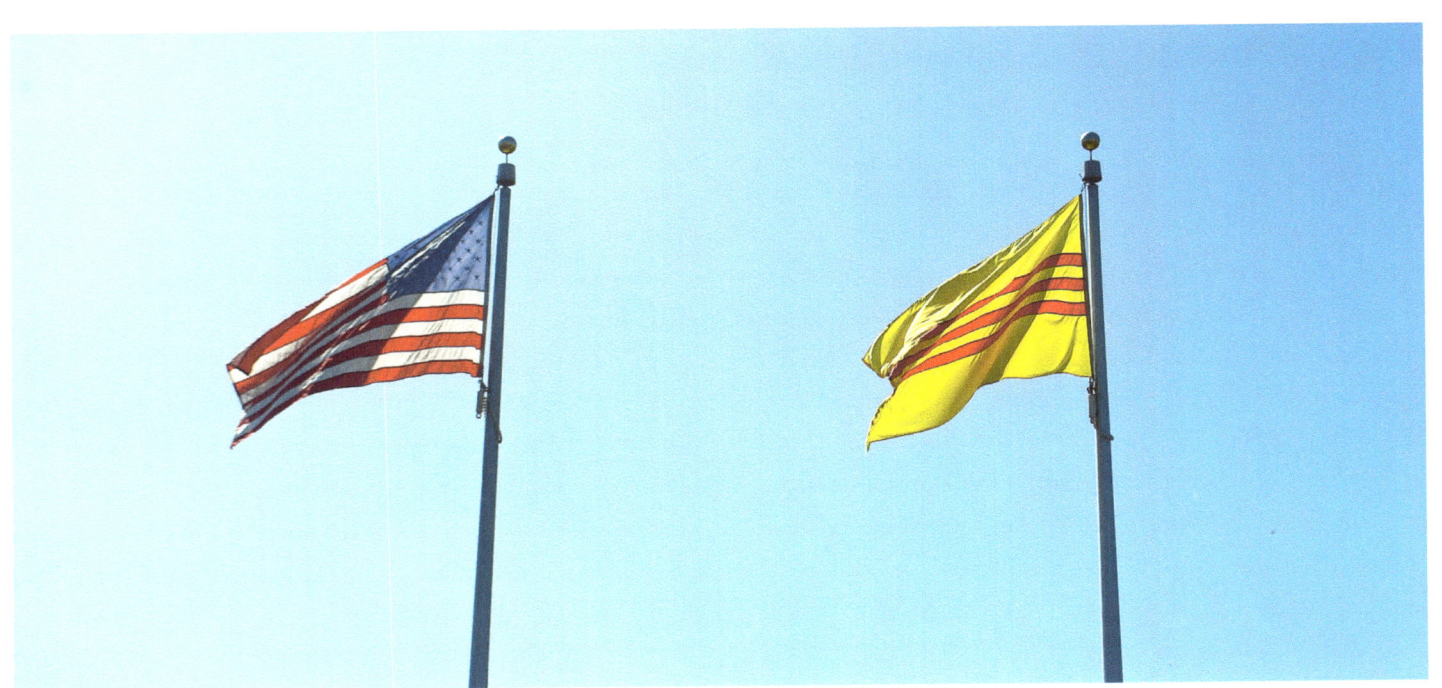

The American Flag and Flag of South Vietnam gently flow in the breeze in Little Saigon, California.

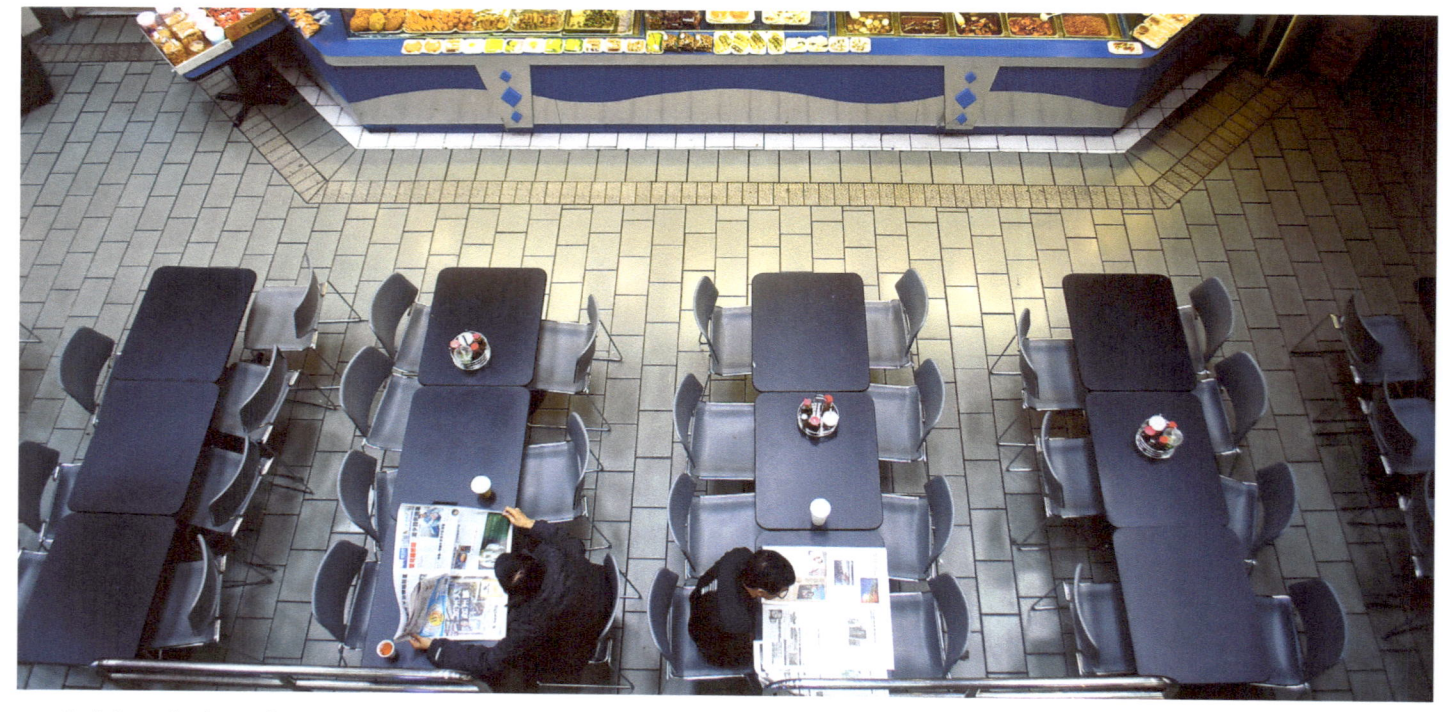

Little Saigon locals sit in front of a food court located in the Asian Garden Mall. Two men sit back-to-back as they read a Vietnamese newspaper while eating lunch.

trash that lined the unpaved streets. Many desired to improve this substandard community and the Public Housing Act eventually provided the funding necessary to construct a new neighborhood called Elysian Park Heights. Los Angeles Dodgers owner Walter O'Malley eventually acquired the property and constructed a new ballpark. After the stadium construction finished, law enforcement swiftly evicted remaining occupants from their home and bulldozed this community. The Dodgers organization currently allows the public to tour their stadium. While most tour the stadium to learn about their favorite ball team, others hope to walk where Chavez Ravine previously existed. Eric Brightwell has cartographed various ethnic enclaves across Los Angeles and said people walk across land where community homes once stood during the stadium tours. He described how it is ironic that the previous generation only sought to tear the establishment down, yet the current generation values its historical significance. "It's not only sad that the communities of Chavez Ravine were displaced, but that the promised public housing never came, largely because providing housing for the old, the poor, and the war veterans was characterized as socialism and therefore, 'unAmerican,' Brightwell said. "There's an irony that it's now a shrine to 'America's pastime.'"

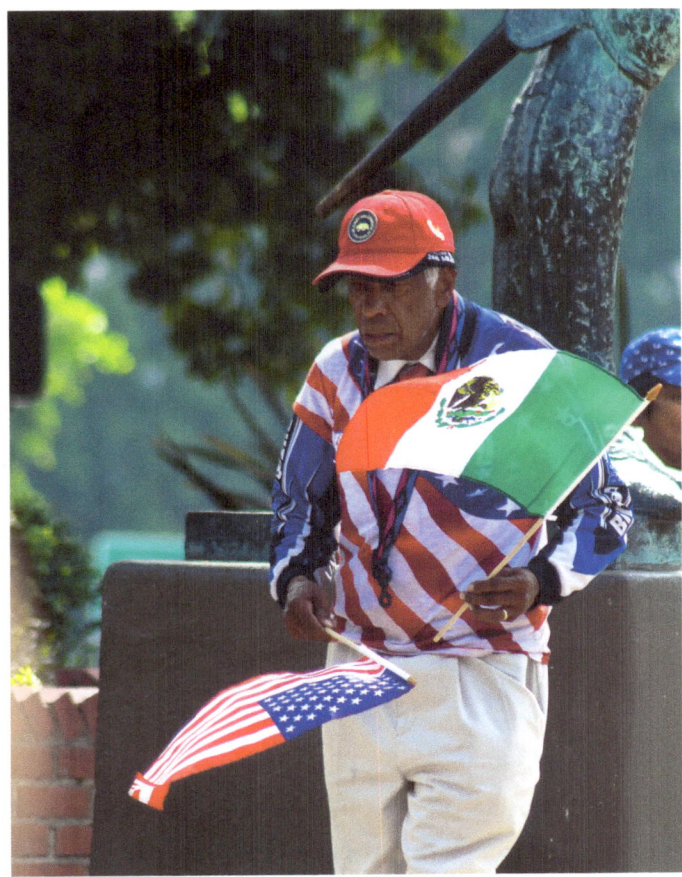

A man parades around El Pueblo waving both American and Mexican flags.

ORANGE COUNTY

The Shoshone Native Americans first settled Orange County, but Spain later colonized the area. Don Gaspar de Portola headed an overland expedition through Orange County in 1769. Father Junipero Serra established Missions San Gabriel and San Juan Capistrano during this time. A cattle rancher from the area named Juan Pablo Peralta received a formal concession to a land east of the Santa Ana River, Rancho Santiago de Santa Ana. This land eventually became the

city of Santa Ana, which features a 78.2 percent Hispanic population today and still functions as a place of refuge for immigrants from Mexico with a 46.7 percent foreign born population. A group of German immigrants in San Francisco later bought a portion of the Rancho land to build a winemaking community and plant vineyards. As evidenced by numerous multi-ethnic shopping centers like Daiso, H-Mart, Diamond DJ Jamboree, and Mitsuwa that have spread across the county, Asian-Americans have also heavily influenced the development of Orange County. Immigrants from various nationalities — Iranians, Armenians, Koreans, Mexicans, Puerto Ricans, Cubans, Dominicans, Filipinos, Cambodians, Laotians, Hmong, Bangladeshi, Asian Indians, Indonesians, Sri Lankans, Thai, Japanese, Chinese, and Vietnamese and several from mixed heritages—constitute about a third of Orange County's overall population today.

THE VIETNAM WAR AND FALL OF SAIGON

The fall of Saigon also spurred a heavy migration of Vietnamese to Orange County, so this group mainly settled in Anaheim, Garden Grove, Santa Ana and Westminster. Tu-Uyen Nguyen, professor of Asian American studies at California State University in Fullerton, was born in Vietnam in 1979. The communist government took over the whole country in 1975 during the Vietnam War and sent anyone not affiliated with the communist government to re-education camps, including her father. The communist government shut down freedom of the press and did not let citizens voice their opinions—freedoms the country still lacks today. Lack of these freedoms and educational opportunities in Vietnam caused her parents and many other Vietnamese refugees to

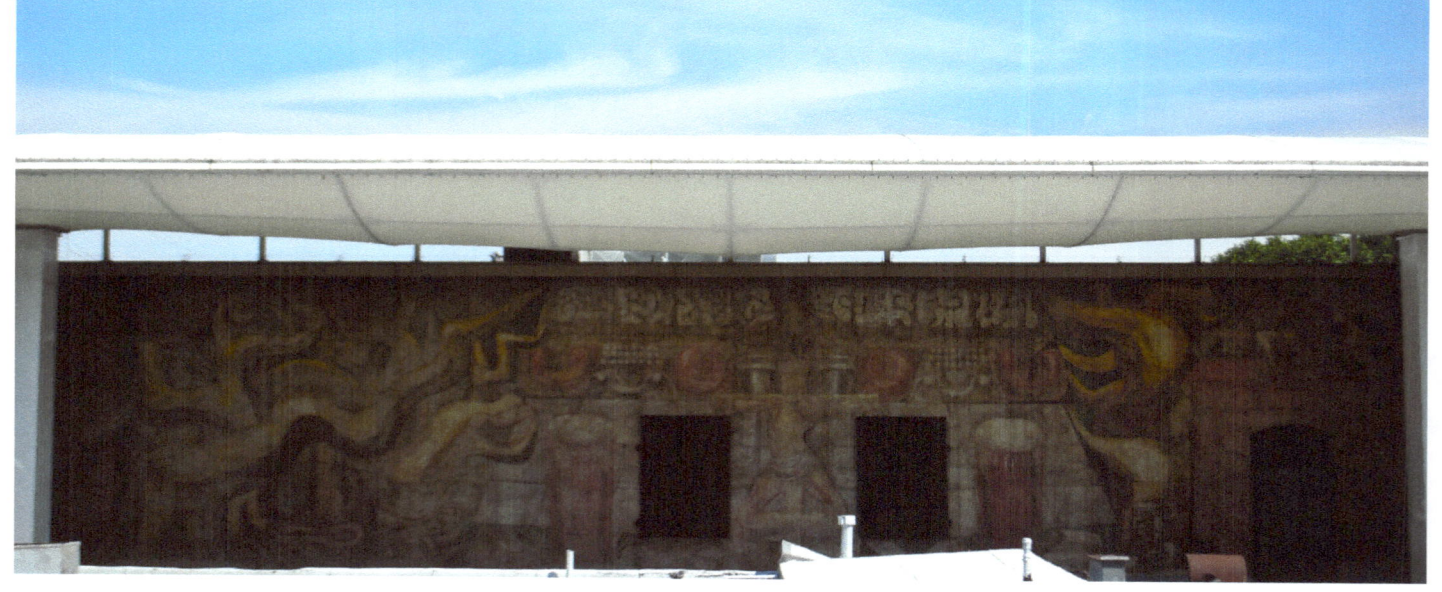

The Siquieros "America Tropical" mural was painted on the wall of the Italian Hall in the 1930's by David Alfaro Siquieros. Depicting a politically radical message, this mural is clearly seen from the second-story balcony at the America Tropical Interpretive Center located in Downtown Los Angeles on Olvera Street.

find a new home in the United States because they wanted to provide a better future for their children. Refugees who escaped from the Vietnam War came in three waves. Nguyen's family falls into the second, which escaped by boat or on foot through jungles in Thailand or Laos. During this journey, people fought for survival and frequently died from starvation or drowning because the fishing boats were rickety and fragile. Pirates also frequently plundered the ships for valuables or raped refugees. The majority of these refugees fled secretly and risked everything they had for a brighter future. Those caught were jailed or killed. People who escaped by boat or land had to first travel through another third-world country, such as Singapore, the Philippines, Malaysia, and Thailand, before they entered a larger country like the U.S. The government screened for refugees versus immigrants during this time, so the Vietnamese had to prove they left Vietnam in fear of persecution from Communist officials. Countries took in refugees, who then went through a screening process and had to get a sponsor that helped them adjust to society once they came to the U.S. Many Vietnamese people could not get through this process and countries repatriated them to their homeland, further halting Vietnamese migration to the U.S. The government set up refugee camps across the United States in Camp Pendleton, Pennsylvania, Arkansas, and Florida. Vietnamese refugees were then set up with families, churches, and charities that wanted to take them in. Nguyen believes the Vietnamese War refugee crisis mirrors today's refugee crisis, such as how

Syrians fled the war like the Vietnamese and how Americans do not readily welcome these refugees because they see them as byproducts of negative wars.

A REFUGEE'S JOURNEY TO AMERICA

Nguyen was seven years old when her family left their homeland and recalls hiding under the bed when bombs struck, yet she did not understand the situation's gravity at first due to her young age. Her mother woke her up in the middle of the night and told her to get dressed because they were going to the beach. They drove up to the beach, where Nguyen saw around 300 people loading onto a boat about 30m long with two levels. She craved her parent's presence as she sat cross-legged on the cramped, dark lower level that

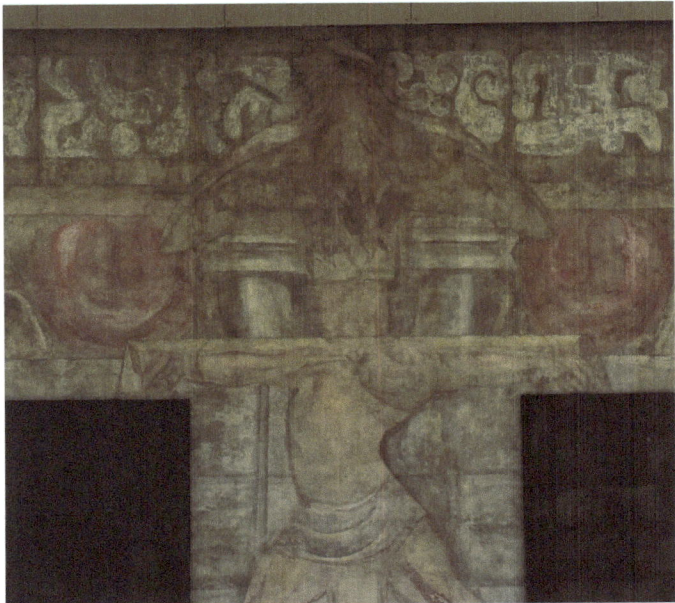

Detail shot of an eagle being poached and an ethnic man being crucified on the Siqueros-America Tropica Mural.

reeked of urine and vomit. Nguyen's younger brother cried and her mom told him not to make any noise so they didn't reveal their location. Her father, who was a dentist, often went on the top deck and checked people on the boat. The family drank water from a bottle cap and ate a tiny bowl of rice soup with jicama each day. After six long days and nights, they landed Indonesia and stayed there for about four months. Her aunt and uncle resettled in Virginia after they came to the United States in the first wave and another family in the Pennsylvania camp previously sponsored them. Nguyen's relatives became established in America through this sponsorship, so they could sponsor her family after they arrived in the U.S. Nguyen stated that California has the largest Vietnamese population due to a second migration where migrants came for great weather, job opportunities, and so they could live with their relatives. The family lived in Virginia for a year and moved to California for these increased job opportunities. Her father could not practice dentistry when he first came due to educational differences, so he worked as a landscaper and saved money to become a recertified dentist. At the same time, Nguyen's mother cleaned houses as a maid and was originally a pharmacist, so she went back to school once her husband finished his recertification. Both parents eventually regained their careers. Nguyen couldn't speak English when she first arrived, so the school placed her in an English as a Second Language class and stuck her in first grade instead of second. As a result, her first grade teacher pulled her aside after school and helped her catch up to her peers. The family later moved to Tustin, then Monterey Park, and finally settled in Irvine when she started high school. Nguyen stayed in California and obtained the education her parents desired.

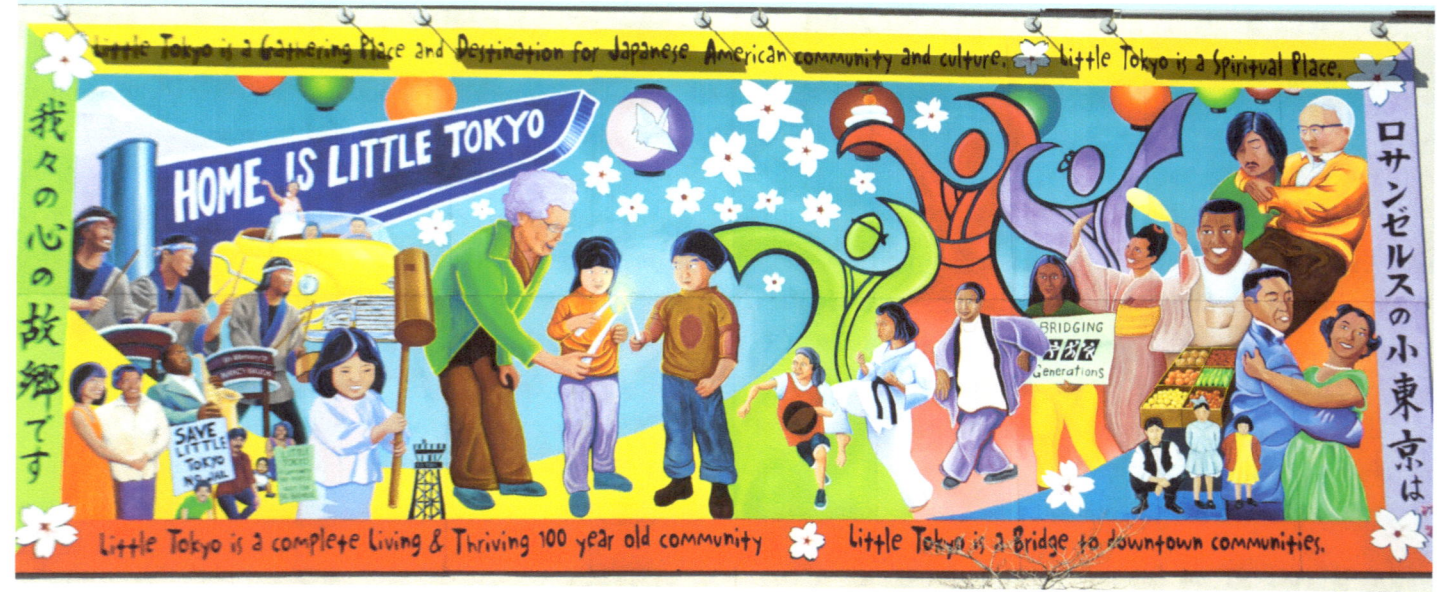

"Home is Little Tokyo" mural located on Central Ave and 1st Street in Downtown Los Angeles. The vibrant mural holds much meaning to locals within the Little Tokyo area as it depicts 110+ years worth of history.

ARTISTIC EXPRESSIONS HINT AT HISTORY

The streets of Los Angeles contain several murals with themes from Mexican-American and Asian-American history, including the "America Tropical" (Tropical America) mural in Olvera Street and the "Home is Little Tokyo" mural in Little Tokyo. Mexican-Americans living in Olvera Street did not share the same optimism Sterling held for the community, including muralist David Alfaro Siquieros, who painted the mural on the wall on the second floor of Olvera Street's Italian Hall in 1932. The artwork's full name, "America Tropical: Oppressed and Destroyed by Imperialism" conveys the difficult circumstances that devastated Mexican-Americans during the Great Depression. Through this mural, Siquieros hoped to illustrate how repressive laws and vigilantes crushed collective bargaining efforts and

how mass deportations affected Mexican nationals. While some identified with the message in his painting, others criticized Siquieros' mural because it contains an image of people pointing rifles at a Native American man crucified on a double cross of imperialism and the Church. Leslie Rainer from the Getty Conservation Institute described how the city whitewashed the mural in 1938 because these images angered many Los Angeles residents and contrasted with the romantic atmosphere Sterling created in Olvera Street. "People were expecting this nice, tranquil scenery of a pastoral kind of Mexico with some senioritas, some guitar, and some fruit hanging from the trees," Rainer said. The lost artwork nearly perished but it lived to tell the important tale of Mexican-American struggles in Los Angeles. According to Rainer, Latino art activist Shifra M. Goldman brought the mural back to life after she began a preservation campaign for "America Tropical" and Siquieros' final piece, "Portrait of Mexico Today." His unique style as well as his use of cement guns and pre-colored cement mortar instead of traditional materials influenced other artists, including Goldman, helped the Chicano Muralist Movement arise in the 1960's, and led to art in the form of social and political expression. The mural was very faded and whitewashed when the Institute first started restorations, but various conservations teams worked on it in three phases, starting 1990 and culminating in 2012. The center opened after this final phase in 2012 and currently houses the restored mural. The Institute currently touches up the mural with modern materials like artist grade conservation grade acrylic or watercolor that they know will remain stable and match the mural's original appearance. Although the conservationists cannot restore Siquieros' artwork with the same paints he used, Rainer said the Institute likes using different materials so people can see the difference between his original materials and their restorations. Guests can walk to the upstairs viewing platform in the America Tropical Interpretive Center, see "America Tropical" from a distance, and hear its incredible story on guided tours. A reading rail on the viewing platform shows a black and white image of when it was intact so people can visualize what it looked originally looked like." We always try to refer back to the way it would have looked at the time without interpreting it on the mural itself," Rainer said.

In the Little Tokyo community nearby, Tony Osumi helped paint the more modern and vividly colorful "Home is Little Tokyo Mural" on the northern half of the Japanese Village Plaza parking structure. Osumi described how the project manager, Nancy Kikuchi, received a grant from the City of Los Angeles' Neighborhood Matching Fund and recruited him to help paint and design the mural along with Sergio and Jorge Diaz. Osumi scheduled community meetings and gathered perspectives from business owners, residents, and youth from the Little Tokyo Service Center's after school program. He wanted a theme of community instead of a collection of images, created a design from all their ideas, and consolidated it into a mural that told the area's history. The mural derives its name from the 1970's group Little Tokyo People's Rights Organization slogan and includes images from several decades of Little Tokyo history: a Nisei couple dancing from the 1940's, a Nisei Week Queen from the 1950's driving a convertible, a little girl pounding a guard tower from a relocation camp instead of mochi, an image from the activist days in the 1970's, an image from the Day of Remembrance, and a Nisei Week parade of characters. It also includes other cultural icons like Charlie Parker playing saxophone, a taiko group, and mystical dancing figures that imitate the Hokusai woodblock print wave. Some of these pictures come from Ichiro Mike Murase's "100 Years of Little Tokyo History in Pictures." Osumi also included an image of a Latino Worker to include other ethnic groups in the area besides Japanese-Americans. Portions of the mural contain a progressive political slant that illustrates ideas of community organizing against big businesses. Four community visions span across the top and bottom while the right and left sides contain Japanese characters that say "Little Tokyo is the 'home sweet home' of our hearts." Over 500 volunteers of all ages and local organizations helped paint the mural for six hours on weekends for about a year. Osumi realized the importance of community and immigrant contributions as he painted this mural. He also noted that each generation of

Little Tokyo residents wanted different images of what was important to them painted. Osumi shared a story about the way two second-generation women repeatedly asked him to paint Mount Fuji, yet a third-generation man and Osumi's father believed he should not put Fuji in there because it was Japanese, not American. They wanted something from Japan that spoke to them, but the third-generation immigrants broke away from their ethnic identity because they did not want to feel like perpetual foreigners in their home country. Some people wanted to see illustrations of Nisei Week, a popular cultural celebration. Despite differences in opinion, Osumi tried to balance each generation's requests. Overall, the mural contains a lot of Asian-American history and struggle as well as Little Tokyo History. "It's kind of a progressive peoples' history of Little Tokyo instead of just purely cultural or purely the rich or purely stuff not connected to peoples' struggles," Osumi said. The process of making the mural was equally important to him as its content because he saw it as a democratic opportunity for the community to express their ideas as opposed to other artists, who leave the community after they finish their job. The volunteers' names inscribed on a plaque below the mural indicate the value he placed on community contributions.

Migrants give back

Osumi noted that although Little Tokyo contains several generations of Japanese-Americans, the first generation residents own businesses and have helped Little Tokyo thrive economically because it started from immigrant labor and still runs on it.

"That's the power of immigrants. When they come, they will often revitalize certain areas, move in and start stuff," Osumi said. "If you deny immigrants to come here, build walls or whatever, you're denying a lot of revitalization throughout America that a lot of small towns are experiencing the positive effects of immigration. "Nguyen described how Little Saigon's exponential growth demonstrates the ways government charity programs, sponsors, and subsidies helped Vietnamese Americans adapt to American Society faster than other migrant groups. Located only a few miles southwest of the Disneyland Resort on Bolsa Ave., Little Saigon contains 4,000 Vietnamese -American businesses and covers three square miles. Nguyen has given back to society as Interim President of the Vietnamese American Arts and Letters Association, which hosts the Vietnamese Film Festival each April that showcases anything related to Vietnamese arts or culture. Nguyen's childhood experiences have helped her understand the importance of diversity and how to include other communities, specifically cancer education and control in the public health industry. Her work focuses on social justice because she desires to help others who lack resources and privileges others around them enjoy. "I know what it's like not to be part of the in-crowd, not to belong to something, not to belong to somewhere," Nguyen said. "I also know what it means to receive compassion from others and to really be able to succeed in life through support from others, who are able to share and who are willing to contribute a little bit of what they have for the betterment of their community."

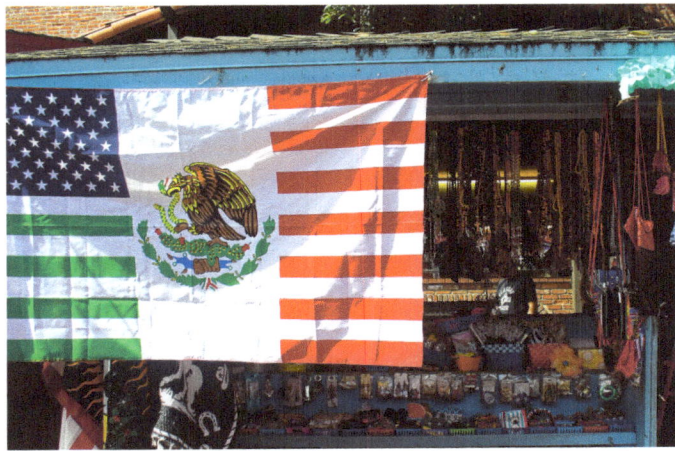

Kiosk on Olvera Street vends vibrant trinkets depicting the colorful culture as well as showing the integration of the Amerian and Mexican flag.

CONCLUSION

Both Mexican-Americans and Asian-Americans have heavily influenced the cultural and geographical development of Los Angeles and Orange County. These communities have left permanent imprints and given back to the new places they called home. Narratives from these two groups are deeply embedded into history of the region, which still contain high percentages of both groups today. The people who came to America as migrants or refugees have transformed the region into a diverse area. This unique world draws visitors across the globe and has contributed to the development of several cultural communities. Even though these places developed many years ago, several still call them home today and share their culture with new generations.

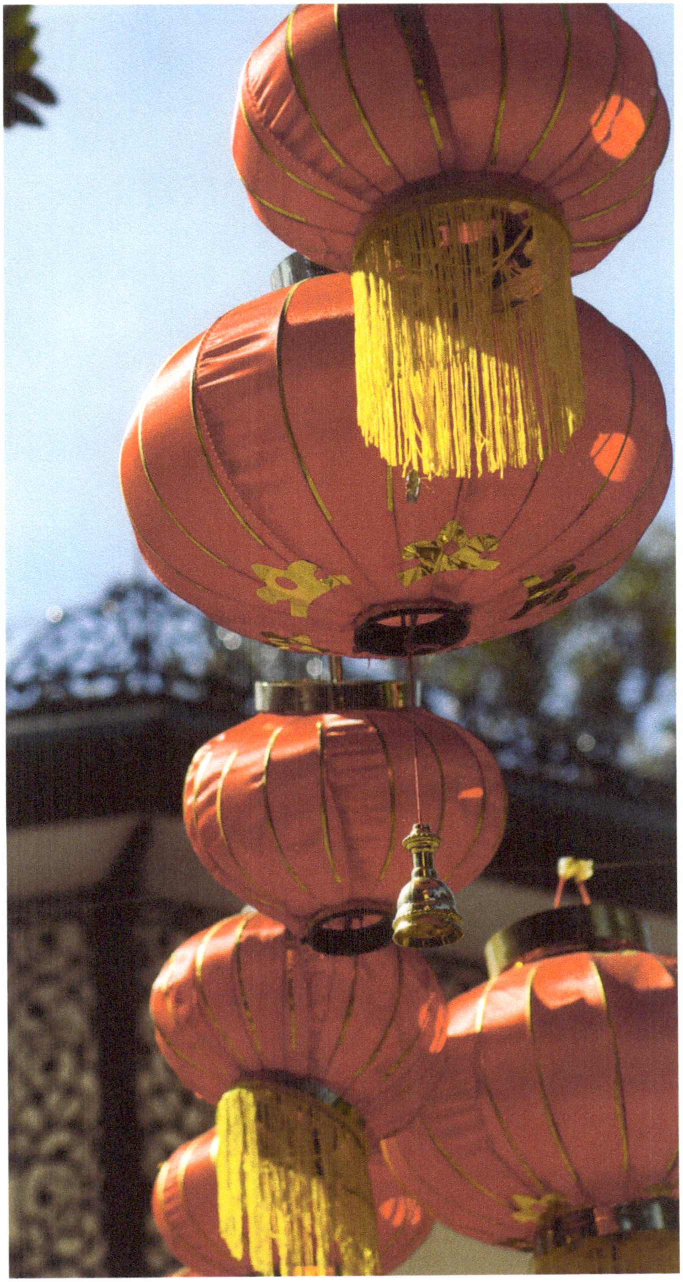

Red and gold lanterns hang in between El Pueblo and Chinatown, as they prepare for the annual Lantern Festival.

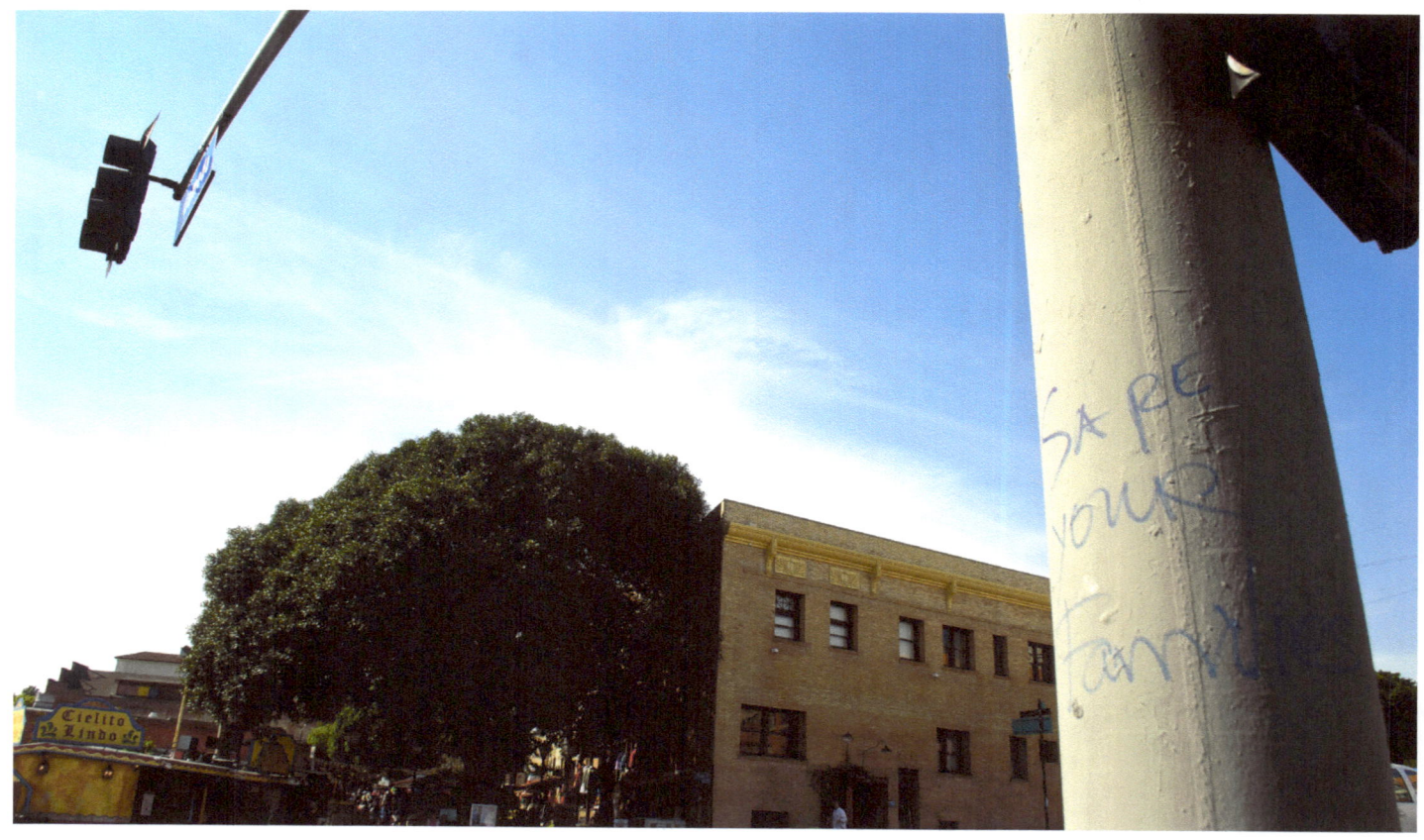

Detail shot of a stoplight pole on the corner of Olvera Street. Pole reads "SAVE YOUR FAMILIES" as Olvera Street culture beats with life in the background.

End Notes

1. "Record 45.5M Tourists Visited Los Angeles Last Year." CBS Los Angeles. Accessed April 08, 2017. http://losangeles.cbslocal.com/2016/01/11/record-number-of-tourists-visited-los-angeles-last-year/.

2. "Population estimates, July 1, 2016, (V2016)," UNITED STATES QuickFacts from the US Census Bureau. Accessed March 29, 2017. https://www.census.gov/quickfacts/table/PST045216/00.

3. "City of Los Angeles Seal El Pueblo De Los Angeles Historical Monument City of Los Angeles Flag." Mexicans : El Pueblo De Los Angeles : The City of Los Angeles. Accessed March 29, 2017, http://elpueblo.lacity.org/HistoryEducation/ElPuebloHistory/Mexicans/index.html.

4. "The First Asian Americans : Asian-Nation : Asian American History, Demographics, & Issues." The First Asian Americans : Asian-Nation :Asian American History, Demographics, & Issues. Accessed March 29, 2017, http://www.asian-nation.org/first.shtml.

5. "Sierra Nevada Geotourism," Wakamatsu Tea and Silk Farm Colony (Nol. 815 California Historical Landmark) - Sierra Nevada Geotourism MapGuide. Accessed March 29, 2017. http://www.sierranevadageotourism.org/content/wakamatsu-tea-and-silk-farm-colony-nol-815-california-historical-landmark/sie9d88cb4e9c47a1027.

6. "Little Tokyo," Historical Background, Little Tokyo, Los Angeles. Accessed March 29, 2017. http://www.publicartinla.com/Downtown/Little_Tokyo/little_tokyo.html.

7. Sidhu, Nancy D. , Ferdinando Guerra, and Kimberly Ritter. "Growing Together Japan and Los Angeles County." Los Angeles County Economic Development Corporation. 2011. Accessed April 8, 2017. http://laedc.org/wp-content/uploads/2012/04/GrowingTogether_Japan_2011.pdf.

8. "Olvera Street - Visit Us." Olvera Street - Visit Us. Accessed April 08, 2017. http://www.olvera-street.com/About-Us/about-us.html.

9. Radio, Southern California Public. "Commemorating LA's Chinese Massacre, possibly the worst lynching in US history." Southern California Public Radio. December 14, 2016. Accessed March 29, 2017. http://www.scpr.org/programs/offramp/2016/10/21/52801/commemorating-la-s-chinese-massacre-possibly-the-w/.

10. Chinese Immigration and the Chinese in the United States." National Archives and Records Administration. Accessed March 29, 2017. https://www.archives.gov/research/chinese-americans/guide.html#uscustoms.

11. "Before It Embraced Immigrants, California Championed the Chinese Exclusion Act of 1882." KCET. February 09, 2017. Accessed March 29, 2017. https://www.kcet.org/shows/lost-la/before-it-embraced-immigrants-california-championed-the-chinese-exclusion-act-of-1882.

12. William Gow, "Building a Chinese Village in Los Angeles: Christine Sterling and the Residents of China City." Gum Saan Journal 32, no. 1 (2010): 2008. accessed March 29, 2017. https://www.chssc.org/History/ChinatownRemembered/Neighborhoods/Residents_of_China_City.aspx

13. Berman, Jay. "The Forgotten 'Repatriation'" Los Angeles Downtown News - For Everything Downtown L.A.! April 17, 2006. Accessed March 29, 2017. http://www.ladowntownnews.com/news/the-forgotten-repatriation/article_50846cb7-21cc-5fa3-bfb2-83247a5f7dc8.html.

14. Los Angeles Conservancy." Japanese American Heritage | Los Angeles Conservancy. Accessed March 29, 2017. https://www.laconservancy.org/japanese-american-heritage.

15. "City of Los Angeles Seal El Pueblo De Los Angeles Historical Monument City of Los Angeles Flag." Mexicans : El Pueblo De Los Angeles : The City of Los Angeles. Accessed March 29, 2017. http://elpueblo.lacity.org/HistoryEducation/ElPuebloHistory/Mexicans/index.html.

16. Andy McCue, "Barrio, Bulldozers, and Baseball: The Destruction of Chavez Ravine." NINE: A Journal of Baseball History and Culture 21, no. 1 (2012). Accessed March 29, 2017. doi:http://muse.jhu.edu/article/503653.

17. "Orange County Historical Society: A Brief History of Orange County, California." Orange County Historical Society: A Brief History of Orange County, California. Accessed April 08, 2017. http://www.orangecountyhistory.org/history-brief.html.

18. "Asian Population by Community." Asian Population by Community. Accessed April 08, 2017. http://www.ocalmanac.com/Population/po16a.htm.

19. Goldman, Shifra M. "Siqueiros and Three Early Murals in Los Angeles." Art Journal 33, no. 4 (1974): 321-27. doi:10.2307/775970.

20. "Little Saigon: The Vietnamese Heart of Orange County." Visit Anaheim. May 02, 2016. Accessed April 08, 2017. http://visitanaheim.org/blog-post/2016/04/12/spotlight-little-saigon.

CENTURIES *of* CHANGE

Pio Pico, the last Mexican governor of California, lamented, "We find ourselves suddenly threatened by hordes of Yankee immigrants...whose progress we cannot arrest."

A group of 11 families comprising 44 Mexicans settles by the river. Felipe de Neve, Governor of Spanish California, names the settlement El Pueblo Sobre el Rio de Nuestra Señora la Reina de los Angeles del Río de Porciúncula. The name is shortened rather quickly.

Los Angeles' first census shows a population of 141. California's first discovery of gold is made at Placerita Canyon, near Mission San Fernando, prompting LA's first population boom.

1781

1841-2

1769

1810

Spanish explorer Gaspar de Portola explores Southern California and establishes the first Spanish settlement in the area. The settlers name the local river Rio de Nuestra Senora la Reina de los Angeles de Porciuncula (River of Our Lady Queen of the Angels of Porciuncula).

Mexico begins an 11-year struggle to successfully achieve independence from Spain.

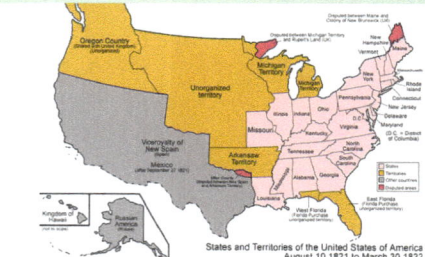

States and Territories of the United States of America
August 10 1821 to March 30 1822

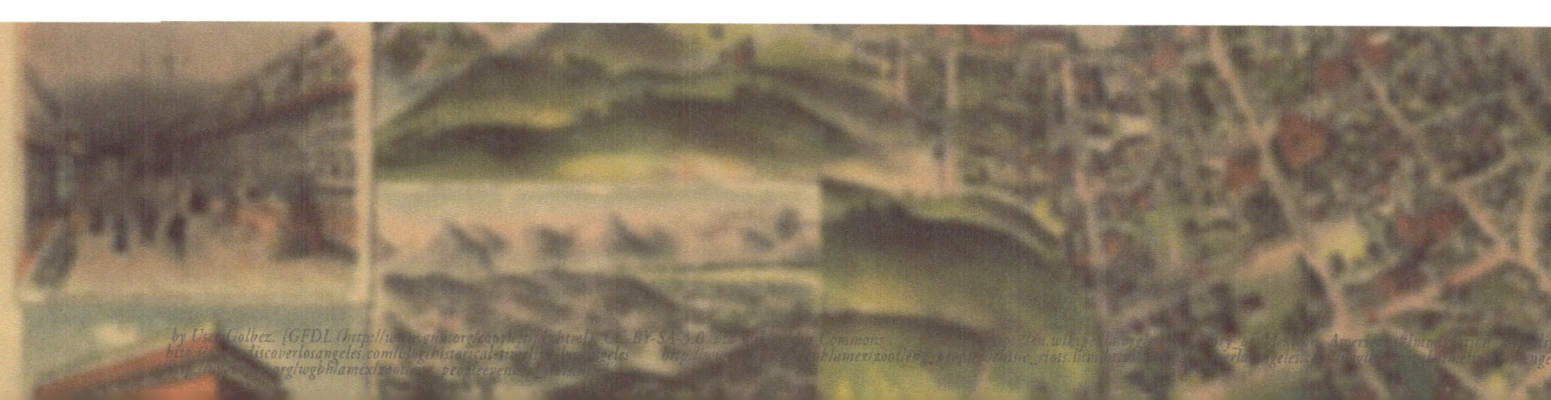

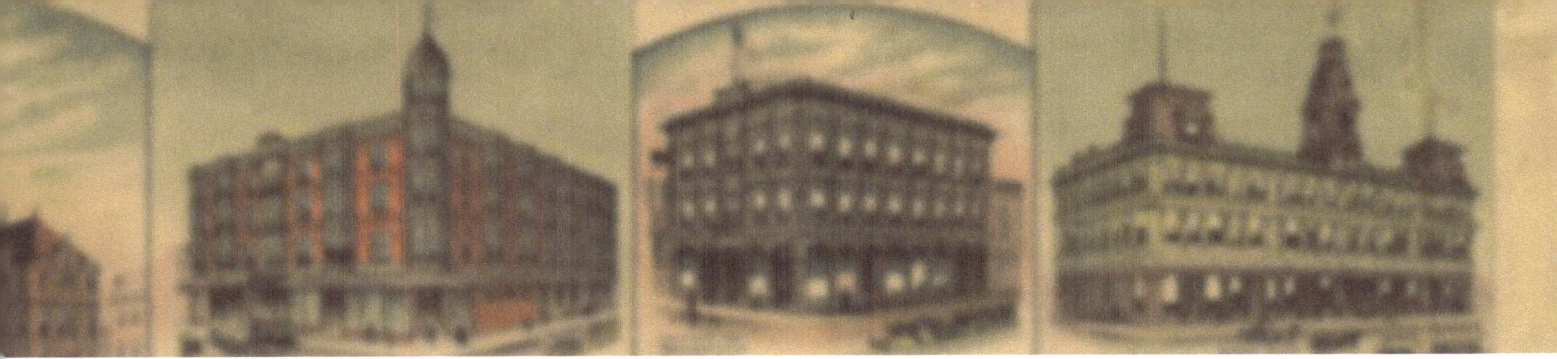

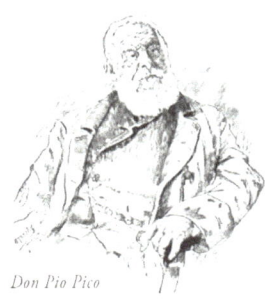

Don Pio Pico

The Immigration Act of 1924 is signed into law. Initially immigration from the other Americas was allowed, but measures were quickly developed to deny legal entry to Mexican laborers.

A Mexican-American was elected to the Los Angeles City Council and it would take litigation to permit a Mexican-American to win election to the Los Angeles County Board of Supervisors in the 1980s, the first Mexican-American to join that body in more than a century.

1924

1986

1846-8

1943

Pio Pico is sworn in as governor of the California, in Los Angeles. Battle of Rio San Gabriel. The United States takes control of Los Angeles. Treaty of Cahuenga is signed in the pass between Los Angeles and the San Fernando Valley. Treaty of Guadalupe Hidalgo. Mexico formally cedes California to the United States, and all residents are made U.S. citizens.

Thousands of Mexican refugees fleeing the Mexican Revolution have made their way to Los Angeles. Racial tensions escalated, resulting a weeklong street fight between sailors on shoreleave and Mexican American boys erupted, known as the Zoot Suit Riots.

Three centuries of Mexican presence in Southern California

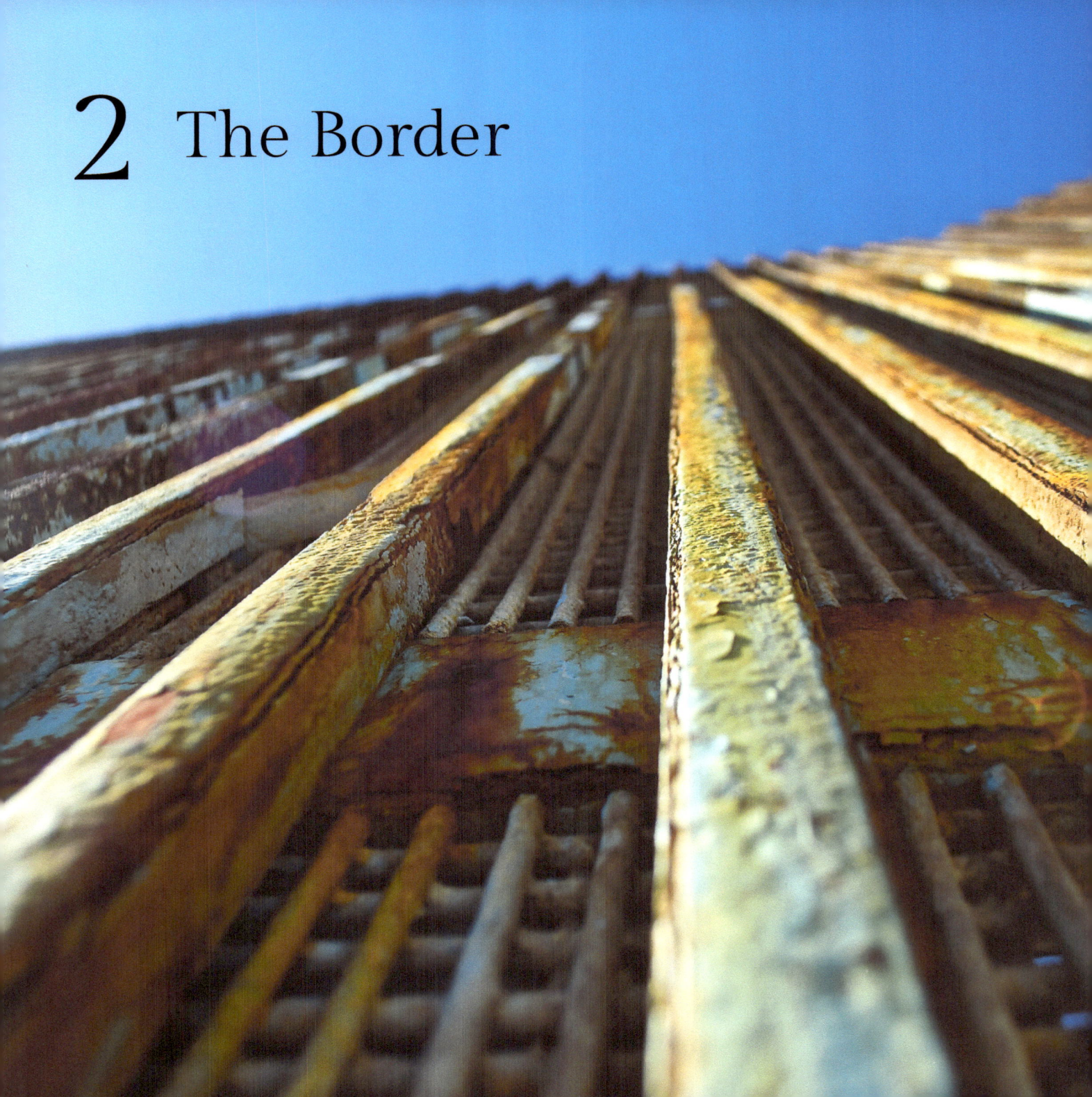

2 The Border

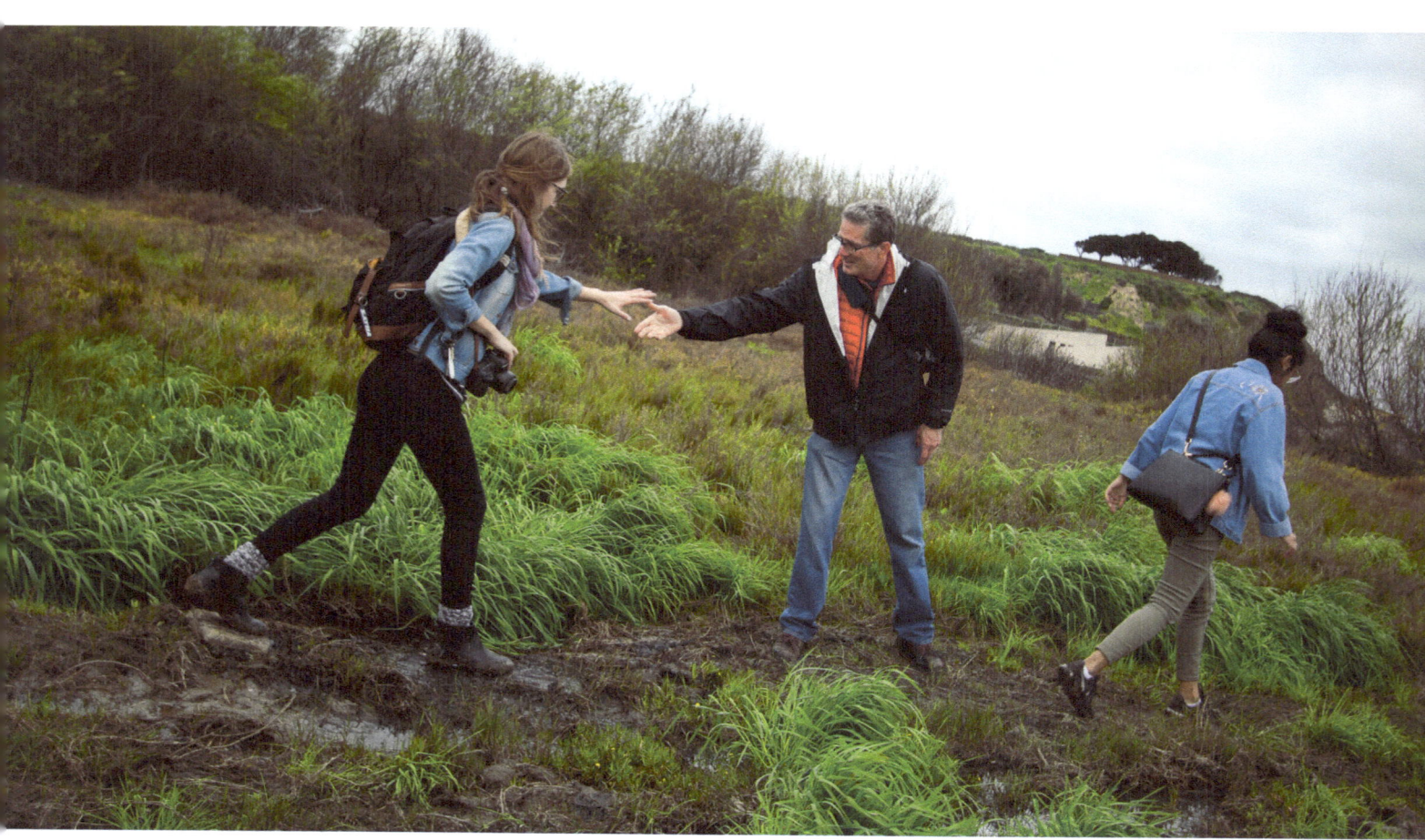

The walk to Border Field State Park on the San Diego side of the U.S.-Mexico border is four-miles roundtrip. A large portion of the surrounding area is filled with sewage, making it difficult for people to reach the border and see their families.

Photo by: Alyssa Yee

Right: The Mexican border looks drastically different in Tijuana. Here, the people have turned the fence into a vast canvas, full of artistic and hopeful expression.

Photo by: Alyssa Yee

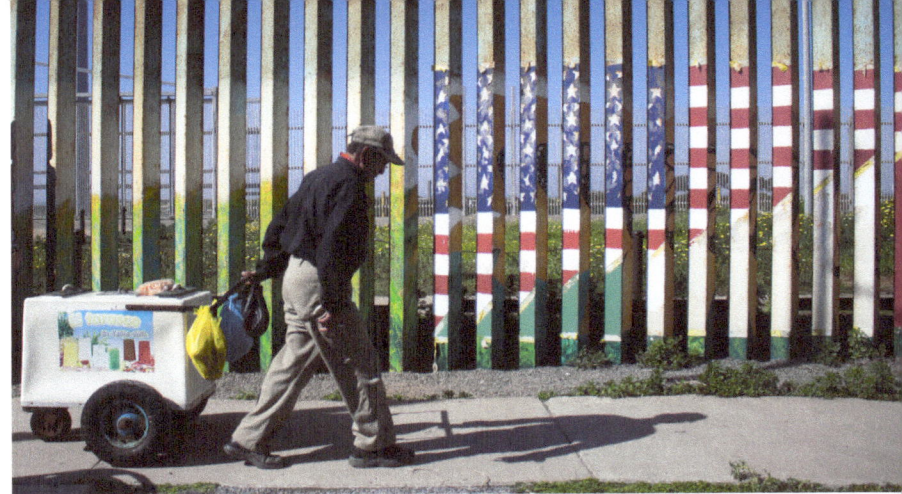

Right: The lighthouse peers over the border from Mexico. The sign, "Abierto," which means "open" in Spanish, belongs to a cafe on the shores of Tijuana.

Photo by: Alyssa Yee

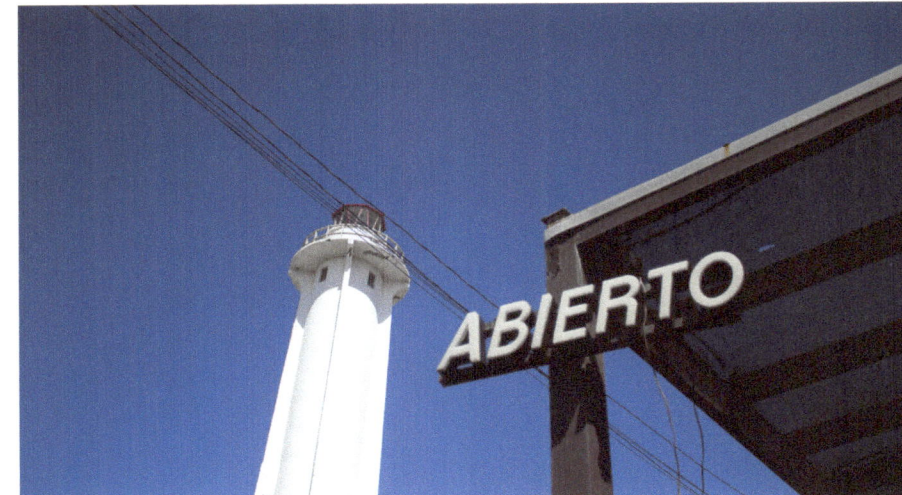

Right: Detail shot of the physical border on the U.S. side, near Friendship Park. "STOP HERE" is painted on a metal beam holding the border fence together.

Photo by: Aili Acone-Chavez

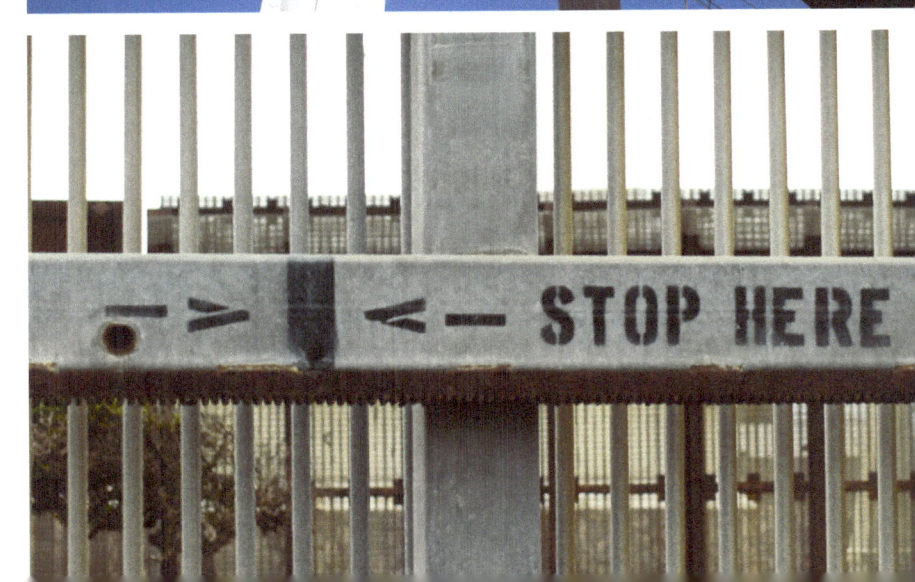

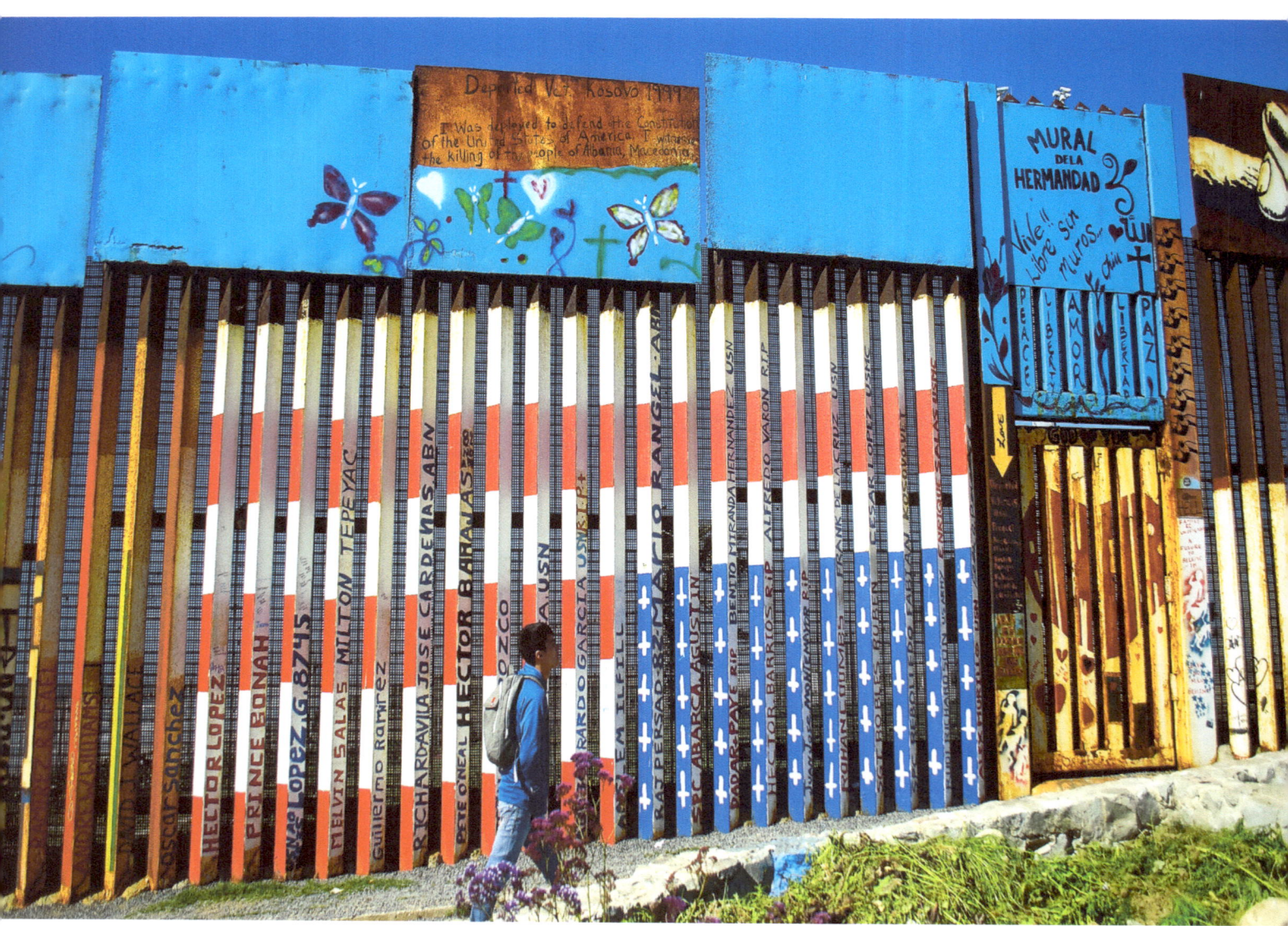

Wide shot of the Mexico side of the border. An upside-down American flag is painted on the rusty metal pillars holding the border fence together. A Mexican boy is seen walking next to the Border in Tijuana, Mexico.

Photo by: Aili Acone-Chavez

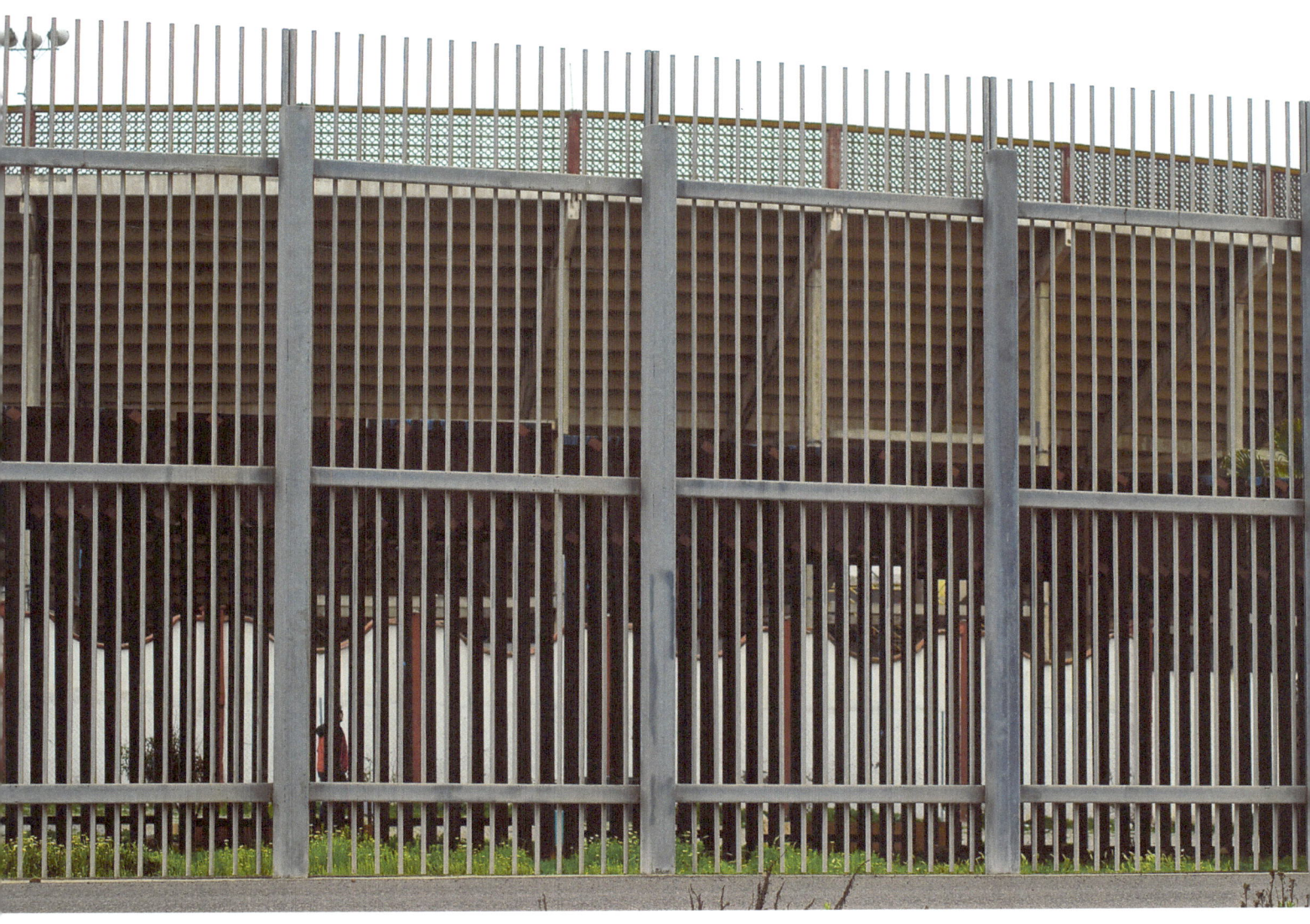

Wide shot of the U.S. side of the border. Seen in the lower left area of convergence is a man in a red hoodie, walking on the Mexico side near Friendship Park.

Photo by: Aili Acone-Chavez

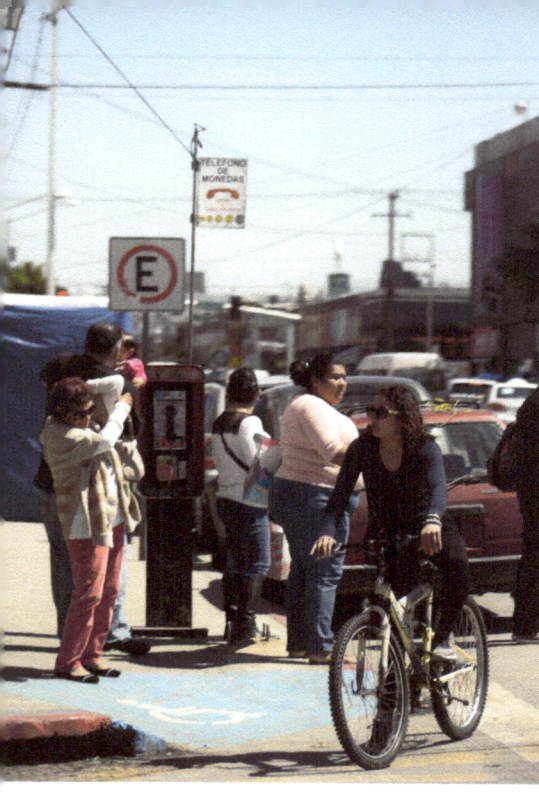

Left: Not far from the border in Mexico, the busy streets of Tijuana are alive with people.

Photo by: Alyssa Yee

Right: In Mexico, two men of varying ethnicity sit on a bench near the walk-across section of the border.

Photo by: Aili Acone-Chavez

Bottom Right: A local man rides to work on a bicycle in Tijuana, Mexico. While maneuvering the bicycle, he holds a bucket filled with supplies.

Photo by: Aili Acone-Chavez

Bottom: Wired posts stand between Border Field State Park and the wall. Civilians are unable to stand within 10 feet of the U.S. border.

Photo by: Alyssa Yee

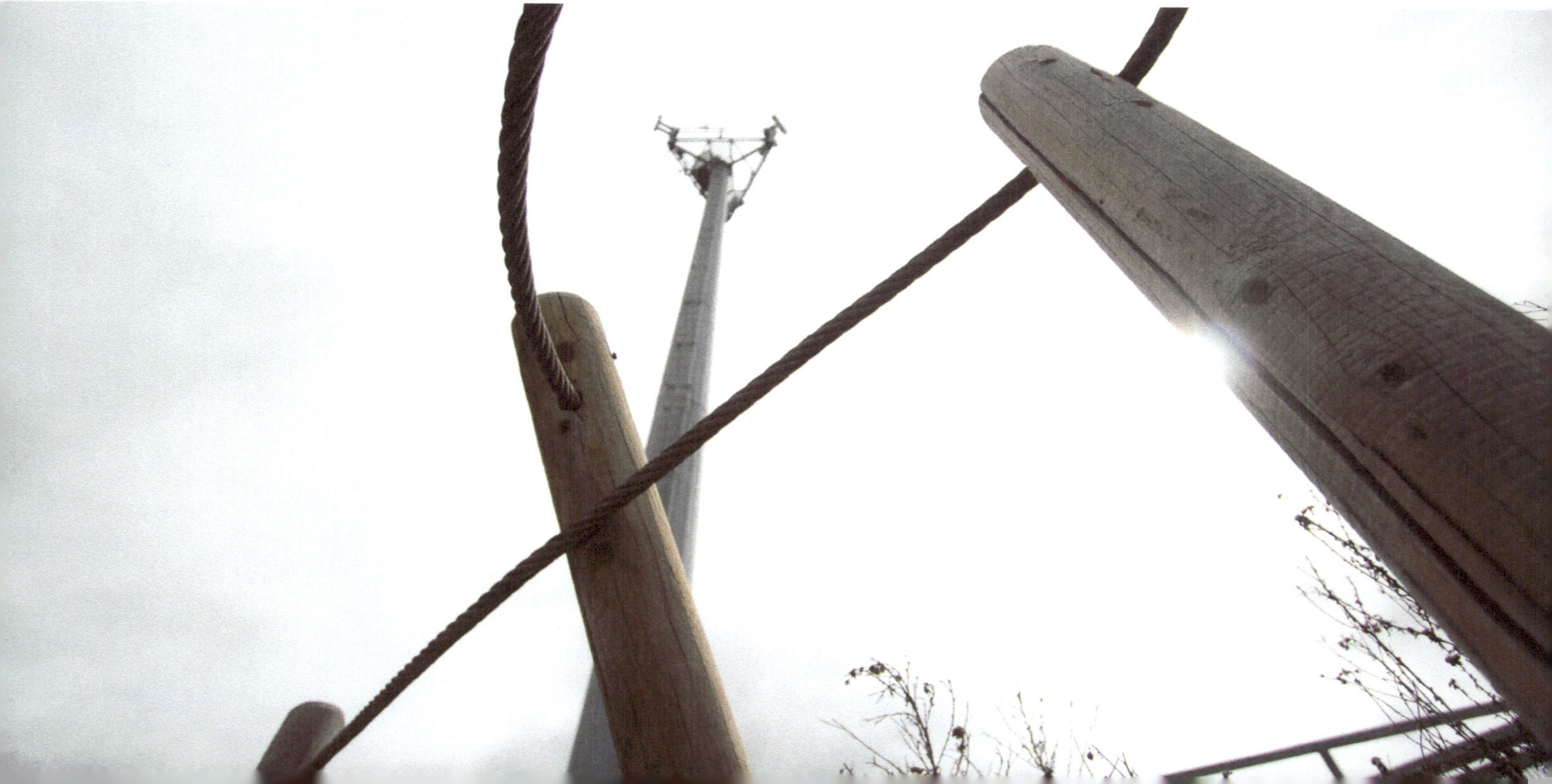

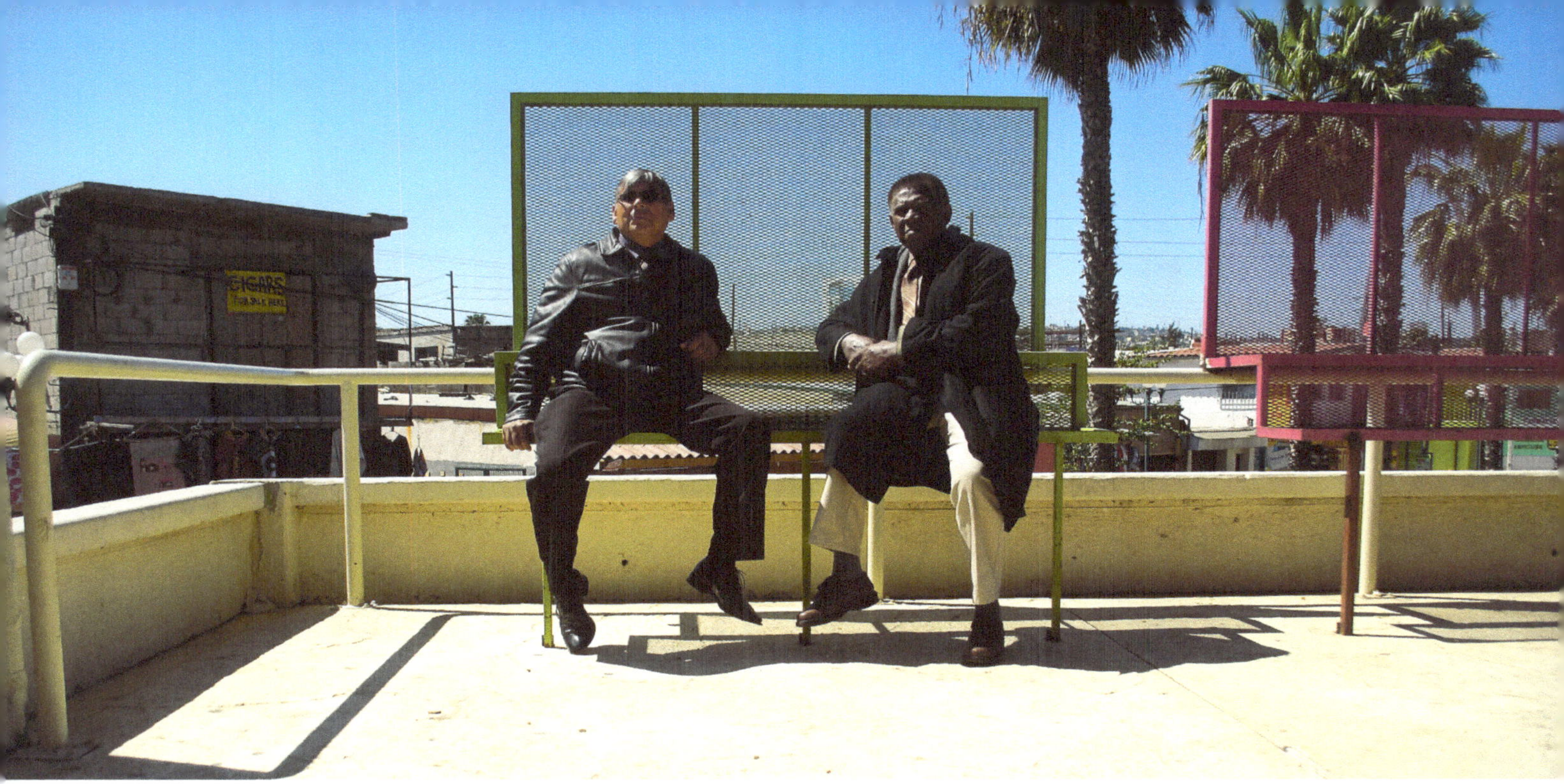
CIGARS

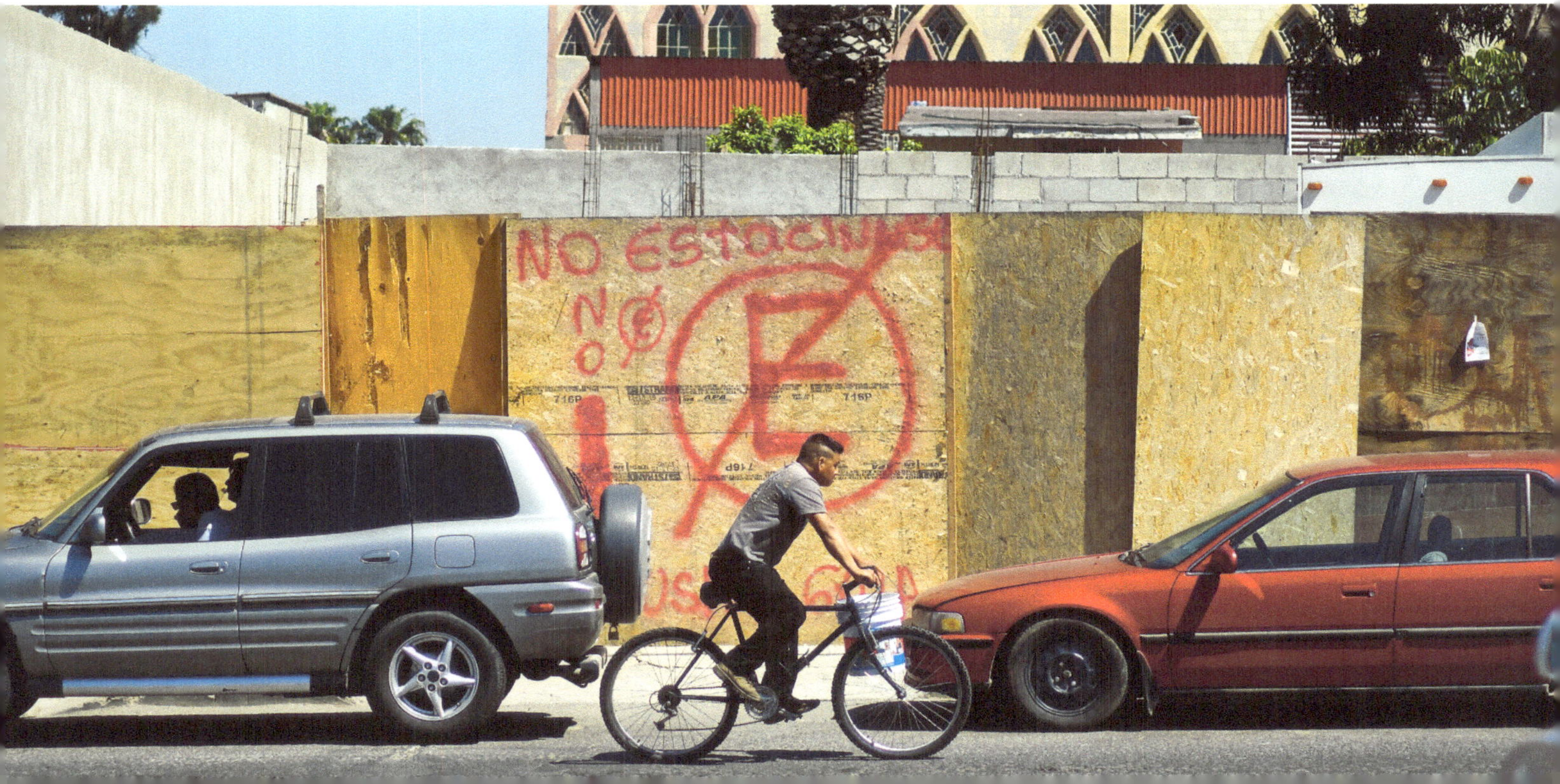
716P

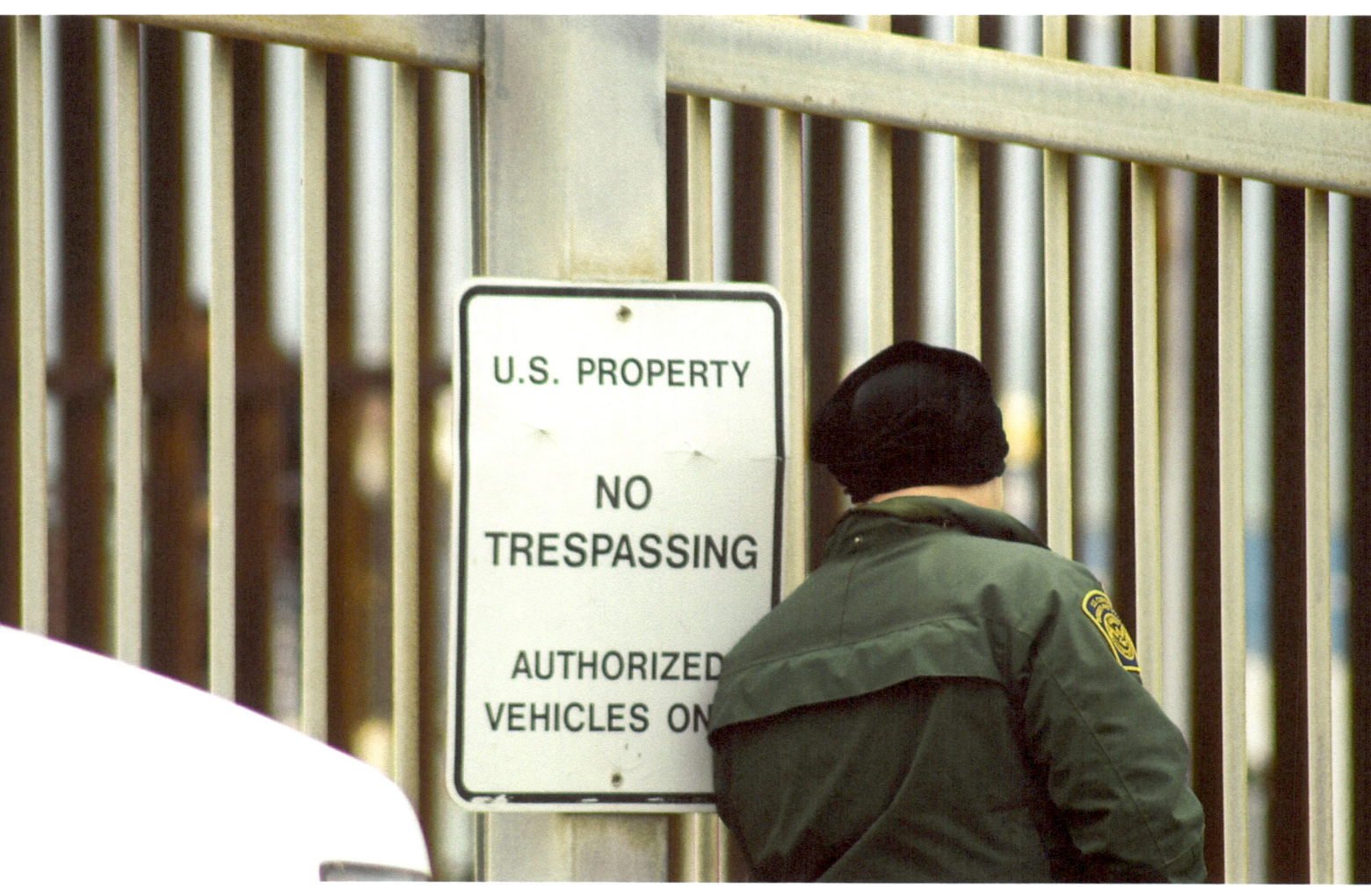

A U.S. border patrol officer leans on the U.S. side of the border near a sign reading, "U.S. PROPERTY NO TRESSPASSING AUTHORIZED VEHICLES ONLY."

Photo by: Aili Acone-Chavez

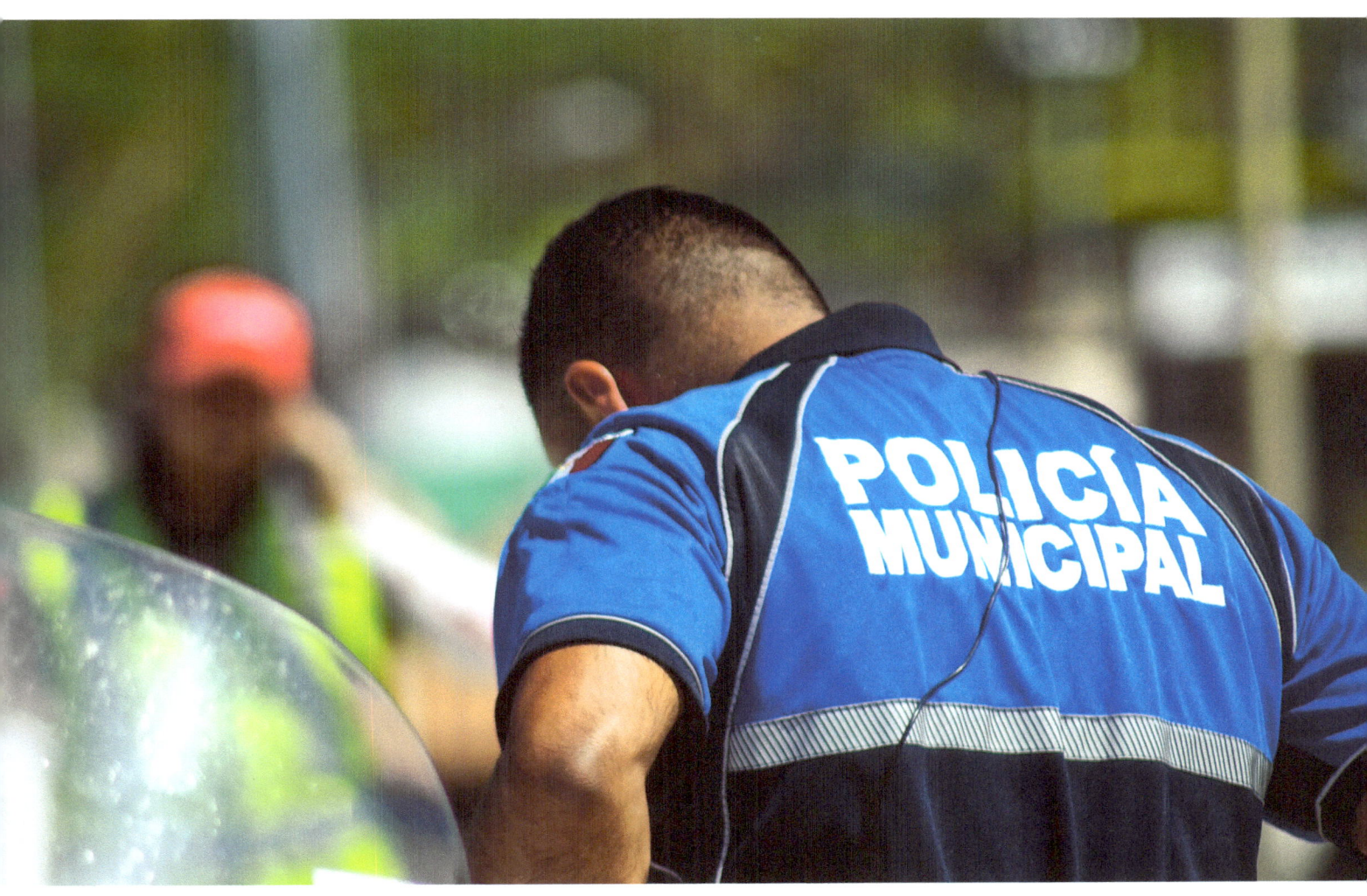

A policia municipal or police officer in Tijuana, Mexico, patrols
the bridge leading to the walk-through border to the U.S.

Photo by: Aili Acone-Chavez

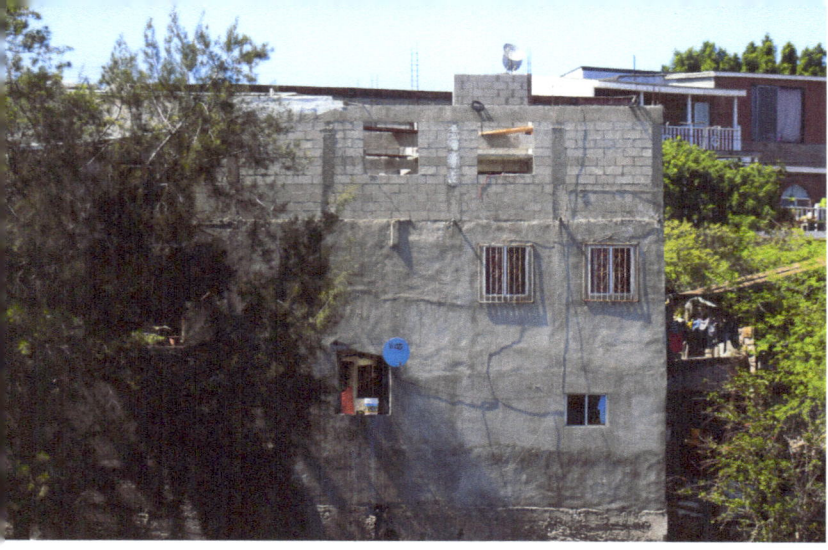

A home in Tijuana, Mexico sits within miles of the U.S. border. On the other side of the wall, miles of desert separate the border from San Diego neighborhoods.

Photo by: Alyssa Yee

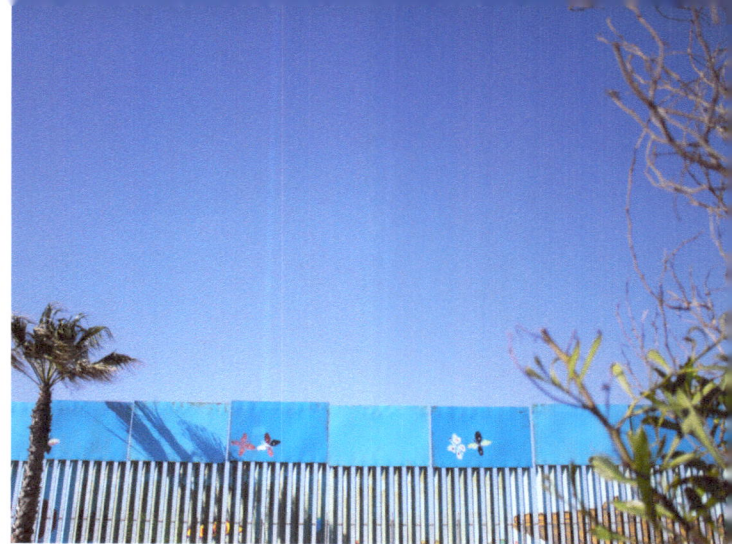

The border in Tijuana sports vibrant banners and childrens' paintings, a symbol of the lively culture.

Photo by: Alyssa Yee

Border Angels in San Diego exists to support migrant families. Their campus' painted pillars mirror the art and culture of the Mexican people.

Photo by: Alyssa Yee

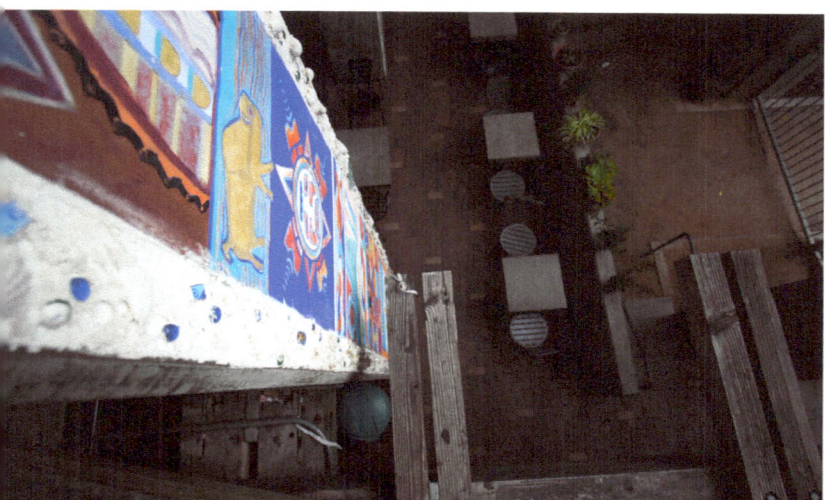

The very posts that separate people from their families are adorned with colorful paintings and phrases of hope.

Photo by: Alyssa Yee

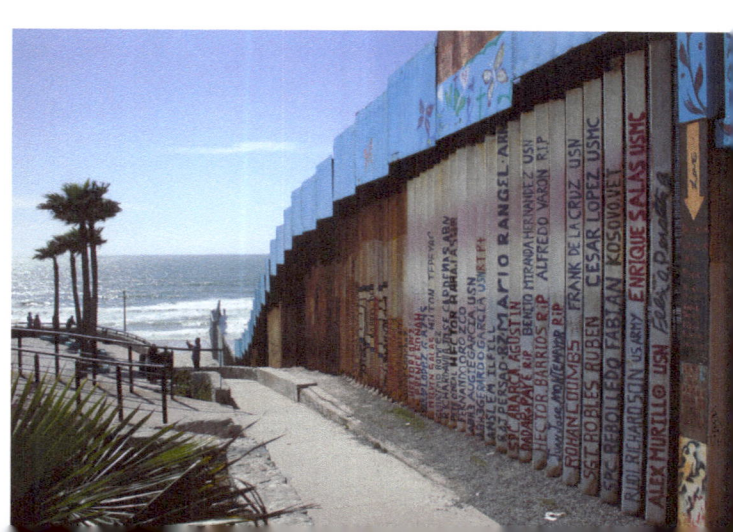

Below: A bridge overlooks the canal where communities
of homeless deportees find shelter.

Photo by: Alyssa Yee

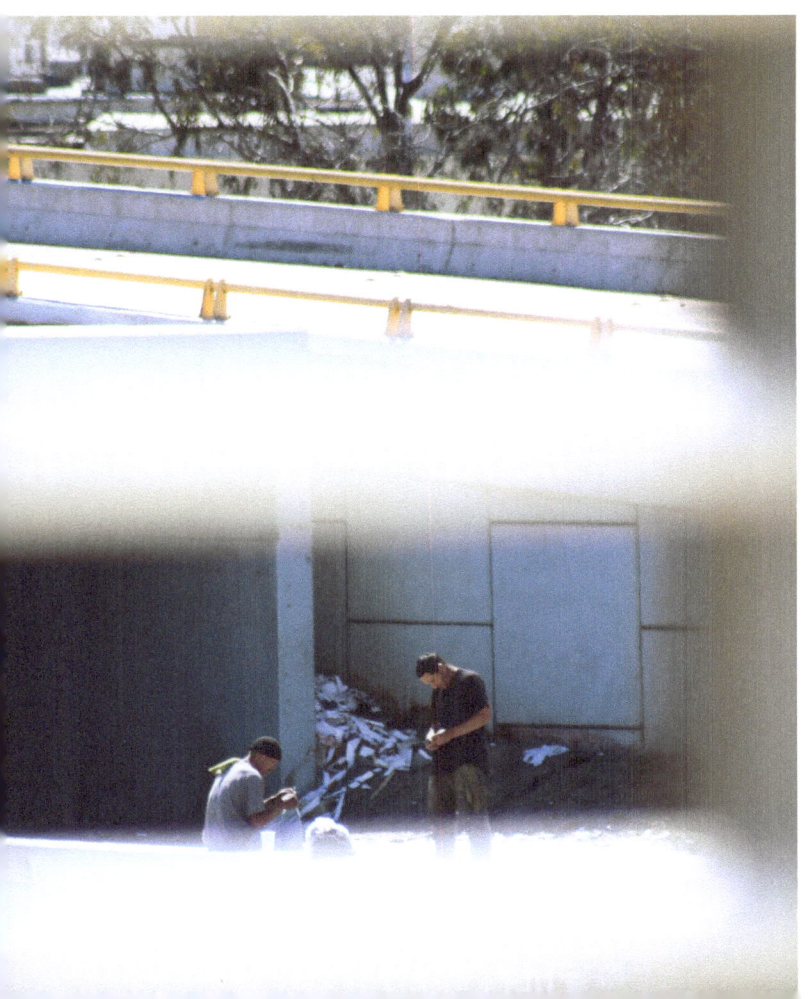

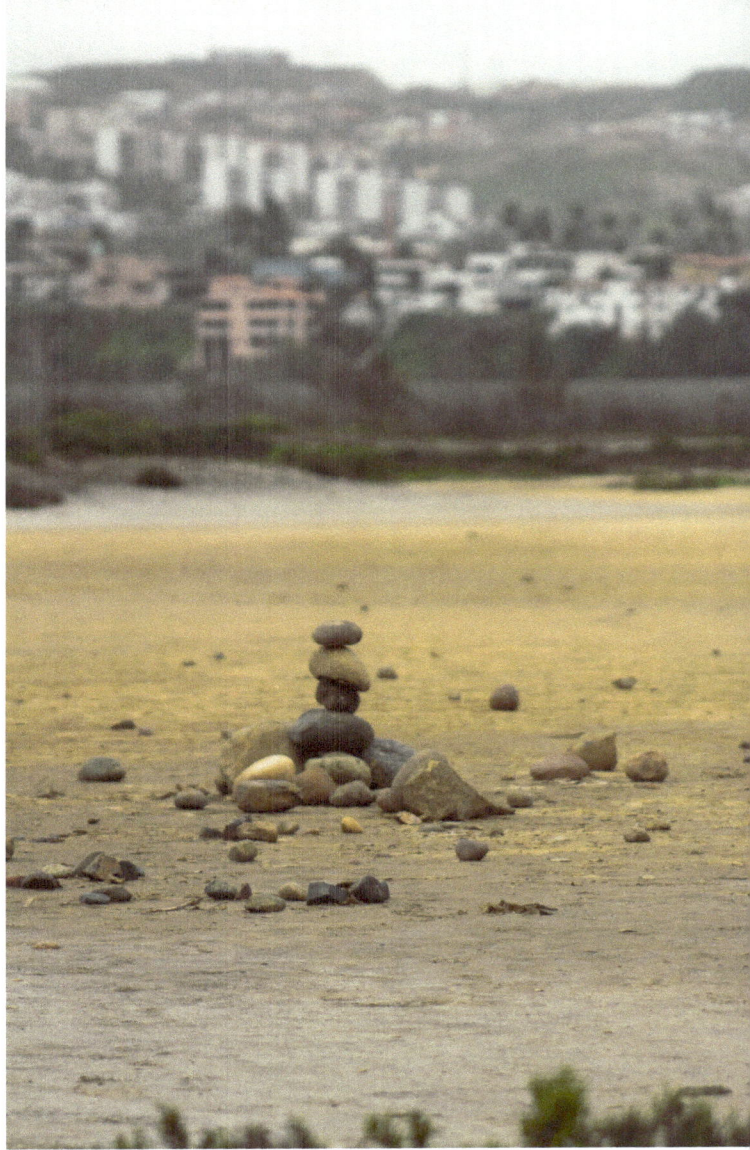

Right: The city of Tijuana can be seen over the wall from
Border Field State Park in San Diego. The distant view fails
to capture the essence of life beyond the border.

Photo by: Alyssa Yee

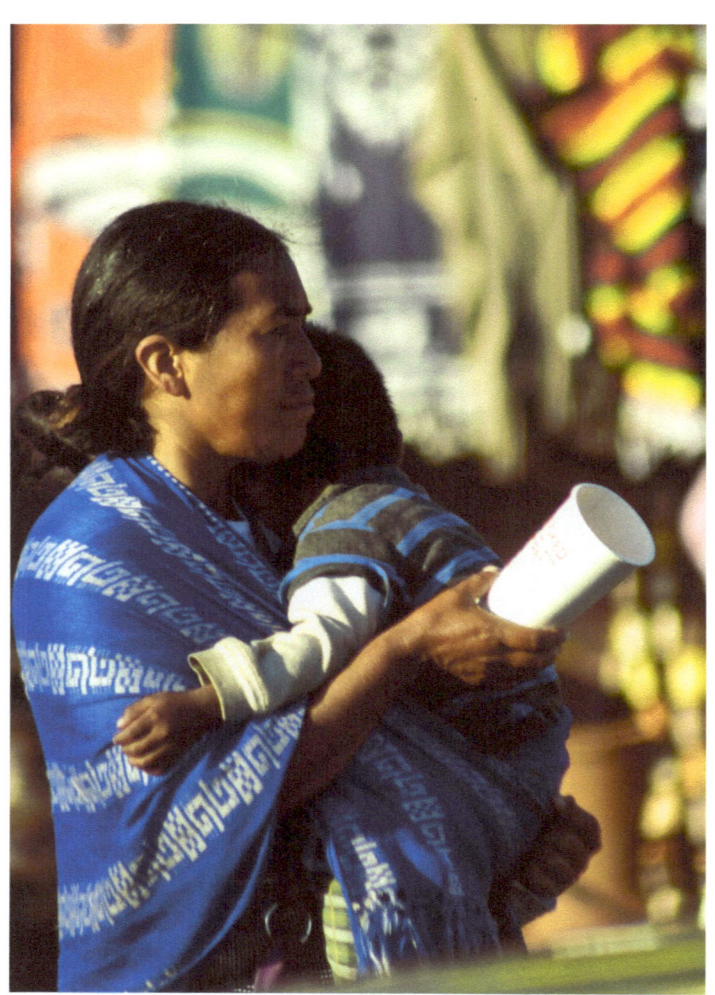

A woman holding her child begs in the middle of the freeway leading toward the CBP (Customs and Border Protection) area on the Mexico side of the border.

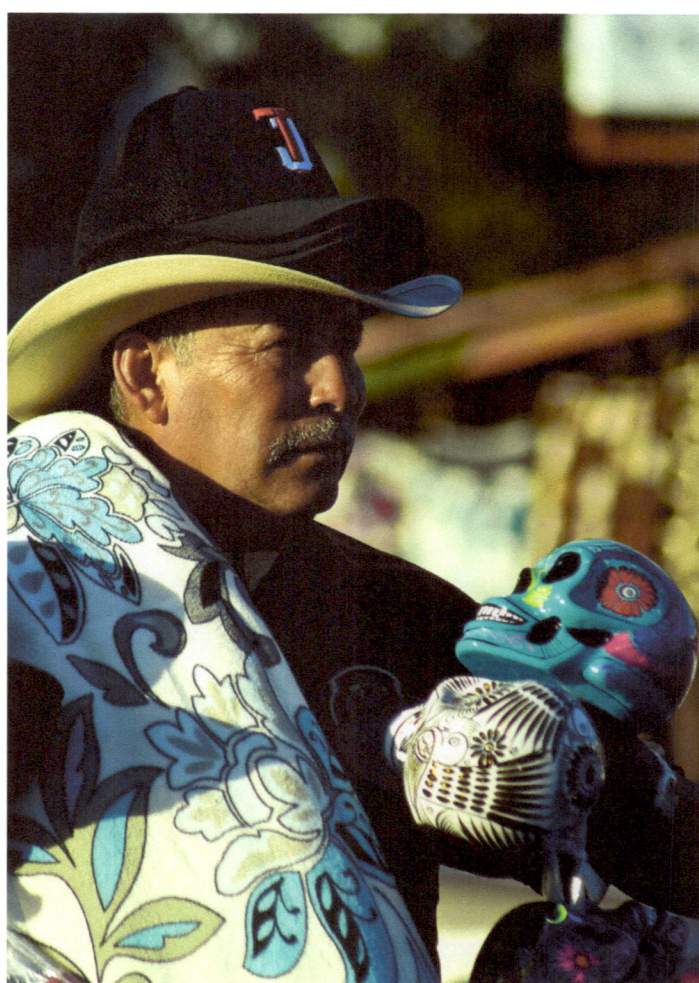

A man sells hats, blankets, and skulls in the middle of the freeway leading toward the CBP area on the Mexico side of the border.

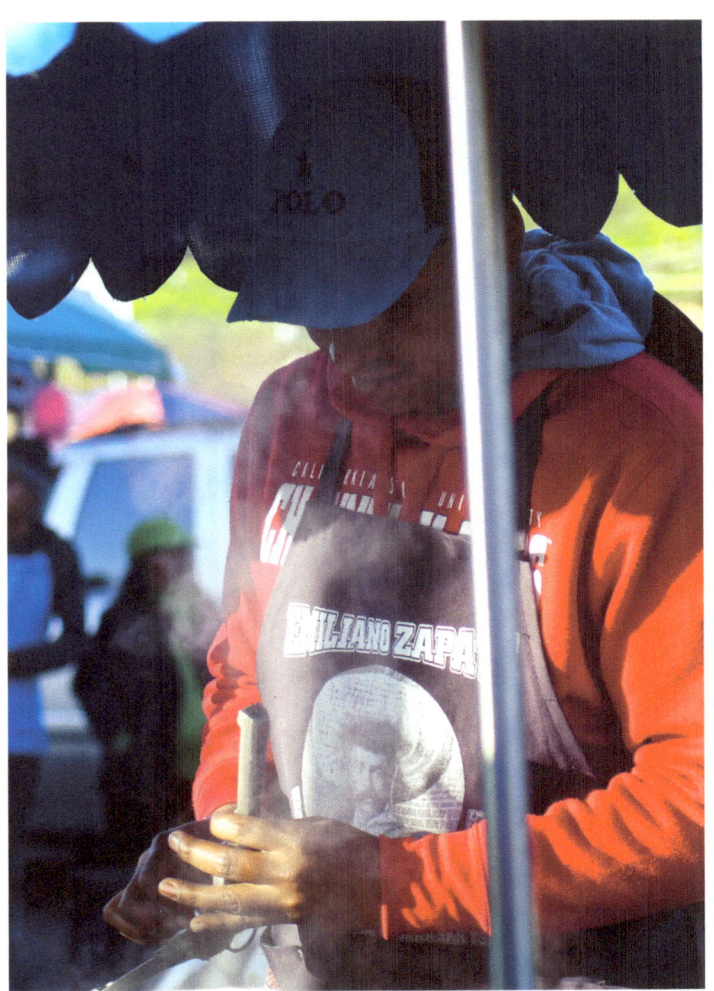

A man cooks on a portable stovetop attached to a kiosk settled in the middle of the freeway leading toward the CBP area on the Mexico side of the Border.

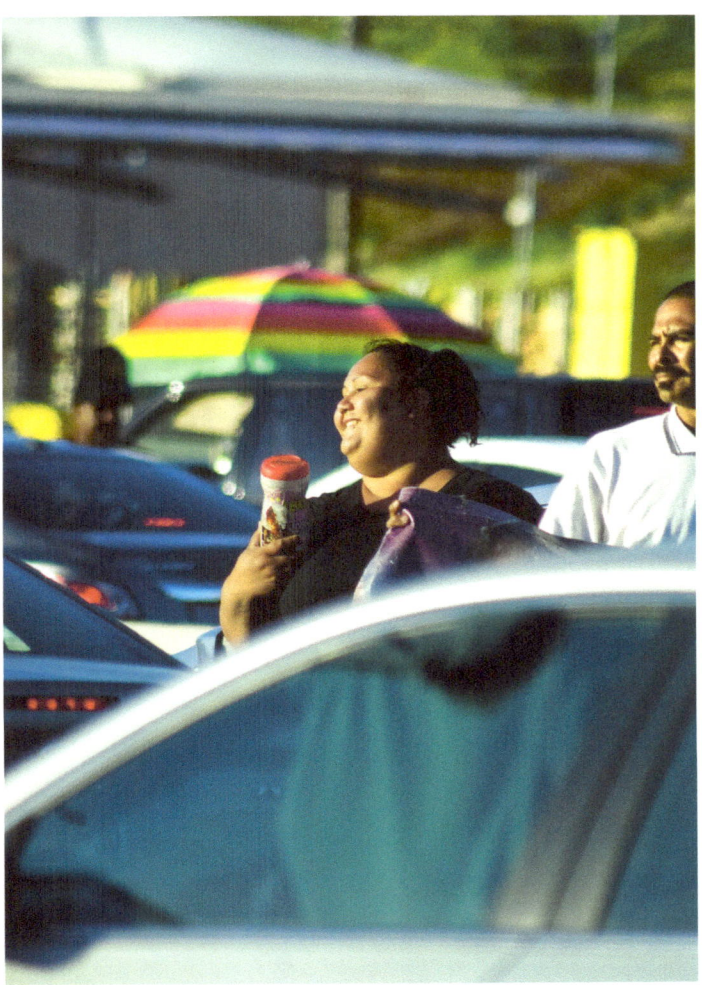

A woman smiles to a friend she is speaking to as they sell goods in the middle of the freeway leading toward the CBP area on the Mexico side of the border.

Photos by: Aili Acone-Chavez

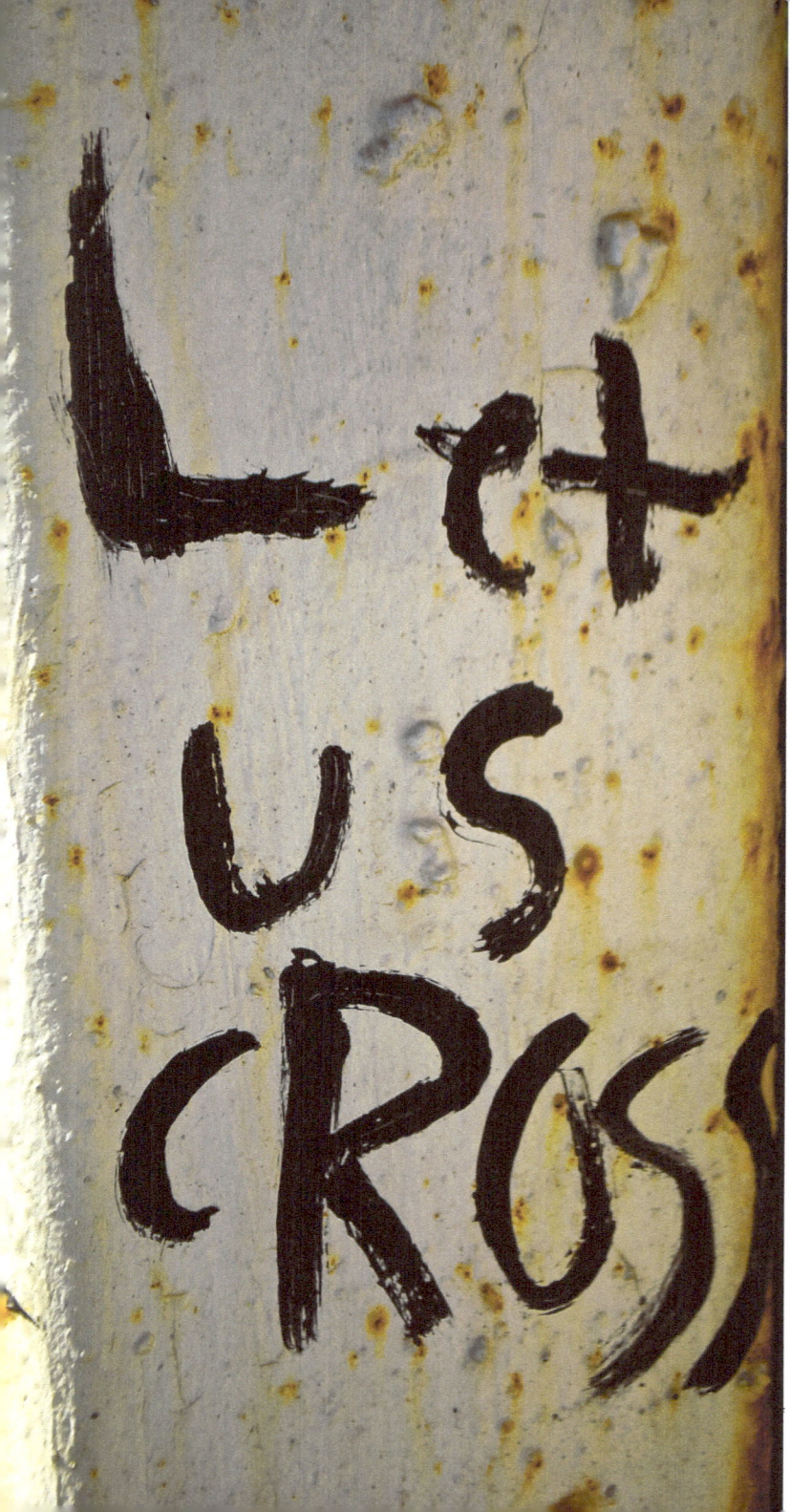

Left: Detail of a provoking message on the Mexico side of the border. "Let us cross" is painted on a rusty metal pillar holding the Mexico border together.

Photo by: Aili Acone-Chavez

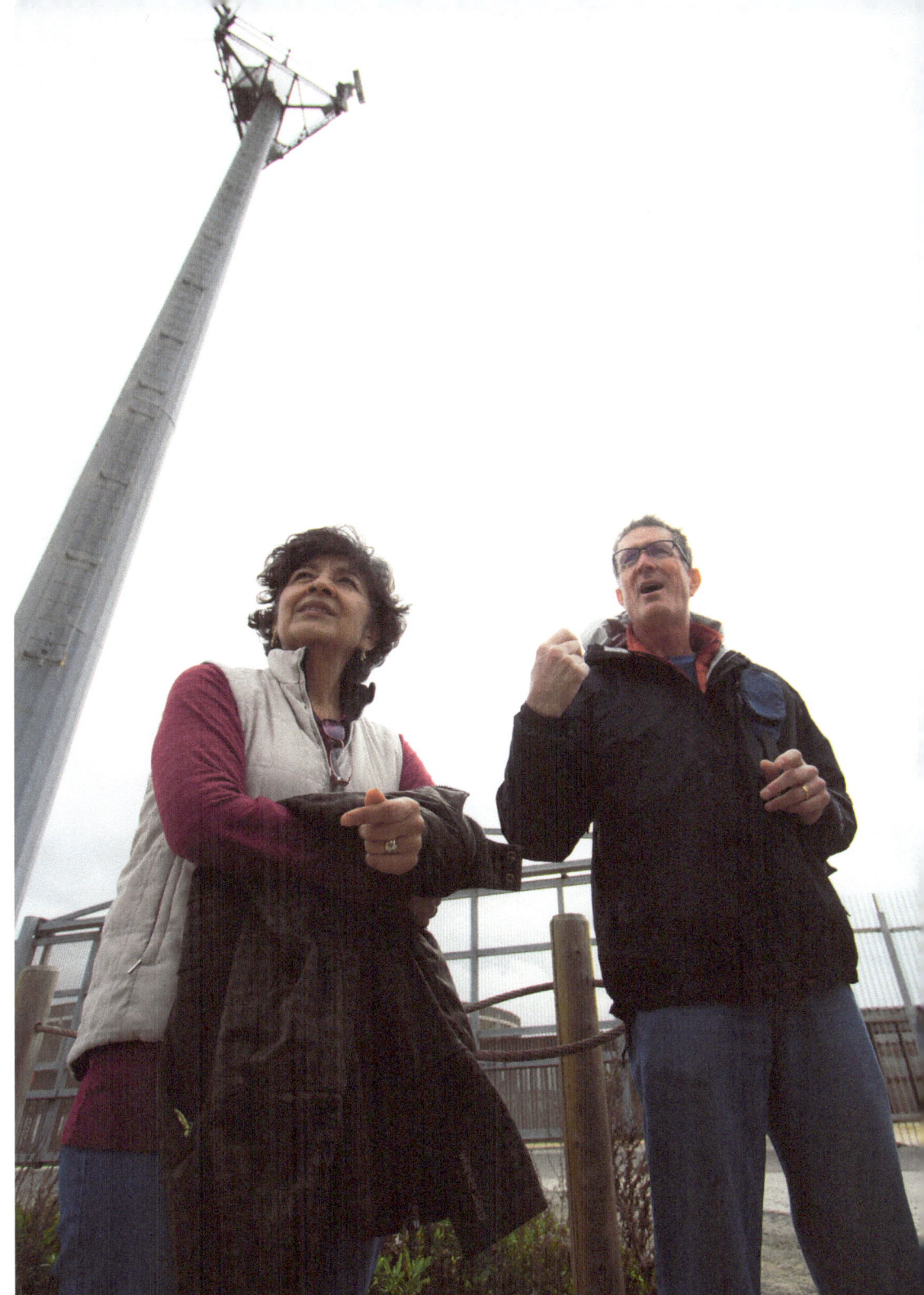

Left: Shaun and Maria Sheahan from Global Immersion Project stand in front of the U.S. border in San Diego. Shaun emphasized the humanity of all parties involved-- both undocumented immigrants and border patrol officers.

Photo by: Alyssa Yee

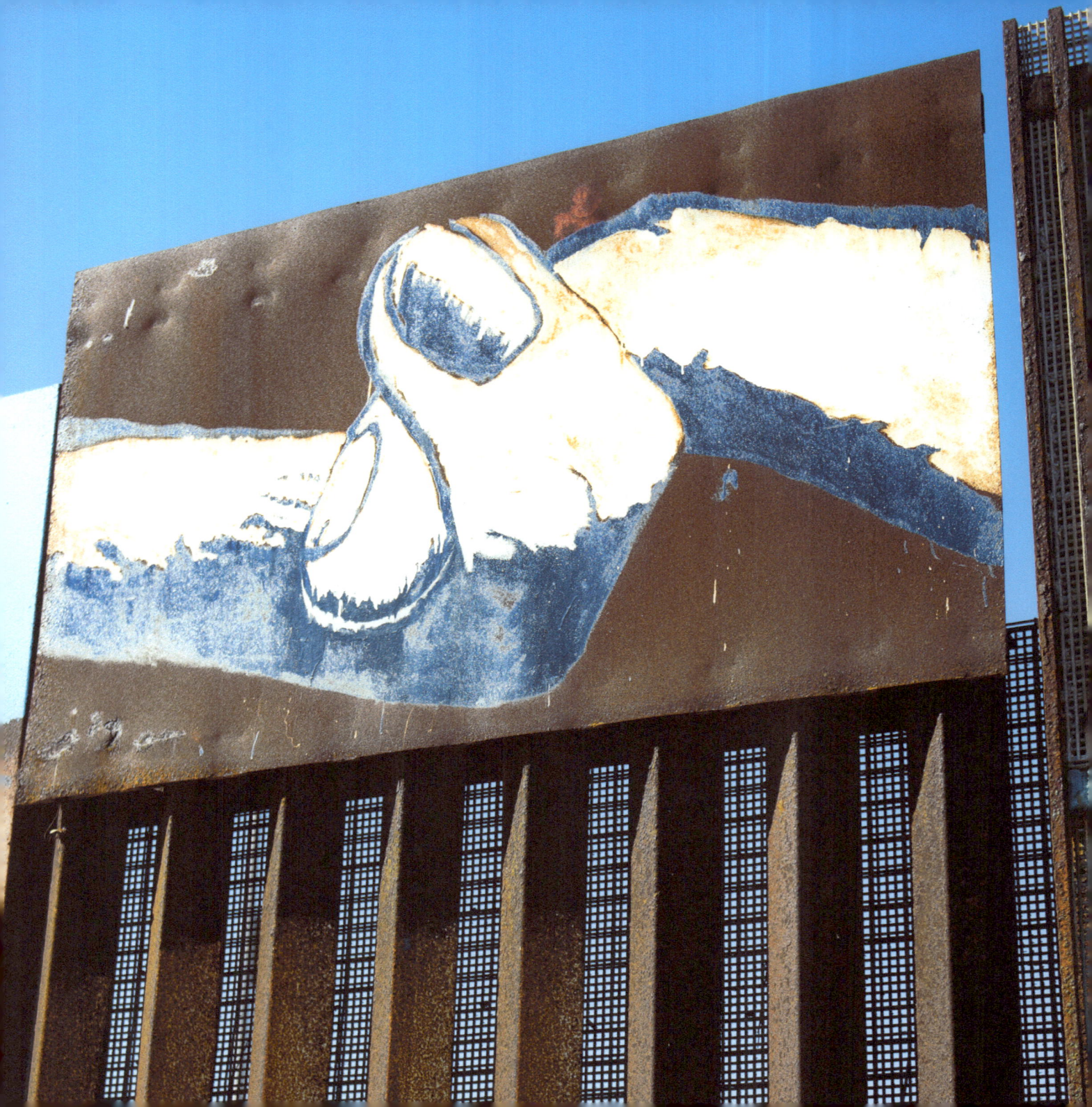

3 Immigration and the Wall

By Jehn Kubiak

Photos taken by Alex Bell and Jenny Oetzell

> " Nearly all Americans have ancestors who braved the oceans – liberty-loving risk takers in search of an ideal – the largest voluntary migrations in recorded history... Immigration is not just a link to America's past; it's also a bridge to America's future. "
>
> George W. Bush

Two different worlds collide in only a pinky's touch through a metal barrier. One world contains a kaleidoscope of colors, hand-painted art, gardens, Scripture, and plenty of penned thoughts. The other remains a blank canvas, completely devoid of color. A 2,000 mile wall of barbed wire, concrete, and steel serves as more than a physical structure separating two nations. It has transformed into a symbolic barrier that divides friends and families, citizens and noncitizens, conservatives and liberals, and even hopefulness from hopelessness. The 2016 Presidential Election and political issues have created contention among many Americans in this nation, including close friends and families. Tensions further flare up as people read headlines about President Donald Trump's latest decisions on their phones or scroll through stories of people who left everything behind in their home country. Some may readily accept those who seek a new beginning, while others live in fear that non-citizens will harm others.

THE FACTS ABOUT THE U.S. IMMIGRANT POPULATION

With such a large immigrant population, a heated debate over illegal immigration has arisen in various areas of the U.S., especially in states along the border region. Around 40 million illegal immigrants reside in the U.S. as a whole and account for 13 percent of the nation's population, according to the Migration Policy Institute. Just under half have gained legal citizenship, and 11.7

million remain unauthorized. They also comprise 18 percent of small business owners and 46 percent work in white collar jobs. In California alone, the population includes 10.68 million immigrants, which make up about 27.3 percent of the population, and 3 million are unauthorized. About 83 percent come from Mexico and Central America, 13 percent from Asia, and the remainder from the Caribbean, South America, Africa, and Europe/ Canada/ Oceania. The majority have lived in the U.S. more than five years, fall between the 25-44 year age range, and are employed in the U.S. workforce.

HISTORY OF THE WALL AND SECURITY IMPROVEMENTS

The U.S. has developed strict security along the border in order to prevent illegal immigration and protect U.S. citizens. The Secure Fence Act of 2006 allowed the Department of Homeland Security to conduct systematic border surveillance through agents and various technologies, including aerial fields, ground-based sensors, satellites, radar coverage, and cameras. The act also includes provisions for physical structure enhancements to prevent unlawful border entry and help U.S. Customs and Border Protection patrol the area. The provisions include additional checkpoints, all-weather access roads, and vehicle barriers. Finally, it defined operational control as prevention of all unlawful entries of people and contraband into the U.S. This act also authorized the construction of new barriers, reinforced fencing, additional roads, lighting, and cameras for all ports of entry. The number of border patrol agents has increased from 11 to 19 thousand after the Secure Fence Act passed in 2006.

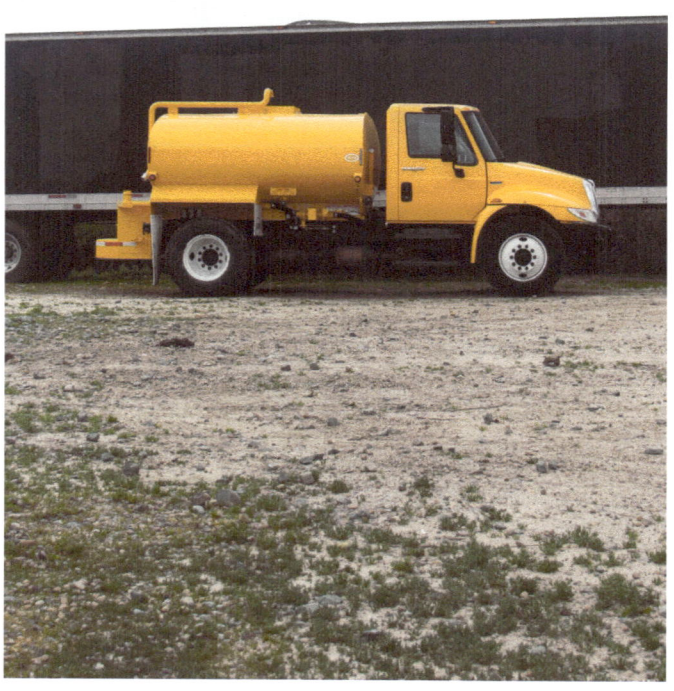

San Diego, California February 17, 2017. A truck lines the pathway to Friendship Park.

Photo by: Alex Bell

Although a border already divides the U.S. and Mexico, Donald Trump called for construction of a new U.S. Mexico border wall as well as an increase in the number of immigrant agents that execute deportations in an executive order issued in January 2017, "Border and Immigration Security Improvements." Furthermore, he asked the government to strip federal funding for sanctuary cities in an additional executive order, "Enhancing Public Safety in the Interior of the U.S." His wall will span about 1,000 miles and Senior Majority Leader Mitch McConnell estimates it will cost $12-$15 billion. The President made the first step to building this wall in February. Since then, the construction project has created division in America. A Pew Research study reports that 62 percent of survey respondents oppose a wall along the entire Mexican border, while 35 percent favor it. About 89 percent of Democrats in the survey oppose the new wall, while 74 percent of Republicans favor it, indicating conflict between the two parties.

Trump's hopes Mexico will pay for the wall, but funding will initially come from U.S. taxpayers. President of Mexico Enrique Pena Nieto did not travel to Washington to meet with President Trump in January due to disagreements regarding who would pay for this wall. His absence further strained the relationship between the U.S. and Mexico, which remains a key trading partner with the U.S. The country trades more than $1 billion worth of goods each day, supplies produce for many American supermarkets and restaurants, and functions as the top export destination for beef, rice, sweeteners, and apples.

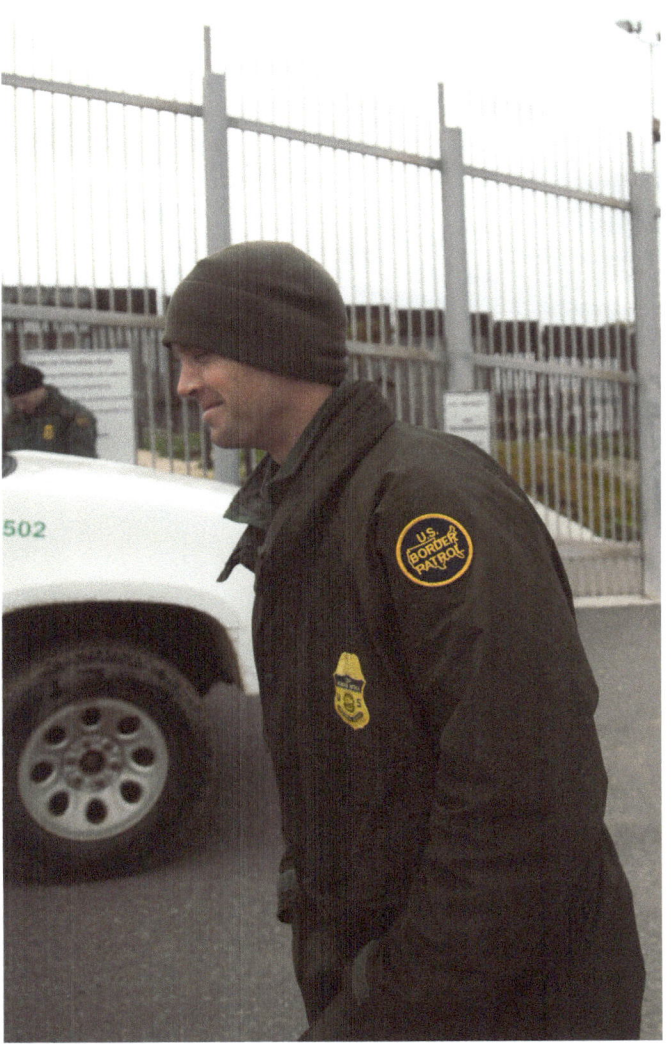

San Diego, California February 17, 2017. A close up of a Border Patrol officer in transition between duties.

Photo by: Alex Bell

Local opposition in California

Opposition to Trump's policies resulted in a national grassroots protest, Day Without Immigrants, that called for immigrants to stay home from work or school, close their business for the day, and refrain from spending at stores. Several businesses in San Francisco, Washington State, Chicago, New York, Los Angeles, and other cities across the U.S. shut their doors. Although a few businesses in Los Angeles remained open, including Northgate Gonzalez Markets, others closed and participated in the protest. Some chose an alternate route and donated all or a portion of their profits to the American Civil Liberties Union or immigrant and refugee rights groups. Taco Maria and Border Grill donated all their profits, while Wilde Wine Bar donated only 20 percent of their revenue. A Taco Maria Facebook post on the day of the protest indicates how the business supports immigrant contributions in America. "Taco María, like so many American Dreams, was built by immigrants and descendants of immigrants. Today, February 16, 2017, we choose to donate 100 percent of profits to the American Civil Liberties Union of Southern California in support of immigrant and civil rights." Hostility also surfaced in Santa Ana, an Orange County city which has become a refuge for immigrants impacted by Trump's executive order on immigration. According to "Unauthorized and Uninsured," undocumented immigrants constitute about 22 percent of Santa Ana residents. Central Santa Ana is also one of the poorest neighborhoods in the county with a poverty rate of about 50 percent for unauthorized immigrants. Many of these immigrants have formed tight-knit communities and have lived in the city for over a

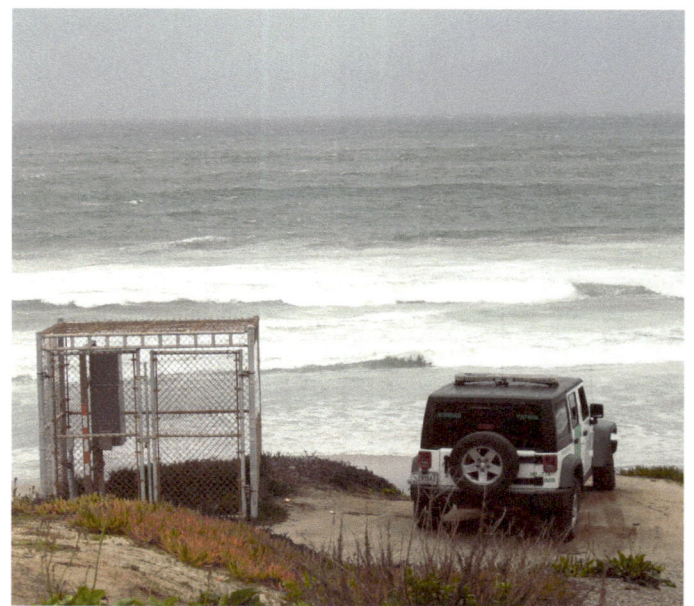

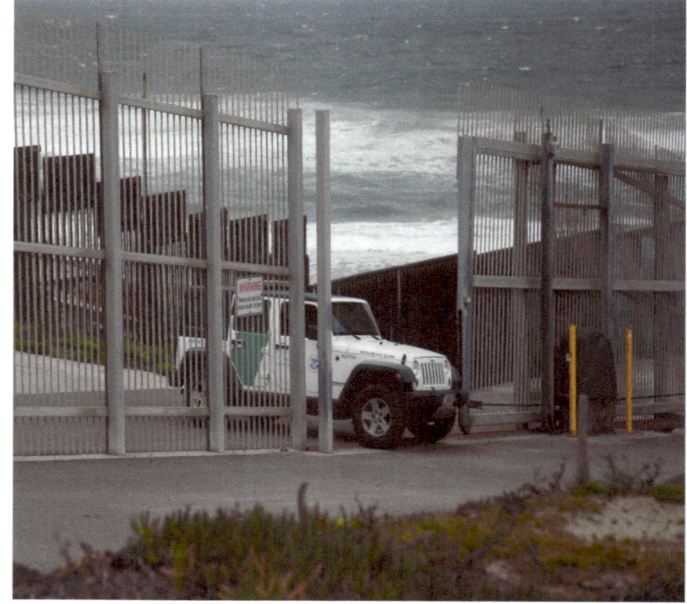

San Diego, California February 17, 2017. The wall opens for a brief moment for a border security Jeep to drive through.

Photos by: Alex Bell

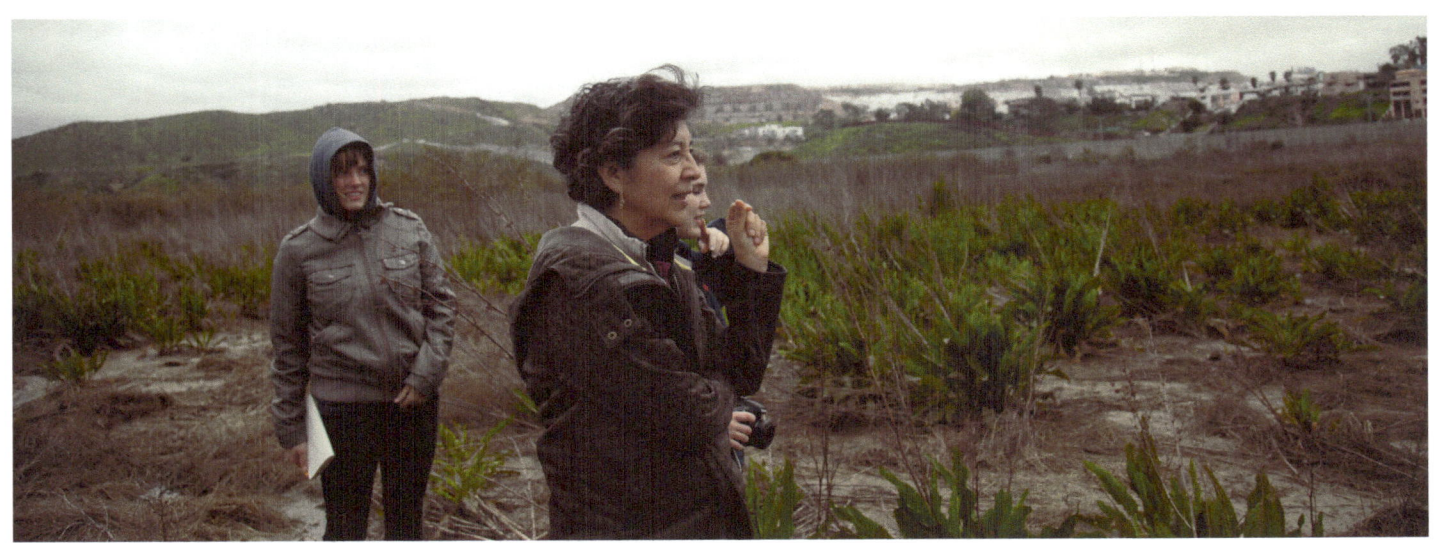

San Diego, California February 17, 2017. Maria and Students cross through a muddy path to make it to Friendship Park.

Photo by: Alex Bell

decade. Approximately 90 percent come from Mexico, while the remaining 10 percent are from Ecuador, El Salvador, Vietnam, and Guatemala. Santa Ana became the first city in Orange County to declare itself a sanctuary city after a city council vote in Dec. 2017. Its identity as a sanctuary city became official on Jan. 18, 2017. Sanctuary cities have laws, ordinances, regulations, policies, or other practices that obstruct immigration enforcement and shield criminals from the U.S. Immigration Customs and Enforcement. Los Angeles, San Bernardino, Santa Ana, and Orange County are all sanctuary counties. Trump's executive orders also spurred immigrant protests in Santa Ana. As a result, Representative Lou Correa organized a Town Hall meeting where he discussed immigrant rights after Trump's executive order halted funding for sanctuary cities. A march outside Santa Ana College followed this

meeting, where people shouted statements like "No ban, no wall, immigration rights for all." Following this Town Hall, the Congressman spoke on the White House floor on Feb.2 and he introduced his first bill, the DACA, Immigrant and Refugee (DIRe) Legal Aid Act. A press release from Correa's website states that the act gives up to $5 million for grant programs for nonprofits that provide immigration legal services to immigrants, refugees and DACA recipients. The bill ensures that immigrants have access to legal resources that help them protect their rights if they are detained with the possibility of deportation. In this speech, he described how the people who gathered exhibited fear about Trump's executive order. "The place was packed with people afraid for their neighbors and afraid for our communities," Correa said. The representative believes Trump challenged the due process

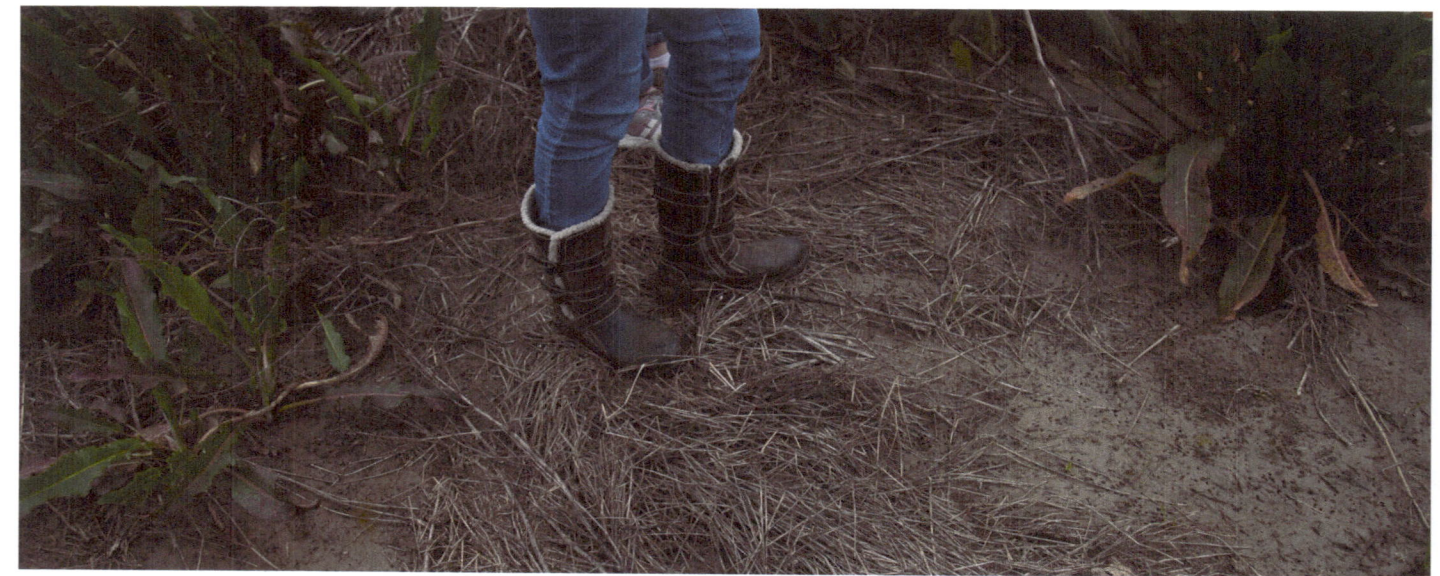

San Diego, California February 17, 2017. Maria and students cross through a muddy path to make it to Friendship Park.

Photo by: Alex Bell

rights the Constitution guarantees for everyone, including DREAMers, immigrants, and refugees. "If we wish to remain a beacon of freedom to the world, we must stand up for immigrants and refugees that look to America as a place of hope," Correa said.

Major issues in the immigration debate

The top 10 major issues in the immigration debate today include: terms used to describe immigrants, amnesty, deportation, the border fence, civilian border patrols, terrorist threats, economic burdens, drivers licenses, border militarization, and state and local law enforcement. Although these are all important issues, amnesty, economics, and environmental impacts have become increasingly prevalent in 2017.

Amnesty

Immigrant amnesty has become a major topic in 1984 after President Ronald Reagan discussed why immigrants who lived in the U.S. for a long time should receive amnesty. The issue became prevalent again in 2014 after President Obama announced the Immigration Accountability Executive Action, which implemented the Deferred Action for Parental Ability (DAPA) program that provides temporary relief from deportation and work authorization for unauthorized parents of U.S. Citizens or Lawful Permanent Residents. The act additionally expanded the Deferred Action for Childhood Arrivals (DACA) policy that provides temporary relief and work authorization for "DREAMers," young people who arrived in the states as children. These grants last for three years and affect around five million immigrants. While some experts note that amnesty could bring economic gain, others believe they must respect the law and should earn their citizenship fairly. The Federation for American Immigration Reform (FAIR) encourages Congress to take up the measures recommended by the U.S. Commission on Immigration Reform (Jordan Commission), the last national commission set up by Congress and chaired by former Congresswoman Barbara Jordan, according to retired diplomat and Federation for American Immigration Reform spokesperson Jack Martin. He explained how the Jordan Commission recommends ending this current practice, where most of the immigration comes from sponsoring earlier immigrants, who then sponsor extended family members. "What the Jordan Commission recommended and what we would recommend is having a system where only the immediate family, spouse, minor children are able to come with an immigrant and the immigrant would no longer be able to sponsor brothers and sisters and adult children and parents," Martin said. President Trump desires to remove anyone who threatens public safety from the U.S., but he softened his stance on amnesty during a news conference on Feb. 16. When the press asked Trump if

Tijuana, Mexico March 24, 2017. The butterfly wall intends to allow butterflies to pass through the border with out harm.

Photo by: Jenny Oetzell

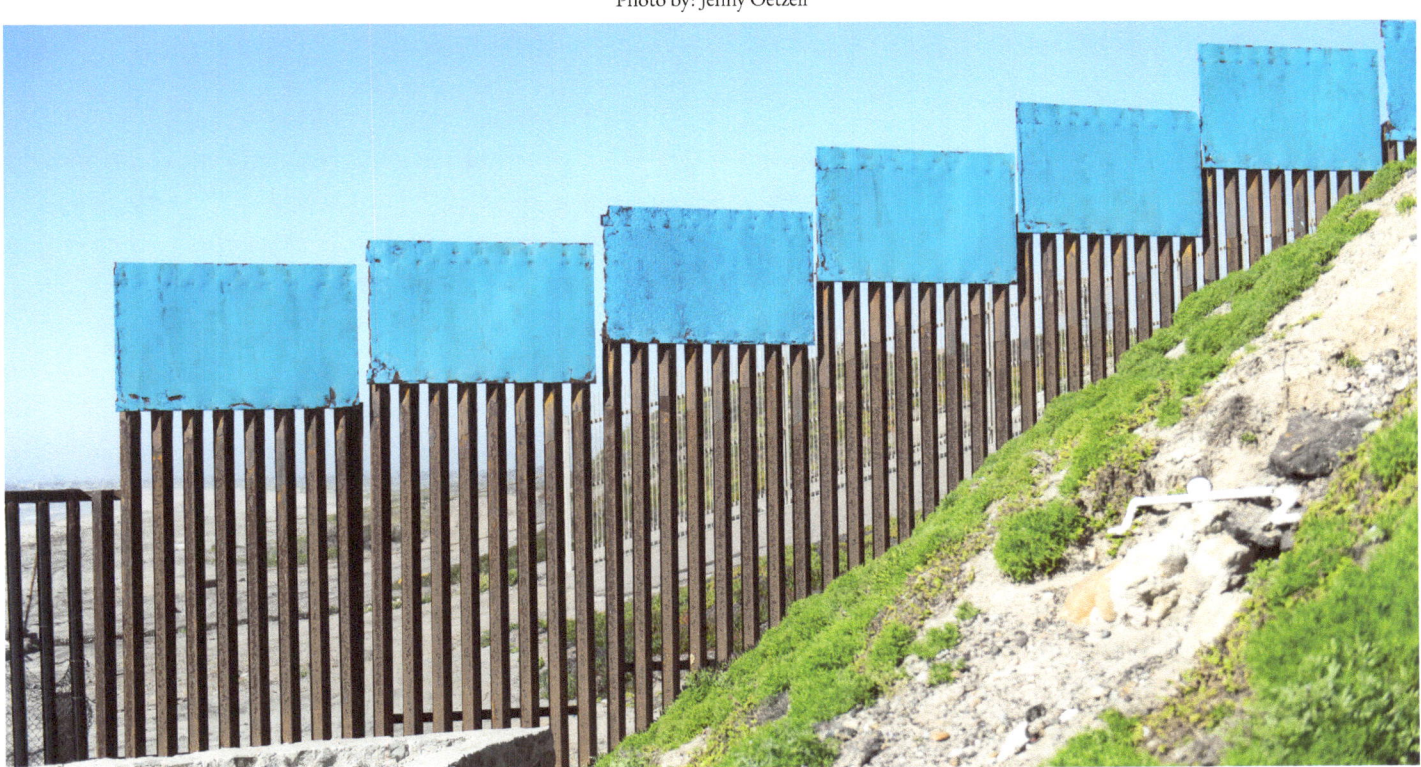

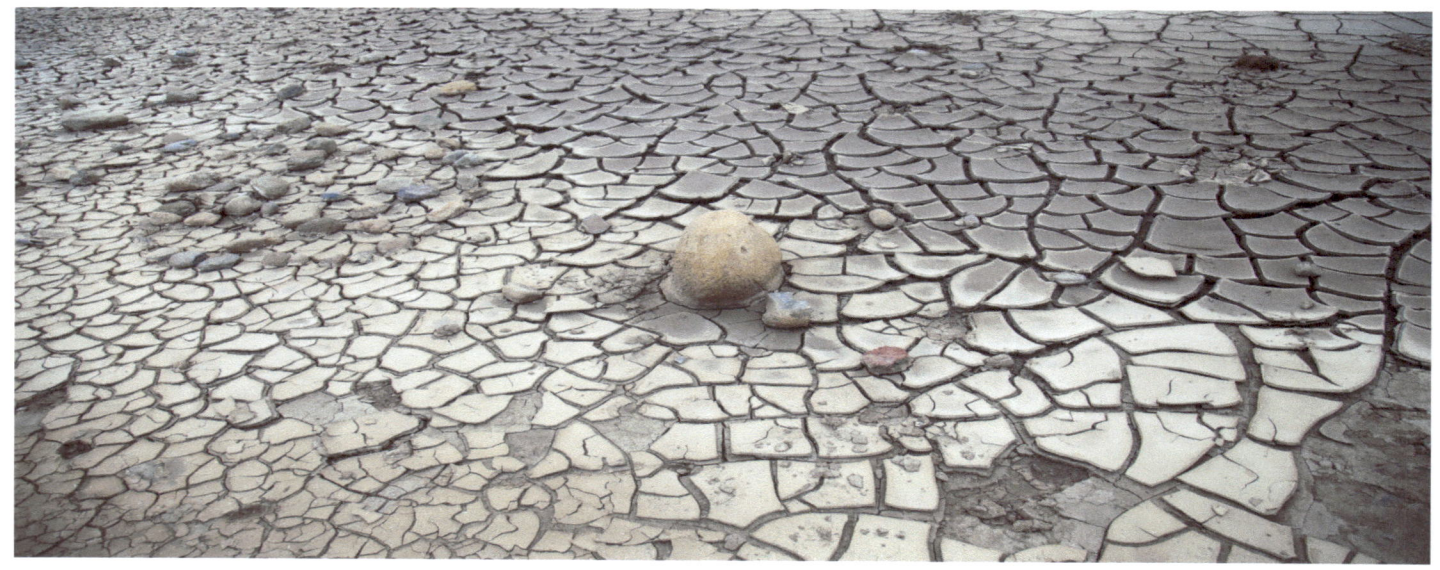

San Diego, California February 17, 2017. The ground on the path to Friendship Park.

Photo by: Alex Bell

he would continue DACA, he said amnesty remains a difficult issue because current amnesty policies can protect dangerous people but affect young children at the same time. "In many cases, not in all cases. And some of the cases, having DACA and they're gang members and they're drug dealers, too. But you have some absolutely, incredible kids, I would say mostly. They were brought here in such a way—it's a very—it's a very, very tough subject," Trump stated.

Economic impacts of immigration

Economic impacts from immigration remain yet another of several contentious issues in America. Tight border security creates long wait times that heavily impact the economy because goods come across the border primarily by trucks and rail. Due to these wait times, companies invest lots of money to ensure that criminals do not intercept their products and they must hold larger inventories. Consumers also pay more for a lower selection of goods, perishable products are put at risk, and both the U.S. and Mexico face higher transportation costs. Immigration holds other costs for U.S. taxpayers. A FAIR USA study reports illegal immigration costs U.S. taxpayers $113 billion a year between the federal, state, and local levels. In addition, the state and local governments pay the majority of these costs. The largest expense includes education for children at $52 million. Furthermore, most illegal immigrants do not pay income taxes. California alone spends about $21 million on illegal immigrants, yet it faced a budget deficit of $14.4 billion between 2010-2011. Amnesty exacerbates the issue, allowing eligibility for programs that many immigrants were previously ineligible for. Conventional belief holds that immigrants take over many jobs. However, a new study from the National Academies of Science, Engineering and Medicine finds that they do not take the majority of jobs, but that many low-skilled, native-born Americans are dropping out of the workforce. The North American Free Trade Agreement (NAFTA) is a trade agreement between the U.S., Mexico, and Canada that President Bill Clinton implemented Jan. 1994, which established a free trade zone and eliminated most tariffs on products the three countries traded. This agreement has become another heavily contentious economic issue in the debate over free trade, causing President Trump to renegotiate the agreement. This further strained tensions between the U.S. and Mexico because NAFTA allows U.S. companies to send materials to Mexico for assembly and eliminates duties on finished goods coming back across the border. The agreement also liberalized trade in agriculture, textiles, and automobile manufacturing. Due to NAFTA, regional trade and cross-border investment between all three countries grew significantly. This agreement has benefitted a Mexican firm, Mabe, which eventually became a leading supplier of household appliances for the U.S. and Canada. The firm and General Electric in the U.S. created a joint venture, causing GE to become a lead gas supplier. Since Mabe's business expanded in North America, they also consolidated operations with a Canadian company, Camco. As a result, these three companies form a strong alliance. Although NAFTA was designed to decrease immigration into the U.S. by raising income and employment in Mexico, the resulting competition with agricultural markets in the U.S. caused many immigrants to leave their home country. Workers in America received large subsidies and could export goods at a lower price. In turn, the lower prices and increased imports from the U.S. caused many farmers to lose their jobs, especially in the corn and meat industries. The trade agreement also prohibited price supports, which made it difficult for farmers to sell their crops and forced them to seek work in the U.S. Sean Sheahan from the Global Immersion Project explained how workers rushed for the border about five years after NAFTA because people in the agricultural industry could not survive in Mexico. "They came over because so many lost their jobs and livelihood. Big corporations took over the whole fields and growing things, and that took the family farms out," Sean Sheahan said. "Little stores—moms and pops—were taken, replaced by Walmarts, by you name it. They had no choice—they didn't know what to do. They came up and they started cropping. " Sean Sheahan also explained how many people come to the U.S. today because they flee violent gangs or political parties, crime, or because they hope to provide a better future for their family. However, several of these immigrants receive deportations that split families apart. "Some of the people we know very well, they're getting hurt, they're getting devastated. Families torn apart at the threat of being deported. I think of the DACA people and the US vets from the war who have gotten deported, who have served and done well, " Sean Sheahan said. "Those are the ones that break my heart most, the second is when families get split apart. That's unimaginably common." Undocumented immigrants are often seen as only criminals due to certain types of crime associated with them, such as drug and gang crimes, smuggling, trafficking, and identity theft. However, Maria Sheahan believes these harmful people, that border patrol officers usually target, make up only a minority of immigrants crossing the border and that the majority seek a brighter future in another country. "Everybody wants to fight crime, but in those cases, it feels like everyone's thrown into that category of crime. When a person that crosses the border without documents –– that's a misdemeanor," Maria Sheahan said. "We don't call a person who runs a stop sign a criminal and yet we call a person who crosses the border a criminal."

Environmental impacts

Tijuana's sewage system does not operate properly, so residents often dig tunnels under the street and make connections to the water mains. Sewage still leaks from houses, through the canyon walls, and down its sides, covering the area with fecal dust and dried urine that carries many diseases. In addition, the large manufacturing industry and increased population have generated several negative environmental problems, according to the Environmental Protection Agency. These negative problems include clean water supply, air pollution, land contamination, environmental health, environment-threatening incidents and response, and industrial environmental stewardship. In light of these circumstances, the EPA has built upon Border 2012 and introduced Border 2020 with updated objectives. According to Martin, the rapid population increase in the U.S. from immigration has created other environmental concerns, such as depletion of natural resources that his organization currently addresses. "The reason we're [FAIR] so focused on the size of the population is because the size of the population impacts the environment in terms of natural resources, such as wilderness areas, as well as agricultural production and non-renewable resources such as petroleum, other fossil fuels, other scarce metals," Martin said. "Things of that nature and in particular with regard to water shortage. It's increasingly becoming a problem."

Facing a greater reality

Despite various stances on immigration, American citizens face the reality that people from another nation live among them. This has created debate across both sides of the aisle, yet several citizens remain uncertain where they stand on the issue. Despite personal views, it is impossible to ignore the issue's significance, so new legislation has arisen under the Obama and Trump administrations. The government continues expanding upon immigration policies and security measures today as more immigrants come across the border and various organizations work together to protect American citizens or provide legal assistance. A new wall may further increase tensions within the nation and with other countries, leading to increased economic, political, and environmental aftereffects.

Endnotes

1. "Frequently Requested Statistics on Immigrants and Immigration in the United States," Migrationpolicy. org, March 21, 2017, , accessed March 30, 2017, http:// www.migrationpolicy.org/article/frequently-requested-statistics-immigrants-and-immigration-united-states.

2. "Profile of the Unauthorized Population - CA," Migrationpolicy.org, December 01, 2016, , accessed March 30, 2017, http://www.migrationpolicy.org/data/ unauthorized-immigrant-population/state/CA.

3. King, Peter. "H.R.6061 - 109th Congress (2005-2006): Secure Fence Act of 2006." Congress.gov. October 26, 2006. Accessed March 30, 2017. https://www. congress.gov/bill/109th-congress/house-bill/6061.

4. Peter King, "H.R.6061 - 109th Congress (2005-2006): Secure Fence Act of 2006," Congress.gov, October 26, 2006, , accessed March 30, 2017, https://www. congress.gov/bill/109th-congress/house-bill/6061.

5. Office of the Press Secretary, "Executive Order: Border Security and Immigration Enforcement Improvements," The White House, February 23, 2017, , accessed March 30, 2017, https://www.whitehouse.gov/the-press-office/2017/01/25/executive-order-border-security-and-immigration-enforcement-improvements.

6. Rob Suls, "Most Americans continue to oppose U.S. border wall, doubt Mexico would pay for it," Pew Research Center, February 24, 2017, , accessed March 30, 2017, http://www.pewresearch.org/fact-tank/2017/02/24/most-americans-continue-to-oppose-u-s-border-wall-doubt-mexico-would-pay-for-it/.

7. Robbins, Liz, and Annie Correal. "On a 'Day Without Immigrants,' Workers Show Their Presence by Staying Home." The New York Times. February 16, 2017. Accessed March 30, 2017. https://www.nytimes.com/2017/02/16/ nyregion/day-without-immigrants-boycott-trump-policy.html.

8. Marcelli, Enricoo A. "Unauthorized and Uninsured: Building Healthy Communities in California > Center for the Study of Immigrant Integration (CSII) at USC > USC Dana and David Dornsife College of Letters, Arts and Sciences." Unauthorized and Uninsured: Building Healthy Communities in California > Center for the Study of Immigrant Integration (CSII) at USC > USC Dana and David Dornsife College of Letters, Arts and Sciences. February 11, 2015. Accessed March 30, 2017. https://dornsife.usc.edu/csii/unauthorized-and-uninsured.

9. Carcamo, Cindy. "Santa Ana declares itself a sanctuary city in defiance of Trump." Los Angeles Times. December 7, 2016. Accessed March 30, 2017. http://www.latimes.com/local/ california/la-me-santa-ana-sanctuary-city-20161206-story.html.

10. "Sanctuary Cities | Center for Immigration Studies." Sanctuary Cities | Center for Immigration Studies. Accessed March 30, 2017. http://cis.org/Sanctuary-Cities.

11. "Map: Sanctuary Cities, Counties, and States." Center for Immigration Studies. July 07, 2015. Accessed March 30, 2017. http://cis.org/Sanctuary-Cities-Map.

12. Kwong, Jessica, and Deepa Bharath. "Orange County locals fear, support Trump's immigration orders." The Orange County Register. January 27, 2017. Accessed March 30, 2017. http://www.ocregister.com/articles/ refugees-742446-immigration-country.html.

13. "U.S. House Debates Bills to Disapprove Federal Regulations." C-SPAN.org. Accessed April 08, 2017. https://www.c-span.org/video/?423409-101%2Fus-house-debates-bills-disapprove-federal-regulations.

14. "Rep. Correa introduces bill to fund legal services for immigrants, refugees, and dreamers." Congressman J. Luis Correa. March 08, 2017. Accessed April 08, 2017. https:// correa.house.gov/media/press-releases/rep-correa-introduces-bill-fund-legal-services-immigrants-refugees-and-dreamers.

15. "Top 10 Pros & Cons - Illegal Immigration - ProCon. org." What are the solutions to illegal immigration in America? Accessed March 30, 2017. http://immigration. procon.org/view.resource.php?resourceID=000842#4.

16. Fuller, Jaime. "The history of 'amnesty' in the immigration debate." The Washington Post. November 21, 2014. Accessed March 30, 2017. https://www.washingtonpost.com/news/ the-fix/wp/2014/11/21/when-did-amnesty-eat-up-the- entire-immigration-debate/?utm_term=.daff2b4a07c0.

17. "US Immigration Amnesty." Immigration | Amnesty in USA - History And Facts. Accessed April 07, 2017. https://www.usamnesty.org/.

18. "Full transcript: President Donald Trump's news conference." CNN. February 17, 2017. Accessed April 07, 2017. http://www.cnn.com/2017/02/16/politics/ donald-trump-news-conference-transcript/.

19. Martin, Jack, and Eric A. Rurak. "The Fiscal Burden of Illegal Immigration on United States Taxpayers." FAIR USA. July 2010. Accessed April 7, 2017. http://www.fairus. org/DocServer/research-pub/USCostStudy_2013upd.pdf.

20. "New Report Assesses the Economic and Fiscal Consequences of Immigration." National Academies Web Server www8.nationalacademies.org. Accessed April 07, 2017. http://www8.nationalacademies.org/ onpinews/newsitem.aspx?RecordID=23550.

21. Mcbride, James, and Mohammed Aly Sergie. "NAFTA's Economic Impact." Council on Foreign Relations. Accessed April 07, 2017. http://www. cfr.org/trade/naftas-economic-impact/p15790.

22. Foreign Affairs and International Trade Canada, and Nafta. "North American Free Trade Agreement." Success Stories | NAFTANow.org. April 01, 2008. Accessed March 30, 2017. http://www.naftanow.org/success/mexico_en.asp.

23. Business Environmental Program. "U.S. – Mexico Border." WSPPN. Accessed March 30, 2017. http:// wsppn.org/resources/u-s-mexico-border/.

24. "What is Border 2020?" EPA. October 24, 2016. Accessed April 07, 2017. https://www. epa.gov/border2020/what-border-2020.

10% of the population of Los Angeles County are illegal immigrants

Out of **3.14** million people in Orange County, roughly **270,000** are undocumented immigrants

Out of **3.211** million people in San Diego County, roughly **207,000** are undocumented immigrants

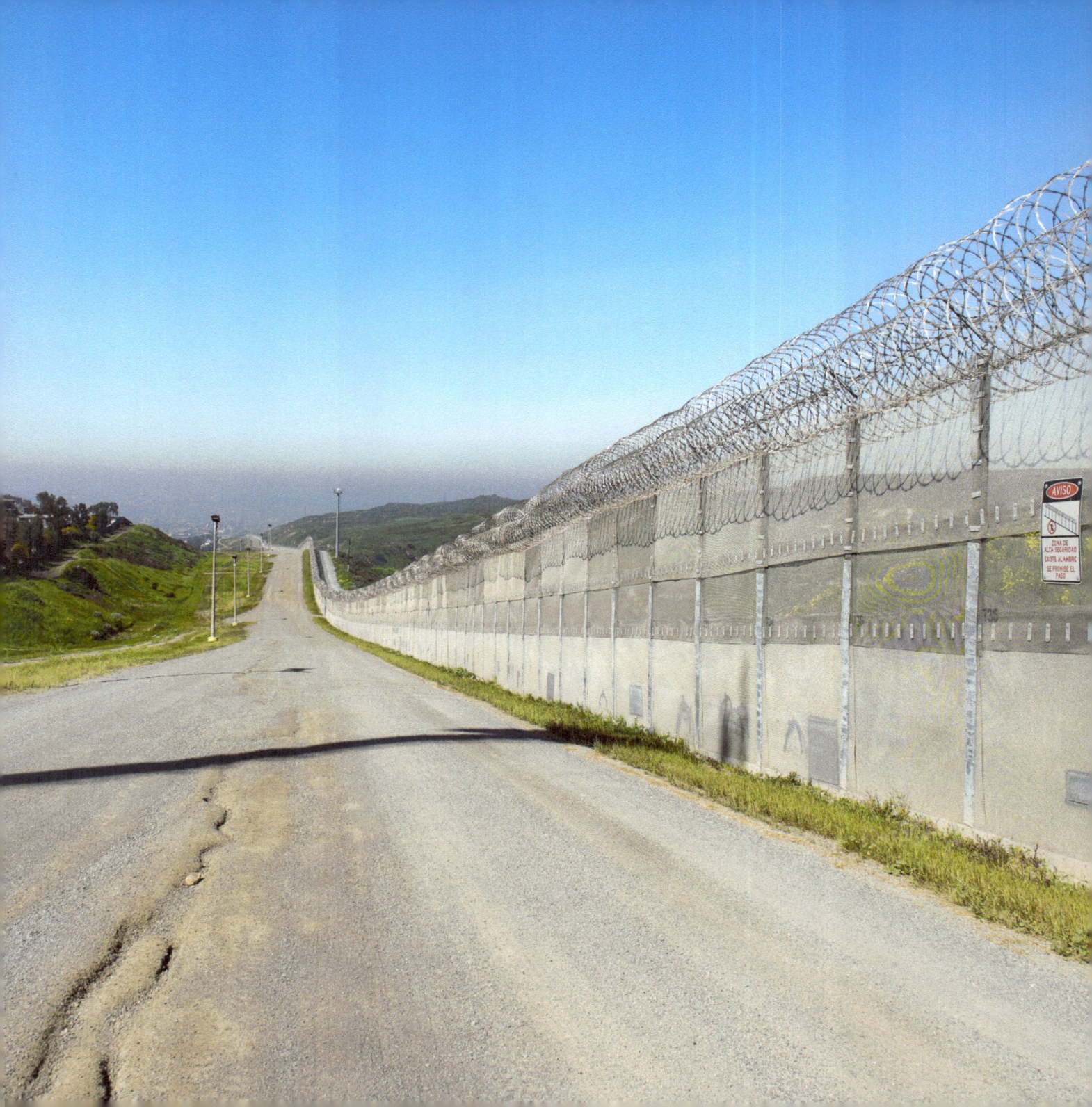

4 ICE and Border Enforcement

By Dayna Bayne and Jennifer Oetzell

Graphics by Dayna Bayne and Anna Warner

" My Border Patrol academy class graduated on September 11, 2001. The attacks on the Twin Towers were at the forefront of my mind as I took the oath of office and vowed to protect the United States '...against all enemies, foreign and domestic.' "

Jose Hernandez

As we came over the top of the hill, I was confronted with a perfect view of the United States–Mexico border. On one side, I saw the transit city of Tijuana, Mexico, and on the other, I saw the immigrant town of San Diego, California. The two were divided on the international border with a primary and secondary border wall built by the U.S Border Patrol agency; the disparity between the two was large.

The Tijuana side was populated with colorful houses crammed together along the hillsides with streets and highways paved right up to the border busy with cars and taxis. The city was populated with pedestrians and people trying to sell souvenirs or local foods like churros and tacos. On the San Diego side there was land, lots and lots of land. There were green hills and plains from the recent rains, a distant hazy skyline from the pollution, a water treatment plant, and the border fences with their accompanying all weather road. Most of the immediate land by the San Diego border is federal land, open to the public but by no means inviting them to come and settle. From the Pacific Ocean, all along the border, there is Border Field State Park, Tijuana River National Estuarine Research Reserve, International Park, Goat Canyon, Tijuana River County Open Space Preserve, and Smuggler Gulch before one would meet the first border checkpoint at San Ysidro. The line drawn by the U.S border patrol's secondary wall was glaring at me, a foreigner, but it was just part of the life for those in Tijuana.

The development of the border happened slowly over time and continues to be developed as the need for securing it continues to change. In 1991, the primary wall was created out of leftover landing strips from the Vietnam war with its main purpose to deter cars and vehicles from crossing the border. (That wall is still there but now has slits cut out at the bottom of the landing pads so that officers can see what activity is happening on the other side. This need grew as assaults on border officers increased. People on the Tijuana side would throw brick sized, or bigger, rocks at the officers as they walked or drove by.) However, it was not until 9/11 that the border received a greater amount of attention. When the tragedy occurred in New York City and Washington, D.C., the government shifted their attention towards securing the borders of the United States. According to the Border Patrol history they stated that "Interest and funding for border security spiked and funding requests and enforcement proposals were reconsidered as lawmakers began to reassess how our nation's borders must be monitored and protected." And so the infrastructure for the secondary wall started with its main purpose to now deter the crossing of pedestrians and vehicles. This was more or less completed in 2010 in the San Diego sector, 1 of 20 sectors along the U.S–Mexico border.

"Since 1924, [when the agency was officially established] Border Patrol has grown from a handful of mounted agents patrolling desolate areas along U.S. borders to today's dynamic work force of over 24,000 agents."

—U.S Customs and Border Protection, Border Patrol History

I got to spend the day with Agent Jose Hernandez and Agent Tekae Michael. They gave me a tour along the physical border whilst explaining what they do and what their job looks like on the California border. Agent Hernandez is 45 years old and has been married over 20 years, together they have two children. He grew up along the southwest border residing in California, Arizona, Texas, and Mexico where he spent school years at different schools in each of these states. He attended a local junior college in the San Diego area where he earned his Associate's Degree and went into sales. He does not plan on retiring any time soon but the company mandates individuals to retire at 57 years of age. Hernandez says, "This career is indeed physically taxing, but I love what I do. I believe in our mission and our purpose and I will probably do it as long as I can." Once he retires he plans on finding a career just keep busy. Agent Hernandez has had over 15 years of service with the U.S. Border Patrol and has worked with their Public Affairs Office, Critical Incident Investigative Team, and the All-Terrain vehicles specialty group. Agent Michael was a teacher before she started to work as a Border Patrol agent nine years ago.

Below is a Q&A conducted with Agent Hernandez.

WHAT DOES YOUR TYPICAL DAY LOOK LIKE?

I am a Border Patrol agent. The U.S. Border Patrol (USBP) is responsible for patrolling the borders in between the ports of entry into the U.S. Typically, we are out in the fields, mountains, and valleys; this includes areas along rivers, lakes and the coastline.

The typical day varies depending upon your assignment in USBP. For the typical line agent who patrols along the

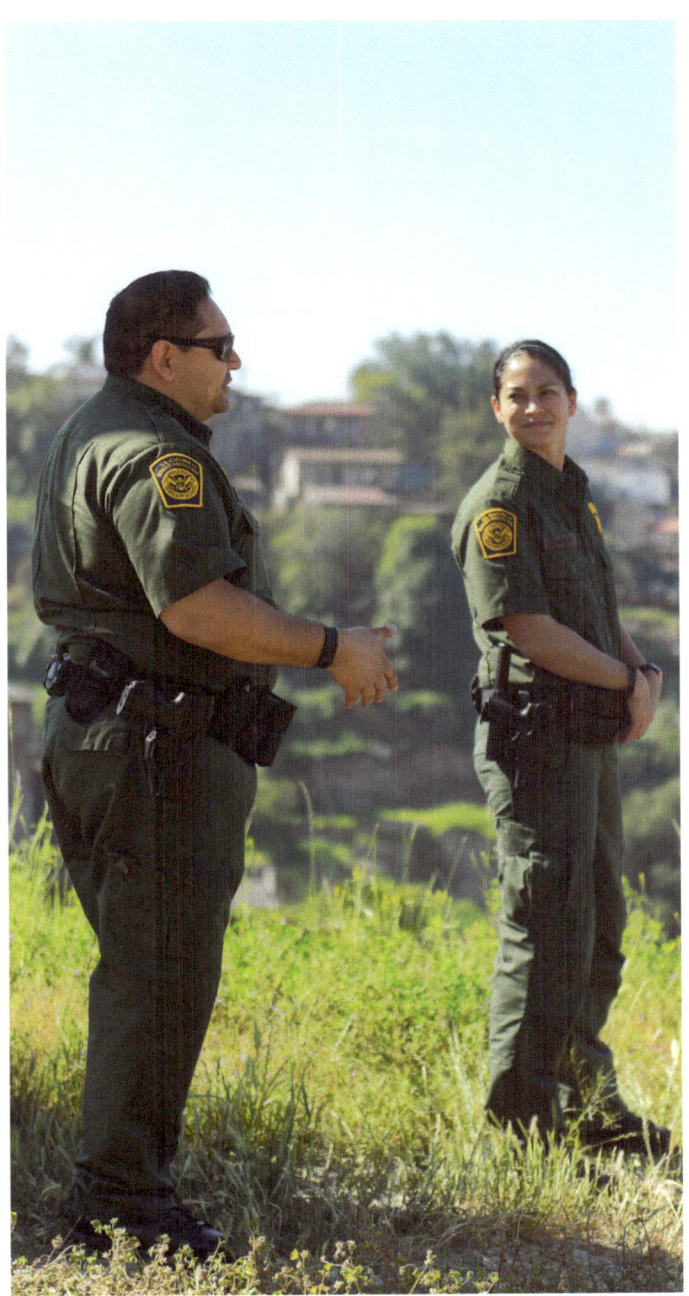

Agents Jose Hernandez and Tekae Michael stand between
the Mexican and U.S. fences along the border.

border, the day starts with a briefing on the current threat assessment. They are assigned to their vehicle and equipment and then set out to patrol the border. Typically, they will drive to their assigned area and begin to search roads near the border area to look for any indication (we refer to it as "sign," i.e., footprints or other indicators of people crossing). Agents will also respond to the activation of seismic intrusion devices (sensors) strategically located through the area of operations and determine what caused the activation. It can be caused by people, animals or vehicles. If the activation was caused by people, the agent will then track the sign to find who caused the activation. At the end of the day, they return to their stations, turn in their equipment and go home.

WHAT RESOURCES DO AGENTS HAVE ACCESS TO?

We have different types of resources. We carry items on our gun belt. Typically, agents will carry their issued sidearm (Heckler & Koch P2000, .40 caliber), a magazine pouch (carrying two extras magazines of ammunition), a handcuff case, a collapsible straight baton (CSB), OC spray (oleo-capsicum spray, commonly referred to as pepper spray) and a flashlight. Agents will also have a Kevlar body armor (ballistic vest).

We mostly use trucks and sport-utility vehicles. We have scope trucks (trucks fitted with daytime and night-vision cameras) and variety of less-lethal weapons beyond the OC spray and CSB. We have a pepper-ball launching system (PLS), which is similar to a paintball gun but fires pellets filled with pepper-spray. We also use an FN-303, which fires a projectile (similar to bean bags) intended to disable, not to kill. We have night-vision goggles, M4 semi-automatic rifles and shotguns.

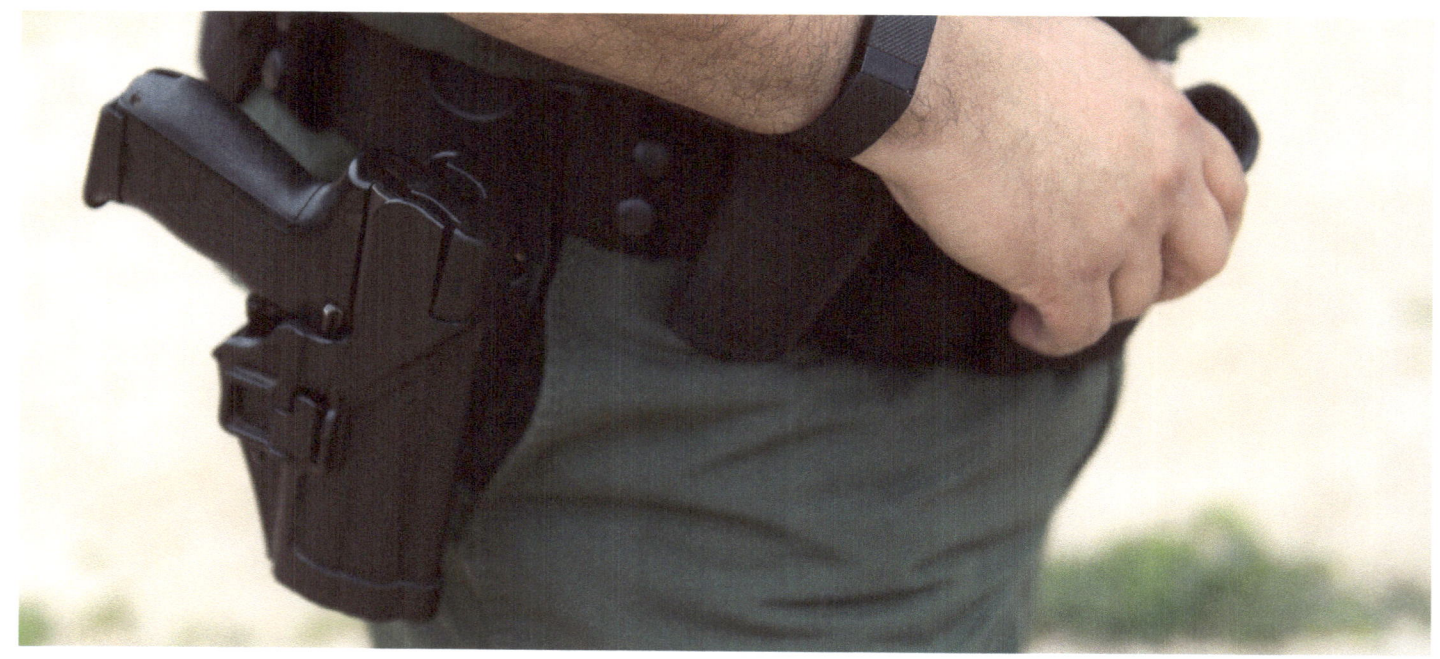

Angent Jose Hernandez grasps his gun belt, which holds the sidearms they are required to carry.

In the San Diego area, we are also supported by infrastructure designed to assist us in detecting and apprehending illegal entries. There is a primary fence, approximately 6-8 feet tall, designed to prevent vehicles from driving illegally across the border. There is a secondary fence, approximately 15-18 feet tall, designed to prevent pedestrians from crossing. We have all-weather roads, stadium lighting, a remote video surveillance system, and sensors.

The officers also explained that with all these weapons they have to be trained and certified to carry them on their gun belt. The training includes having the weapon used against them so that they can understand what it feels like. Agent Hernandez after having the OC spray sprayed on his face prefers not to carry that spray on his gun belt. Both

agents Hernandez and Michael decided against using a Taser as they do not want to go through the training as it meant being tased.

How often is there a crossing/ how many do you get in a day?

In the San Diego Sector, we apprehend approximately 95 people a day attempting to enter the U.S. illegally.
Hernandez and Michael later expressed that they used to apprehend on average 300 or more people per single 8-hour shift. When I asked them why the significant change they mentioned three things:

The first was how the Cartel and other drug gangs now control the border turf and routes coming north. He explained that in the past, about a decade ago, undocumented persons from Mexico might cross back and forth a couple times a year depending on the holidays and family events. For those individuals, they knew how to cross the border independently and thus could do it with almost no financial cost or use of coyotes. (Coyotes are a group of paid human smugglers that facilitate willing individuals in crossing international borders.) Now, however, even if crossing the border independently one has to pay a fee to the Cartel or other drug gang in order to cross 'their turf.' This has in turn reduced the amount of crossing undocumented immigrants attempt to make back and forth.

Secondly, was how the murder of Agent Robert Rosas on July 23rd, 2009 just East of San Diego affected the number of crossings. While on duty the officer responded to some suspicious activity and called for backup. It ended with the officer being shot a total of eight times, with four shots to the head, three to the torso and once in the neck after a robbery had gone wrong. When the news about the murder had spread border crossings drastically slowed down. Hernandez explained that the amount of activity since from undocumented immigrants trying to cross has never bounced back.

And thirdly, Hernandez commented on the overall increase in proper infrastructure, technology and resources and manpower at the San Diego sector. It is one of the better developed sectors when compared to the Arizona and Texas sectors.

HOW MANY PEOPLE WOULD YOU SAY MAKE IT ACROSS/WHAT IS THE PROBABILITY IN MAKING IT ACROSS THE BORDER WITHOUT BEING CAUGHT?

This question is a little more difficult to answer. There are a number of people who make it across the border that go undetected. Of the ones that are detected, we (in San Diego Sector) have an effectiveness of approximately 90%. Effectiveness takes into consideration how many we apprehended, how many got away, and how many were deterred (those who attempt to cross and turn around for whatever reason). With respect to those who are undetected, this is an unknowable quantity.

The Pew Research Center, in their article, 5 Facts about illegal immigration in the U.S. published on November 3rd, 2016, estimated that Mexicans made up 52% (5.8 million) of the 11.1 million unauthorized immigrants living in the United States (the greatest number recorded being 2009 was 6.4 million unauthorized immigrants living in the United States). However, while the number of unauthorized Mexican immigrants living in the United States decreasing there is an increase of illegal immigrants coming from different nationalities. Border Patrol uses the term otoms (other than Mexicans) when referencing these people. Between 2009 and 2014 the increase of otoms jumped by 325,000. Thus, the estimated amount of otoms living illegally in the United States in 2014 is 5.3 million.

Agent Hernandez illustrated this with an example from the 2012–2013 fiscal year when the percentage of otoms caught entering in the U.S. illegally increased by 55%. The number of illegal immigrants apprehended from China in 2014 was five, in 2015 they apprehended 54, and in 2016 they apprehended 881. Overall there are 144 different countries recorded.

What happens when you guys catch someone?

"When someone is apprehended, they are searched (for officer safety) and transported to a Border Patrol station for processing. They are fingerprinted and photographed. Their biographical information is entered into a database. Their information is searched through multiple national and international databases to search for prior previous arrests and convictions (if any). If no criminal history is found, they can be charged criminally, turned over to another agency or simply processed as an expedited removal and barred from re-entry for five years (on the first offense) [before] returned to their home country. This process can take as little as 24 hours or many days, depending upon their country of citizenship. Mexican nationals are returned more quickly due to its proximity. Those who are otoms take longer depending upon how long it takes to acquire travel documents for that individual."

How do these people typically attempt to cross?

Most people crossing the border illegally will do so on foot somewhere in between the ports of entry. They will use many methods (across mountains, swimming across rivers, etc.). They will go over, through or under fences. Many also cross through the ports of entry as well. Methods are only limited by your imagination and creativity. I've seen people smuggled in gas tanks, under seats of vehicles, in the seats of vehicles, engine compartment and even in dashboards.

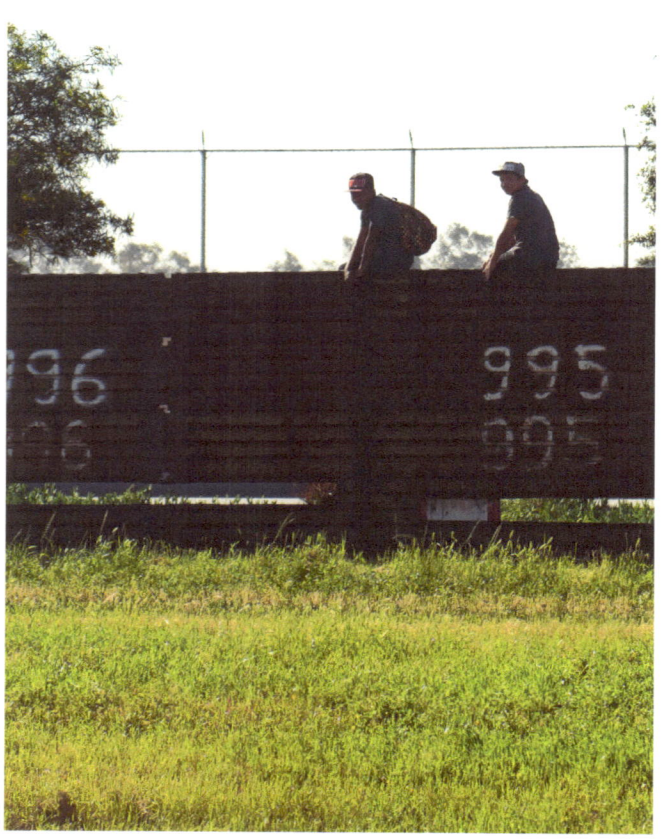

Two young Mexican men sit on top of the Mexican border fence outside the Tijuana International Airport. Each metal panel is numbered to help the U.S. Border Patrol authorities quickly locate each area.

What happens when you apprehend an individual crossing the border illegally?

When someone is apprehended, they are searched (for officer safety) and transported to a Border Patrol station for processing. They are fingerprinted, photographed and their biographical information is entered into a database. Their information is searched through multiple national and international databases to search for prior previous arrests and convictions (if any). About 17% of apprehended aliens attempting to cross the border have a criminal record. If no criminal history is found, they can be charged criminally, turned over to another agency or simply processed as an expedited removal and barred from re-entry for five years (on the first offense) [before] returned to their home country. This process can take as little as 24 hours or many days depending upon their country of citizenship. Mexican nationals are returned more quickly due to its proximity. Those who are otoms take longer depending on how long it takes to acquire travel documents for that individual.

Agent Jose Hernandez stands in front of a poster highlighting the exciting aspects of a Border Patrol Agent's job.

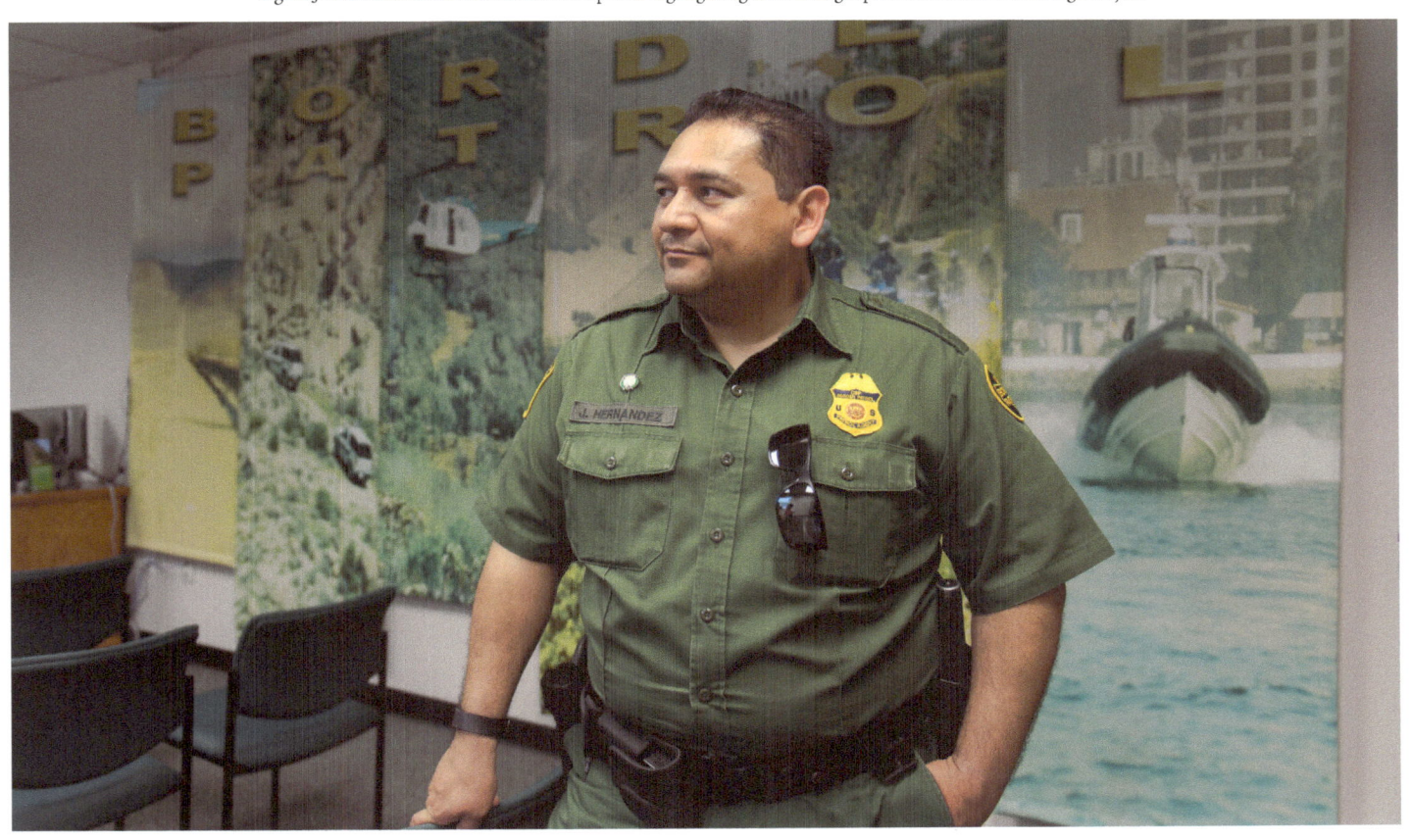

AND WHAT HAPPENS WHEN YOU APPREHEND UNACCOMPANIED MINORS?

With respect to juveniles, it depends. Accompanied juveniles are returned to their home country with the person traveling with them. Mexican unaccompanied juveniles are turned over to Mexican consular officials who then find a family member to turn them over to in Mexico. Other than Mexican unaccompanied juveniles are turned over to an immediate family member sponsor in the United Stated pending further proceedings.

WHAT ARE THESE INTERACTIONS TYPICALLY LIKE?

Typically, most of the people we apprehend for illegal entry in the San Diego Sector are compliant. Many run and hide but are eventually taken into custody without incident. However, we are seeing an increase in assaults on agents. Former Border Patrol Chief Mark A. Morgan said, "...the United States Border Patrol agents are among the most assaulted law enforcement personnel in the country. There have been 7,542 assaults against agents since 2006, and 30 agents have died in the line of duty since 2003."

When I was on the border tour Hernandez pointed out a change they had to make to the border fence due to the increase of assaults on agents. The barbed wire at the top of the fence used to be at a horizontal slant to make it harder for individuals to climb up and over it. However, those who did manage to get over used to sit on top of the fence and throw rocks at the agents. After this repeatedly happening the barbed wire at the top of the border fence is now the more traditional large barbed wire coils.

WHAT HAPPENS IF THE PERSON IS INJURED WHEN YOU CATCH THEM?

If someone is injured, we render medical aid. That may be as simple as providing basic first aid, calling one of our agents who is cross-trained as an emergency medical technician or taking them to the hospital for more urgent care.

The agents explained to me how they try to avoid injury in the strategies that they use. When it comes to the infrastructure they make the areas with the more dangerous terrain much harder to cross. For example, in an area that had cliffs about 100 feet after the border fence on the U.S. side, they added extra barbed wire to the top and bottom of the fence. This was to ensure that those trying to cross, which happens more typically at night, would not cut passages in the fence in this area and try to run down this type of terrain. If they were to do so the drop would be fatal.

Another example that I noticed was in their technique of apprehending boats transporting undocumented immigrants and drugs. They explained the tactic that the coyotes or drug smugglers use is promising the immigrants a ride across the border on a luxury boat. However, once they get the money and everyone boards the boat they take them to some islands just off the Mexican coast and put everyone in smaller pirogue boats. Hernandez explained that if they spotted a boat and then tried to pursue it the drug smugglers would push everyone off the boat into the water, women and children included. The smugglers would then speed off to try and save their drugs. For the Border Patrol this would mean their task has now turned into a rescue mission to try and help all the immigrants in the water. If someone was injured and needed to go to the hospital, Border Patrol has to assign two agents per one undocumented immigrant. Instead they

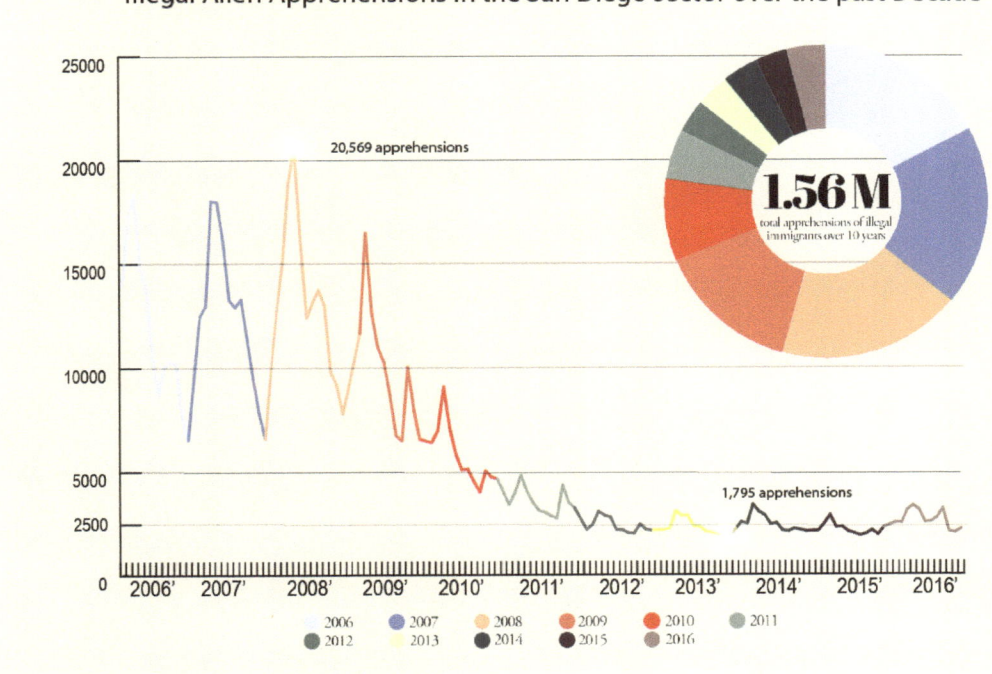

Illegal Alien Apprehensions in the San Diego sector over the past Decade

20,569 apprehensions

1.56 M
total apprehensions of illegal
immigrants over 10 years

1,795 apprehensions

2006 2007 2008 2009 2010 2011
2012 2013 2014 2015 2016

Data from the US Border Patrol. Graphic by: Dayna Bayne and Anna Warner

would try and intersect the drug smuggling boats when the boat reaches land further up the coast.

WHAT IS THE ORDER OF COMMAND/ WHERE DO ORDERS COME FROM?

We are a paramilitary organization. We have a defined command structure. With respect to 'orders,' it depends on what you consider orders to be. If you mean agency-wide policy, that is determined at the headquarters level. If you are referring to

commands given on a daily basis affecting local operations, orders can come from any superior officer, supervisor or above.

WITH ALL THE CONTROVERSY AROUND THIS JOB PUBLICALLY WHAT MOTIVATES PEOPLE TO WANT TO WORK HERE?

I cannot speak as to why others are willing to do this job despite the controversy, but I can tell you why I do this. I have been working with the federal government in immigration since 1996, and as a Border Patrol agent, specifically, since 2001.

Coincidentally, my Border Patrol academy class graduated on September 11, 2001. The attacks on the Twin Towers were at the forefront of my mind as I took the oath of office and vowed to protect the United States '...against all enemies, foreign and domestic.' I have dedicated nearly half my life to protecting our borders. It is a responsibility I take very seriously. I love my country and will do all that I can to protect her. I think of it as my home and I simply want to know who is coming into my home and why. Regardless of public opinion or perception, we need to do this with those who are coming into America.

WHAT ARE THE HARDEST THINGS ABOUT THIS JOB?

There are a couple of things that could apply. Physically, the job is very demanding. We are frequently in remote locations, arresting numerous groups of people at a time, and often by ourselves. It is very common for an agent to arrest a group of five to ten people at a time, but it is also common that a single agent would apprehend a group of 50 or more. When the San Diego area was very busy (leading the nation in highest number of apprehensions in the 80s and 90s) it was very common to arrest groups of 100 or more. Another difficult aspect is the negativity involved with fulfilling our mission. There are portions of our community who advocate for open borders where anyone can cross the border at will with no inspection or impediment. Those who espouse this dangerous mentality often attempt to vilify us (agents and the agency as a whole) to promote their personal agenda. They say we are 'dream killers' who rob immigrants of their dreams. This only foments a negative attitude towards us and allows them to ignore the very positive and necessary things we do.

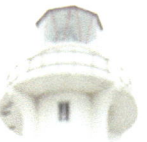

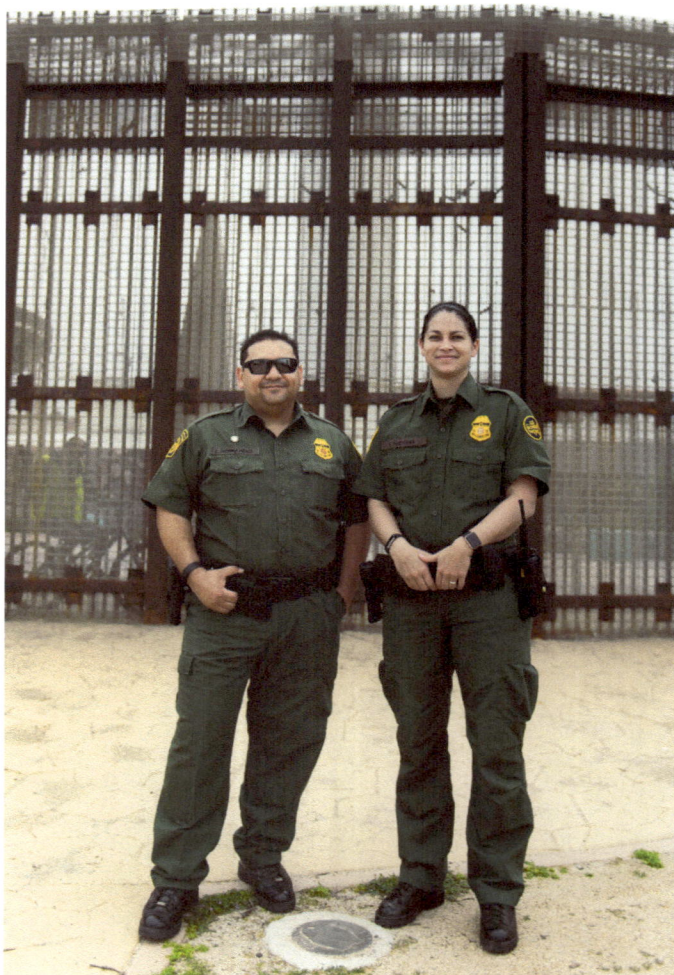

Agents Hernandez and Michael pose in front of the border at Frendship Park, between Tijuana, Mexico and San Diego, California.

Hernandez also expressed to me the he and his family live further north but still at a distance where he can commute to work because of the harassment that they or their children might receive in the San Diego community. Michael described that they cannot go into certain restaurants with their uniforms on because they may not be treated fairly. They also know of other agents whose kids get harassed and bullied at school because of their parent's job.

What are the best things about this job?

For me, the best part of my job is the satisfaction of a job well done. I know that by protecting our borders, we are protecting our communities and keeping them safe. Though a significant majority of those who cross the border illegally are not criminals, there is also a significant percentage who are coming here to prey on others. Knowing that we have prevented those who would do us harm from entering is very satisfying.

Have you ever felt conflicted following orders?

No, not really. I haven't liked every order I've been given, but at the same time, I understand the chain of command.

Do you have a couple stories you can share with us?

While working in Arizona, I was tracking a large group but I couldn't tell how many there were. When I caught up to them, I discovered a group of 37 hiding in a wash in the desert (a wash is a dry desert stream or creek bed). Assistance was approximately 10 min away so I had to apprehend and maintain control by myself in the middle of the night until backup arrived.

In another instance, while working at a checkpoint, a man driving an 18-wheeler tractor trailer presented himself for inspection. He was unclear about what he was transporting or where he was going. When I opened the trailer to inspect it, it looked like there were crushed boxes inside, but it did not look like other loads of crushed boxes I had seen before. I tried to look over and behind the piles of boxes. The moment my head went over the piles I could feel intense humid heat (much like a steam room or sauna). As I went further behind the pile, I discovered a group of 67 concealed behind the boxes. The driver was arrested, prosecuted and convicted for alien smuggling.

How do you feel about how the media portrays this job? Is it fair?

We don't really have any control over how the media chooses to report stories related to the USBP. What we can focus on is getting our message out to our community that what we do makes our communities stronger and safer. Many of us live within these communities and have a vested interested in protecting them. Though many who are coming here illegally may not mean us any harm, there is a significant danger of those who do mean to hurt and kill Americans are crossing with them. Therefore, we must be vigilant and do what we can to secure our borders.

These agents love protecting their country and its borders. Their job however has a black and white view. The social issues surrounding the border are not black and white, they are a web of grey.

5 East Coachella Valley

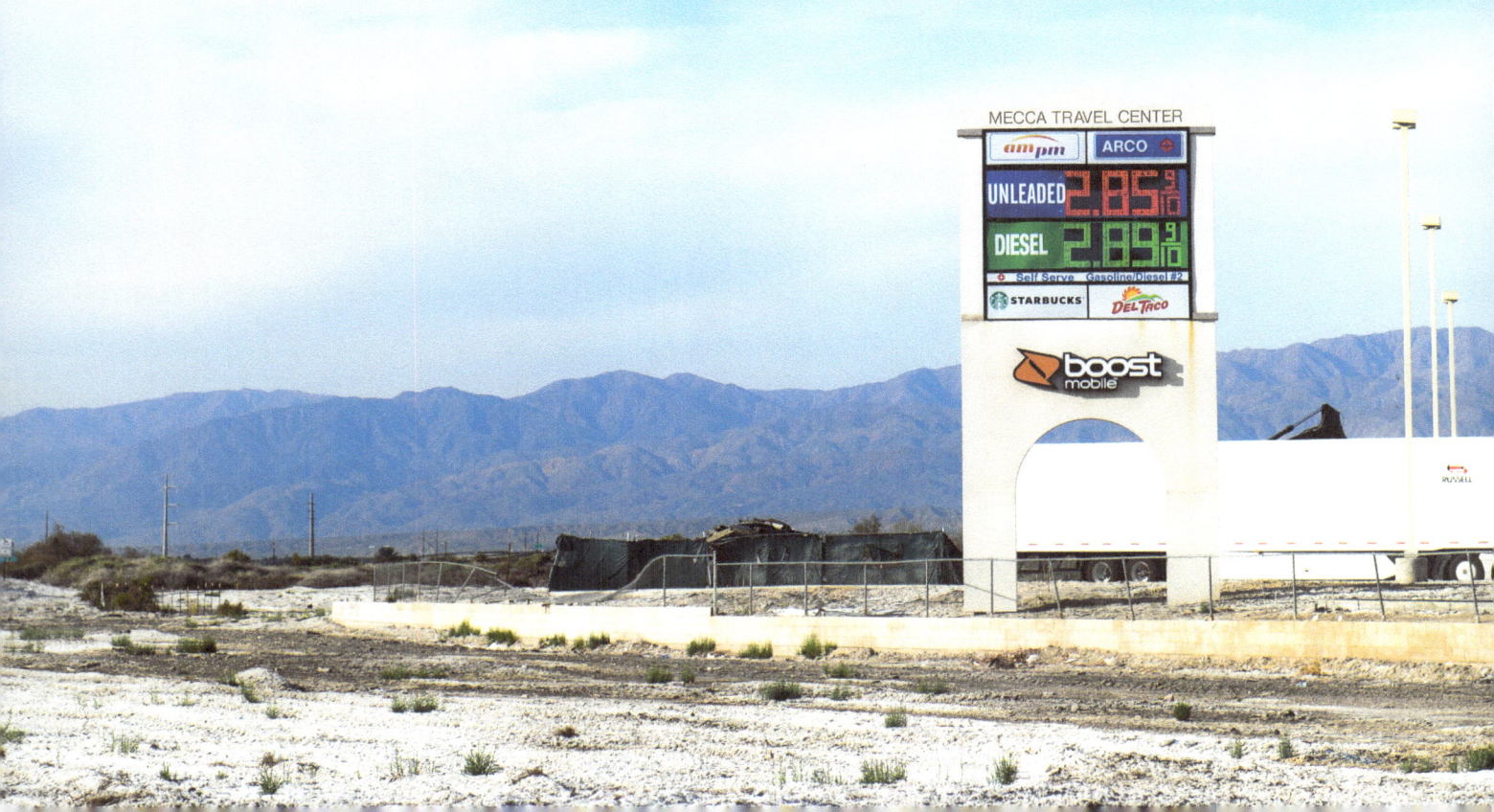

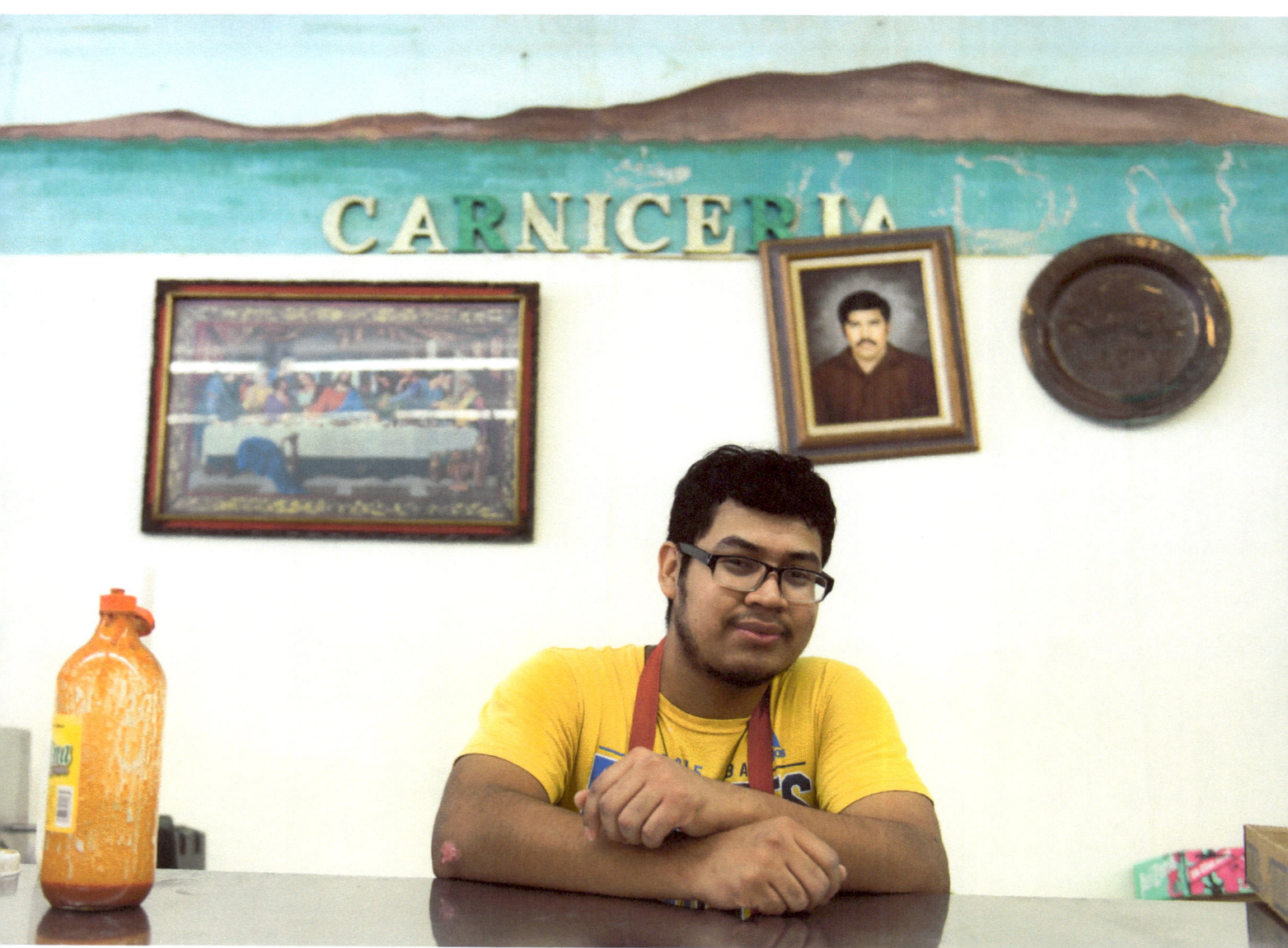

Greg Barragan works at the local butcher shop in Coachella. He is one of the only workers at the store who speaks and understands English.

Photo by: Jenny Oetzell

Cover Photo by: Jenny Oetzell

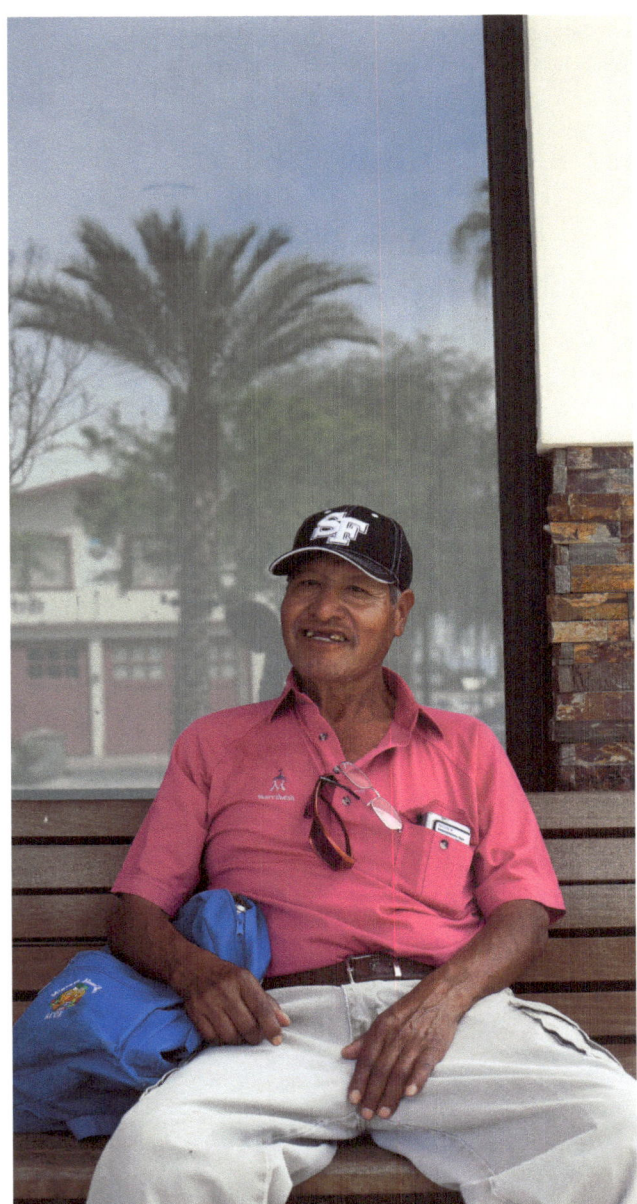

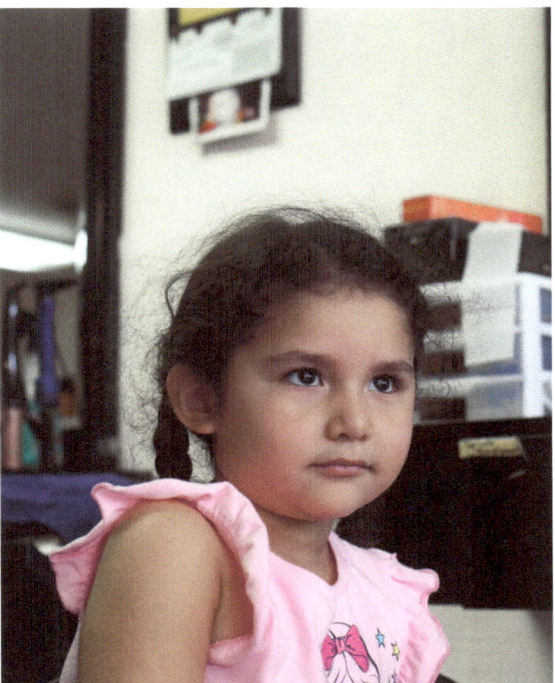

In Coachella, three year-old Ashley sits patiently at a hair salon while her mother gets a haircut.

Photo: Alex Bell

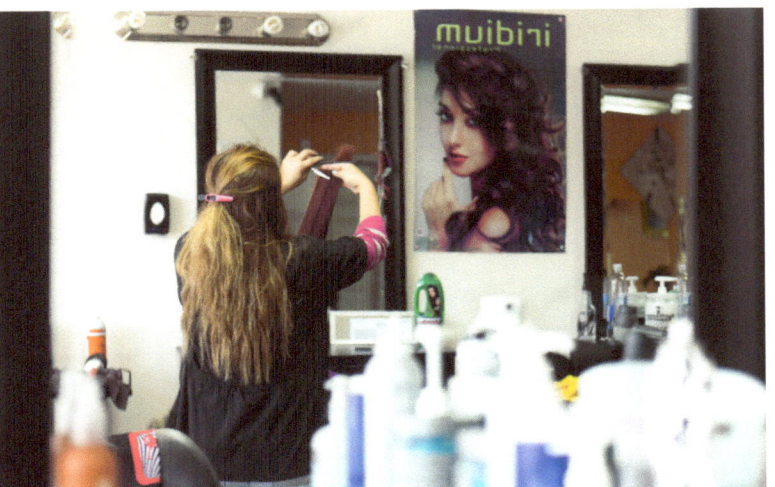

An elderly man sits on a city bench in Coachella.

Photo by: Alex Bell

A local hairdresser cuts the hair of a customer on a quiet afternoon in Coachella.

Photo by: Jenny Oetzell

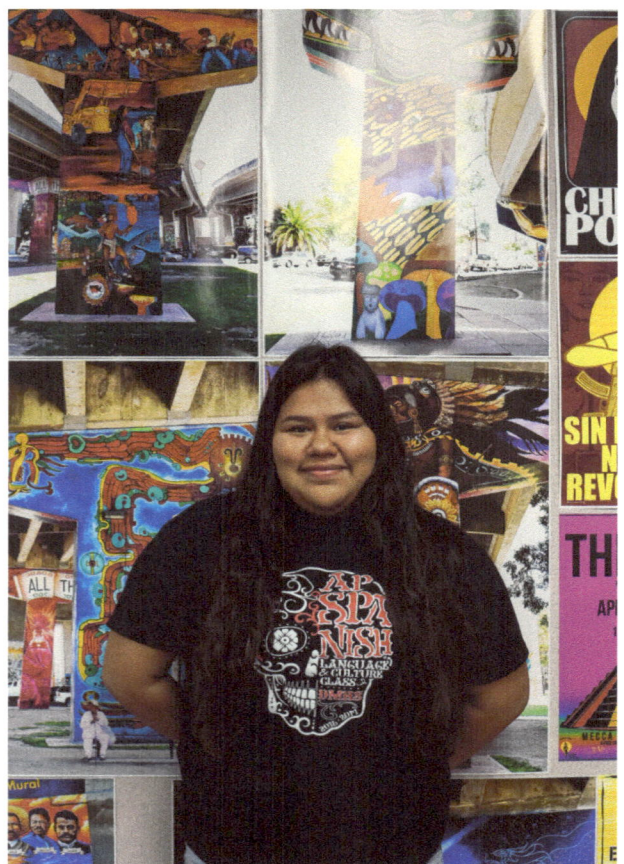

Left: Guadelupe, a student at Desert Mirage High School, wants to make a difference in her community, to give her younger siblings a brighter future.

Photo: Alex Bell

Below: Students of all grades listen as the director of Coachella Unincorporated gives them instruction during their twenty-minute lunch period at Desert Mirage High School.

Photo: Alex Bell

Bottom: Paper maché skulls, decorated for Día de los Muertos, the Mexican Day of the Dead, line the front of a classroom at Desert Mirage High School.

Photo: Jenny Oetzell

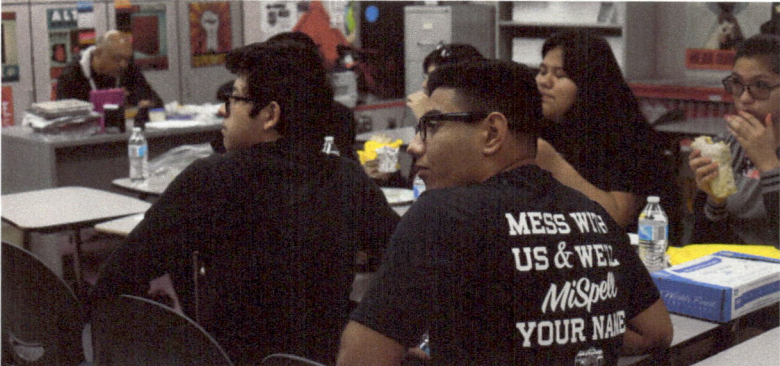

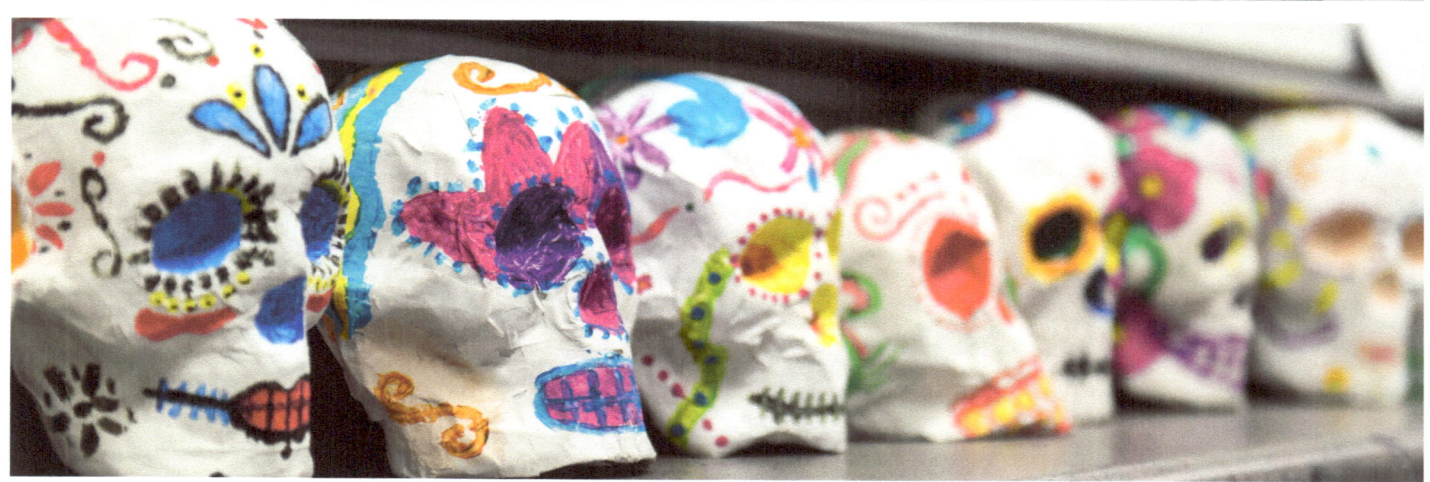

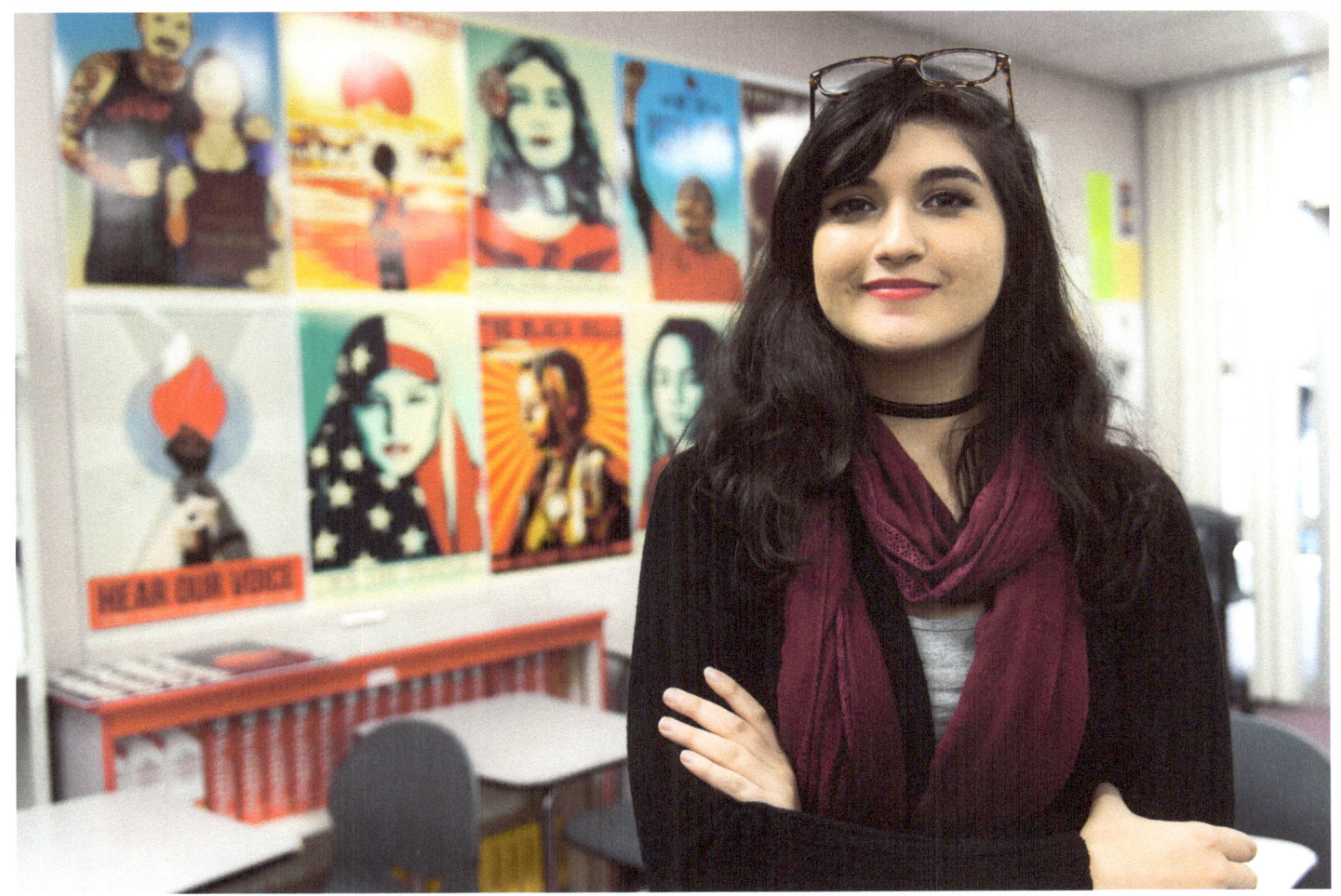

Above: "Bear," senior at Desert Mirage High School in Thermal, CA, stands proudly in front of activist posters in the classroom where Coachella Unincorporated meets. She spoke with confidence about her duty to tell the stories of the people in the Coachella Valley.

Photo: Jenny Oetzell

COACHELLA UNINCORPERATED

High school students in the Eastern Coachella Valley have a unique opportunity to tell the stories of their community through Coachella Unincorporated. This youth-led journalism program and media-training project teaches students how to report on the stories that are happening around them. The main goal of the program is to equip youth with the tools and skills to build a healthy community in the Eastern Coachella Valley.

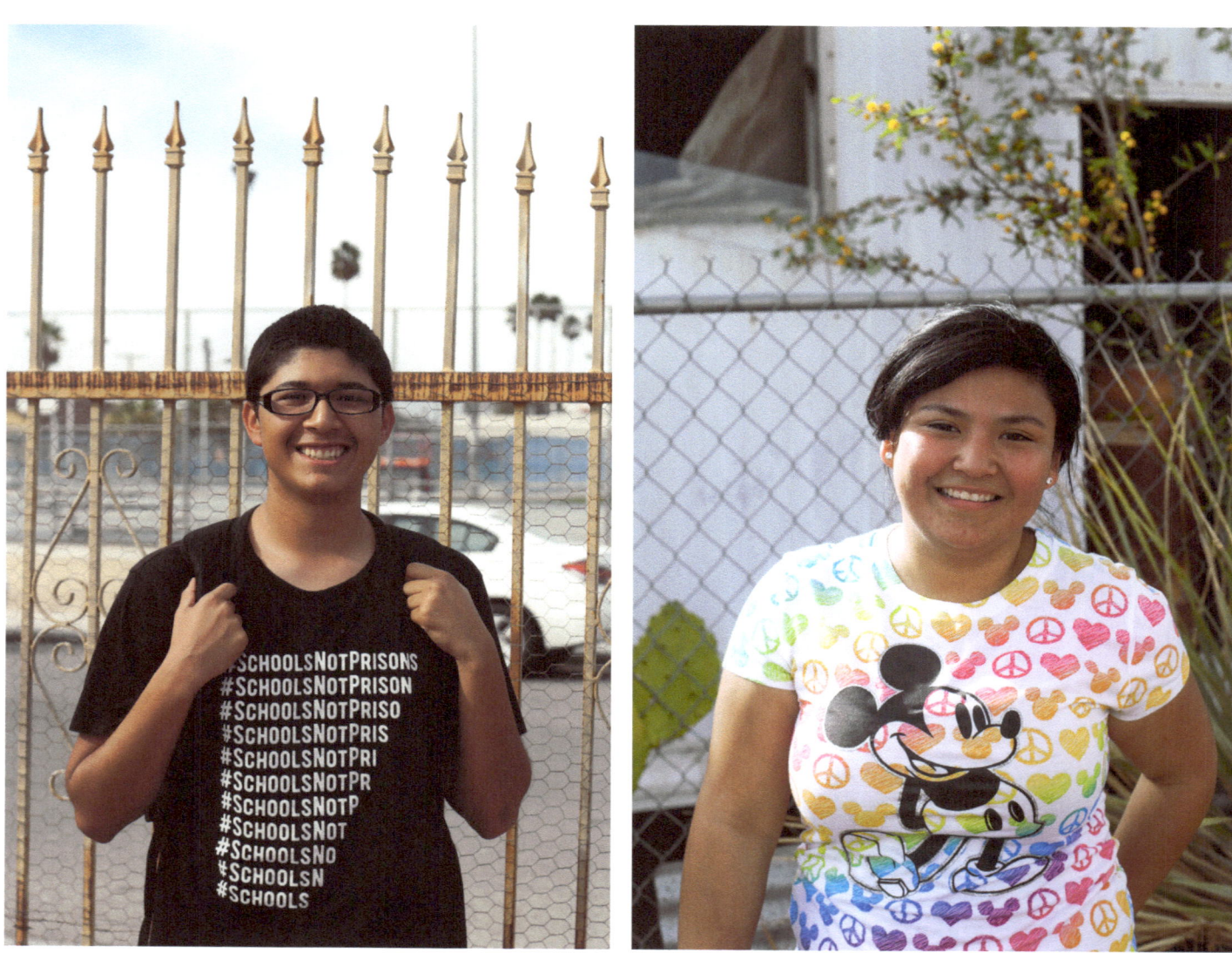

Emmanuel and Gabby, two high school students from Coachella Valley, are part of a team planning The Hue, a local music and arts festival. The event is completely organized by youth in the area.

Photos: Alex Bell

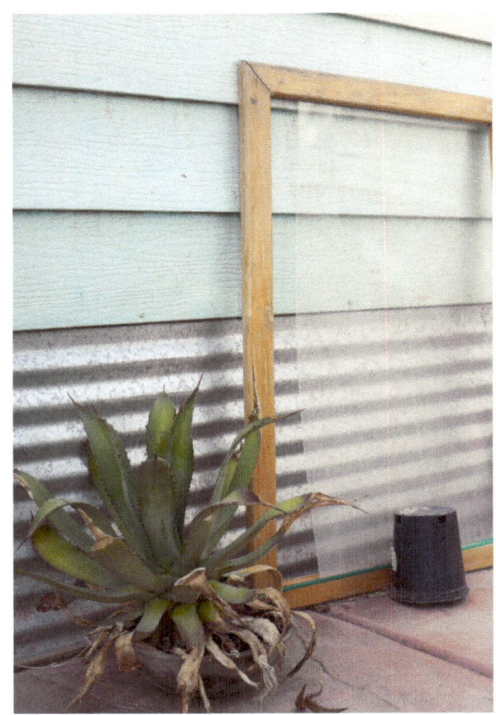

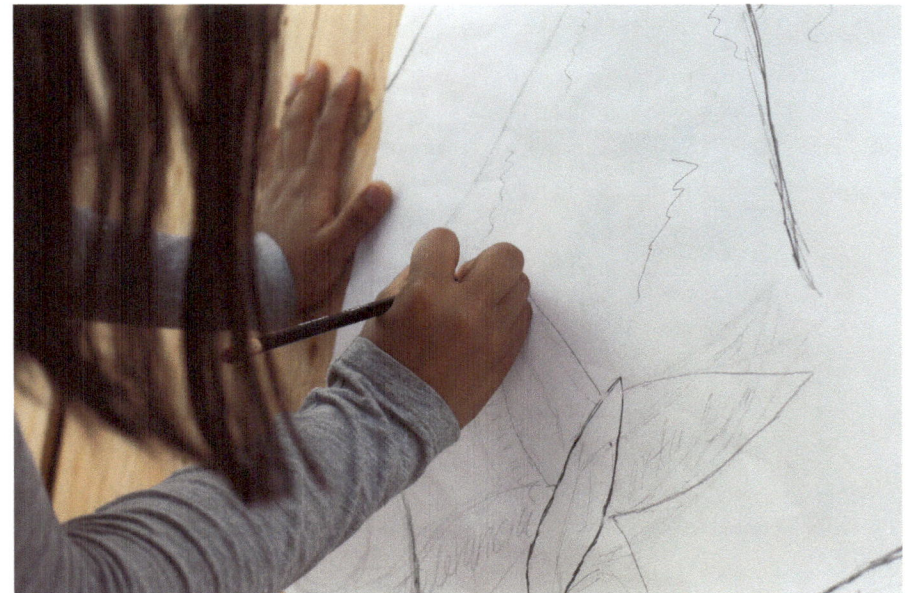

The Hue

In the East Coachella Valley, students have a deep passion for their neighbor. They are willing to sacrifice hours after a long day at school to plan a music and arts festival they call The Hue. The young high school students do not gain anything academically or monetarily from planning this event. They simply love local artists in their community and want their voices, through art and music, to be heard.

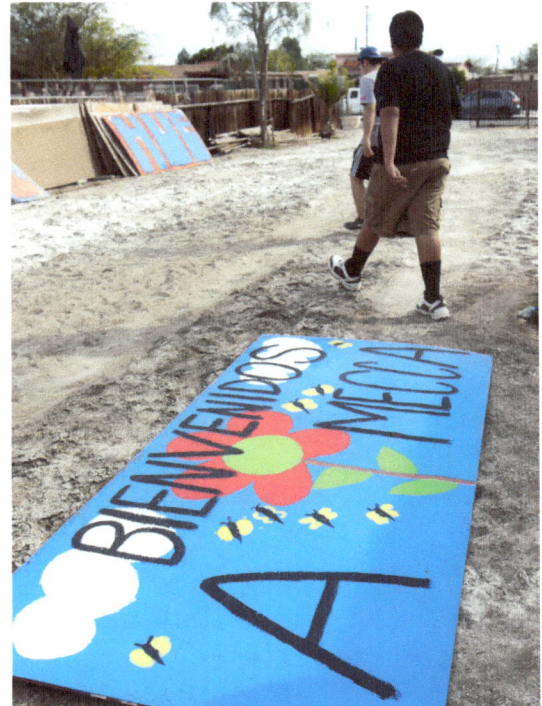

Far Left: A broken frame lies against the portable trailer where the high school students meet to plan The Hue.

Photo: Alex Bell

Below, left: Students prepare signs and artwork for The Hue music and arts festival. "Bienvenidos a Mecca" translates to "Welcome to Mecca".

Photo: Jenny Oetzell

Above: A student sketches butterflies. which will be painted onto a sign for The Hue.

Photo: Alex Bell

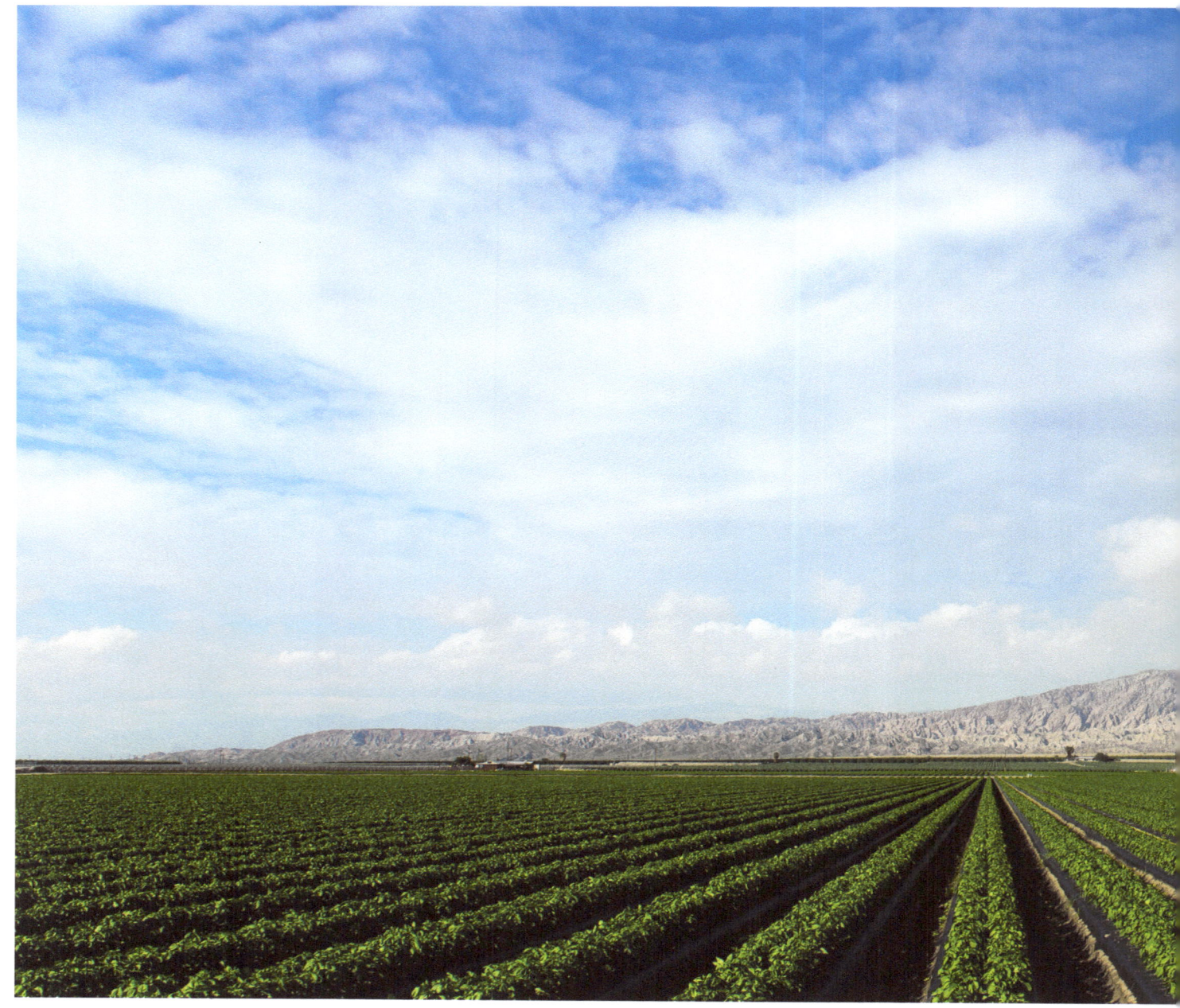

Vast strawberry fields extend toward the mountains. The East Coachella Valley is home to acres of produce fields where migrant farmworkers labor.

Photo: Jenny Oetzell

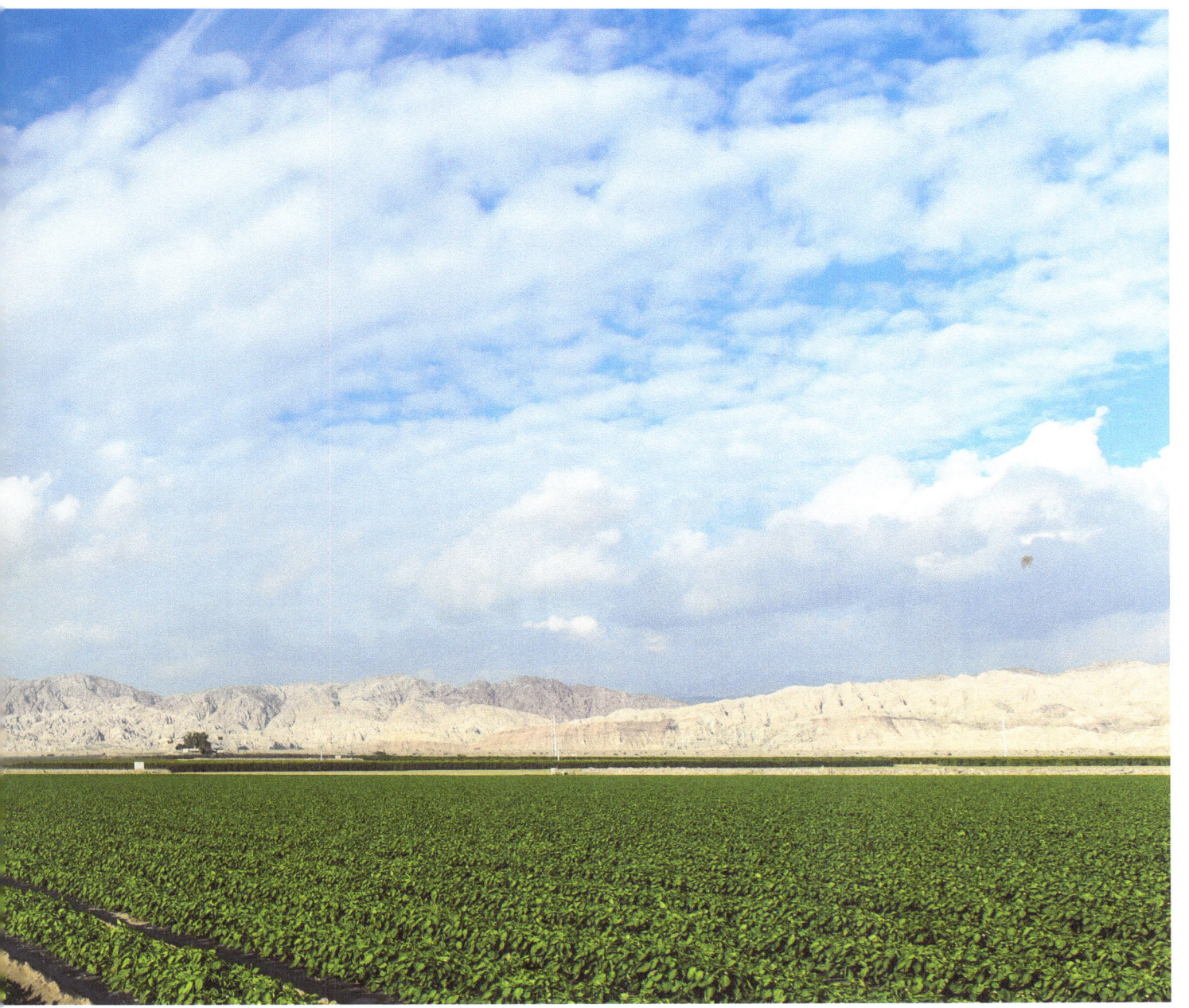

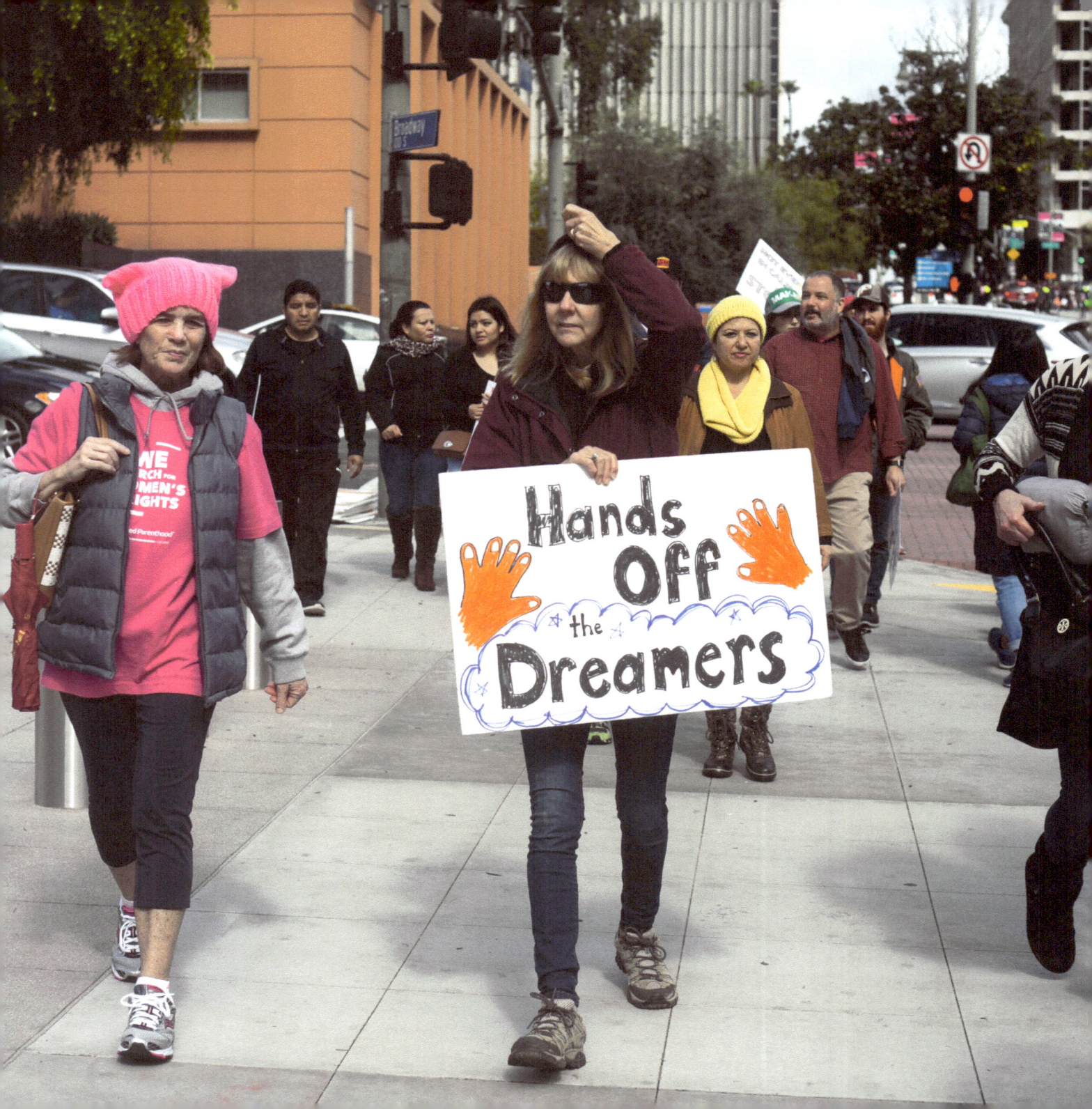

6 Migrants, the DREAM Act and DACA

By Jubilee Pham

Photos by Molli Kaptein, Jenny Oetzell & Anastasia Waltschew

> " Have faith in your dreams and someday
> Your rainbow will come smiling through
> No matter how your heart is grieving
> If you keep on believing
> The dream that you wish will come true "

"A Dream is A Wish Your Heart Makes," Cinderella

When she was three years old, Berania illegally crossed the U.S.-Mexico border. Known by friends and family as Bear, the high school senior has a similar larger-than-life presence to her animal counterpart that commands attention. When she stands, she stands tall, and when she speaks, she speaks with equal parts passion and eloquence.

However, living life as an undocumented student proves difficult. Her community in the East Coachella Valley know about her status, but she explains how she doesn't go outside when it's dark, how her parents are afraid to take her to after-school activities. Her fear of deportation is real and unavoidable with immigration officers strategically lingering in different parts of town.

"I'm not a criminal," Bear states, her voice shaking slightly as tears fill her eyes. The fact that she feels like she lives like one goes unspoken.

Photo by: Molli Kaptein

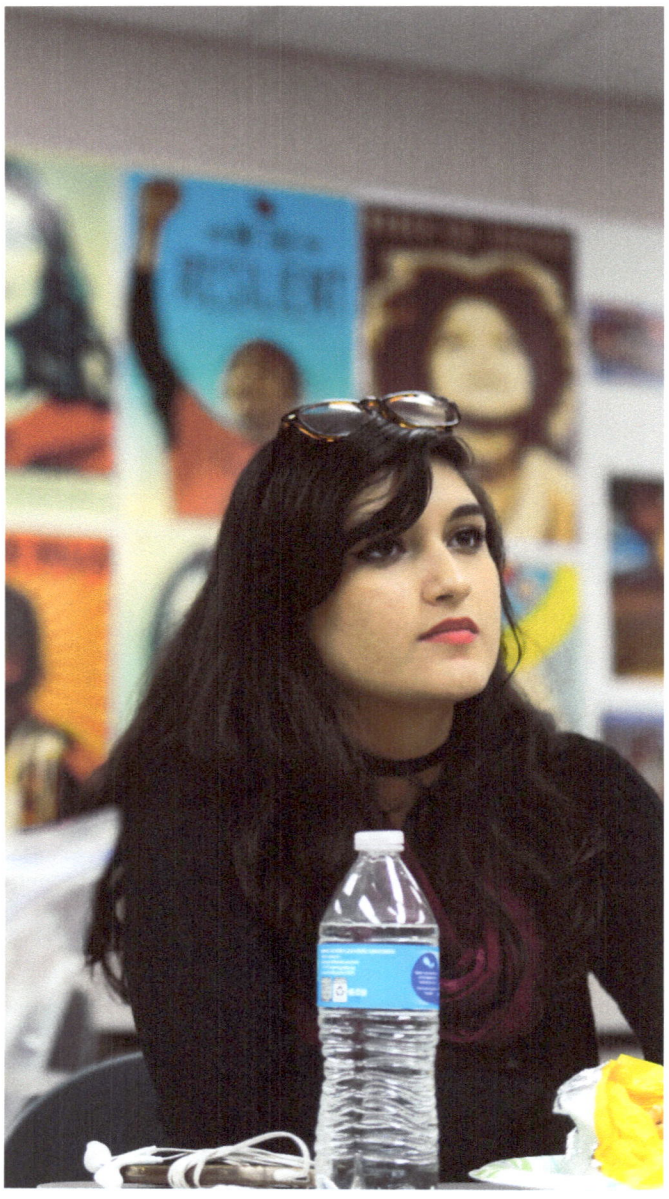

Bear, a DREAMer from East Coachella Valley, discusses the fear she feels on behalf of her family, as well as her aspirations to advocate for the people of her community.

Photo by: Jenny Oetzell

However, other undocumented students actually are treated like criminals.

On February 10, 2017, 23-year-old Daniel Ramirez Medina was arrested by ICE agents when they entered his home in Seattle, Washington with a warrant for his father's arrest but brought him in instead. He's been held in an immigration detention center for over a month.

Only a couple weeks after that, 22-year-old Daniela Vargas publicly spoke to the media about her family's detention. Hours later, she was brought into custody.

While all three people are undocumented, they are not criminals. They are DREAMers.

Who are the DREAMers?

The term "DREAMers" was a direct result of the Development, Relief and Education for Alien Minors Act. Commonly known as the DREAM Act for short, it is a piece of legislation that was first introduced to Congress in 2001. According to the American Immigration Council, the DREAM Act is specifically geared towards young, undocumented immigrants like Bear, Ramirez and Vargas who grew up in the U.S., want to go to college and want to legally work in America. If passed, the DREAM Act would allow current, former and future undocumented high school graduates a way to become U.S. citizens through higher education or the military.

The DREAM Act has caused worry, giving way to myths and misconceptions, such as that DREAM Act recipients will be able to "cut in line" to become U.S. citizens or that it will simply grant amnesty to millions of undocumented immigrants no matter how old they are.

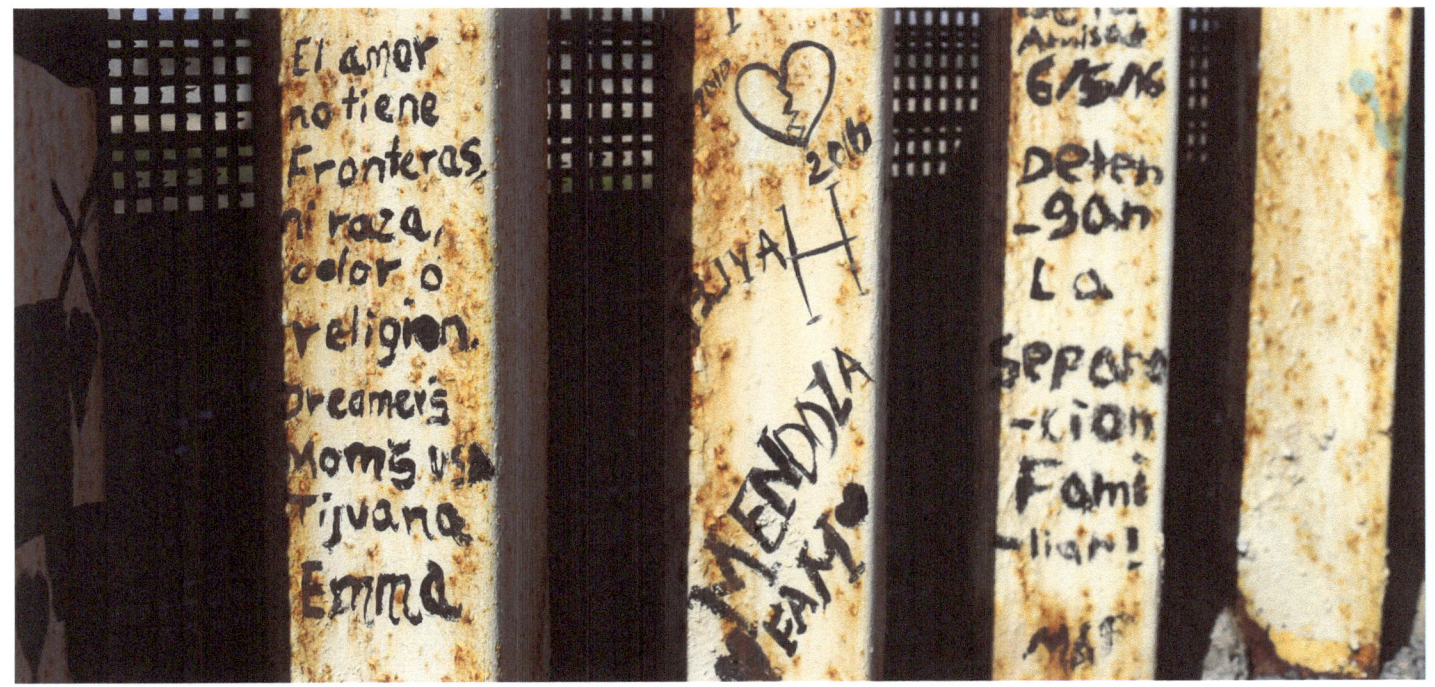

A member of DREAMers Moms expresses that "love has no borders" on the Tijuana side of the U.S-Mexico Border.

Photo by: Anastasia Waltschew

However, the DREAM Act is more complex than that. It provides a clearly-defined process to legalize undocumented students who grew up in America and are committed to their education, as well as maintaining good moral character. The list of qualifications that the DREAM Act presents is long and therefore narrowly tailored. The National Immigration Law Center states that the benefits of the DREAM Act are limited to undocumented students aged 35 years or younger who have either graduated from high school or earned a GED. If they fit these criteria, they would then apply for a six-year conditional status and complete two years of higher education or military service.

The profits that could be reaped through the DREAM Act would be huge for undocumented students, American higher education and even the American economy.

As of 2017 though, the DREAM Act has not been passed.

The bill was reintroduced many times throughout 2002-2006 to no avail. When the latest reiteration of the DREAM Act was introduced again in 2010, it was passed by the House but fell short by only five votes when it reached Senate on December 18, 2010.

The fight continues.

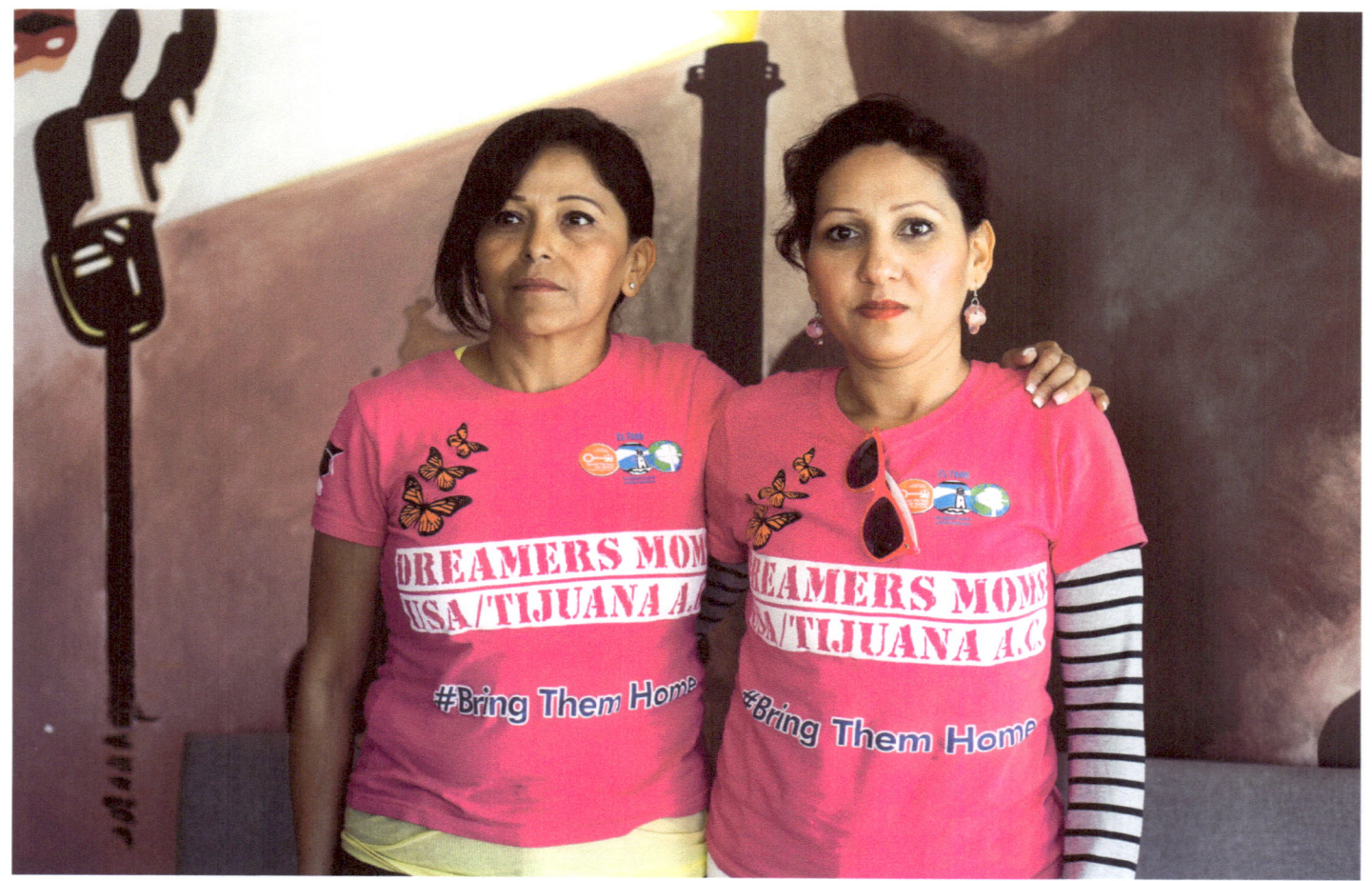

Yolanda Varona and Emma Sanchez Paulsen, director and member of DREAMers Moms, share the hopes and fears they have for their children that remain in the U.S.

Photo by: Molli Kaptein

A New Hope with DACA

In 2012, President Barack Obama issued an executive order to pass the Deferred Action for Childhood Arrivals Act. Many undocumented students who would have been eligible for the DREAM Act if it passed are also eligible for DACA. The Colorado Alliance for Immigration Reform states that DACA recipients "are offered two years of amnesty ('deferred action'—meaning a stay of deportation), are given a social security number, and are allowed to apply for a work permit." And in a memo released by the Department of Homeland Security concerning DACA on June 15, 2012, Secretary Janet Napolitano stated, "Our Nation's immigration laws must be enforced in a strong and sensible manner. They are not designed to be blindly enforced without consideration given to the individual circumstances of each case. Nor are they designed to remove productive young people to countries where they may not have lived or even speak the language. Indeed, many of these young people have already contributed to our country in significant ways."

According to a national survey conducted in 2016 by Latino Decisions, a research center that specializes in Latino political opinion, one out of every three Latino voters know DACA applicants. In a study released by the Pew Research Center in January 2017, around 750,000 undocumented immigrants have benefitted from DACA. In California alone, there are over 200,000 DACA recipients, the most out of any state.

However, while the DREAM Act provides a clear path to citizenship, DACA does not and is only seen as a temporary measure by DREAMers who are still waiting to apply for citizenship.

"It's kind of like residency," explained Bear, who recently applied for DACA. "[Except] citizens don't have to worry about getting a ticket and then being deported."

The Other Side of the Border

Although the DREAM Act and DACA provide hope for younger undocumented immigrants, immigration is inherently a familial issue that crosses different generations. The parents of DREAMers also face the possibility of deportation but don't have DACA to fall back on. As a result, some DREAMers also have to deal with being separated from deported family members.

DREAMers Moms of Tijuana is a group comprised of deported mothers—and a handful of fathers—whose children are U.S. citizens and DREAMers. Their main goal is to help members reunite with their families legally.

In 1994, DREAMers Moms founder and director Yolanda Varona came to America with her two young children. In 2010, she was deported and has been in Tijuana ever since. Her son was able to become a U.S. citizen, and although her daughter has a permit that allows her to stay in the U.S., if she ever crosses the border, she won't be able to return to America. "The only reason I want to go back is because my family is up there," Yolanda said in Spanish. "I know I made a mistake. I was conscious of the fact that I was undocumented."

Emma Sanchez Paulsen, another member of DREAMers Moms, was barred from entering the U.S. while attempting to process her visa paperwork despite her marriage to a U.S. Marine Corps veteran and being the mother of three children who are all U.S. citizens. She has been separated from her family for eleven years.

"My kids come to visit me on weekends," Sanchez said with the help of a translator. "I try to give everything I can." It's clear that both Varona and Sanchez still struggle to tell their stories even though they have been raising awareness for DREAMer Moms for several years. But they know it's important for others to try to feel their pain and understand their situation. They also know it helps bring attention to the struggles that the younger generation of undocumented immigrants face, and they do their best to preach empathy.

"Don't discriminate against undocumented students," advised Sanchez. "They are studying and they have high aspirations. Just help them out however you can."

Fear and Hope

When DACA was passed, it gave a small measure of comfort and relief to undocumented students throughout the nation. Immigration reform is still a hotly debated topic though, and fear and tension has only increased with the possibility that DACA might be repealed and that the DREAM Act will never be passed.

"Many undocumented students are living under stress because they don't know if DACA is going to disappear," commented Varona. "They're on edge and don't know what's going to happen tomorrow. There's definitely more fear now than there was five months ago."

For DACA recipients like Ramirez and Vargas, their fear has become reality simply because of their existence.

"I was supposed to be one of the lucky ones," Ramirez said in an essay he wrote for the Washington Post while in detainment. "I was treated [by ICE] as though my DACA status and my work authorization meant nothing."

"I was brought here. I didn't choose to be here," Vargas commented shortly after her arrest in a statement that appeared in Huffington Post. "I strongly feel that I belong here and I strongly feel that I should be given a chance to be here and do something good and work in this economy."

For both the DREAMers and the DREAMers Moms, there's solidarity in banding together and educating themselves and others about what they can do about their situation.

"Our hope is for the laws to change," Varona said. "If we all speak as one strong force, it's possible for this to happen."

In Bear's case, she remains optimistic about her future.

"To me, 'DREAMer' means opportunity, a chance to prove myself. I'm worth so much more," Bear said. "I feel like I want to make a good example. The moment I stand up for myself, I'm standing up for everyone else."

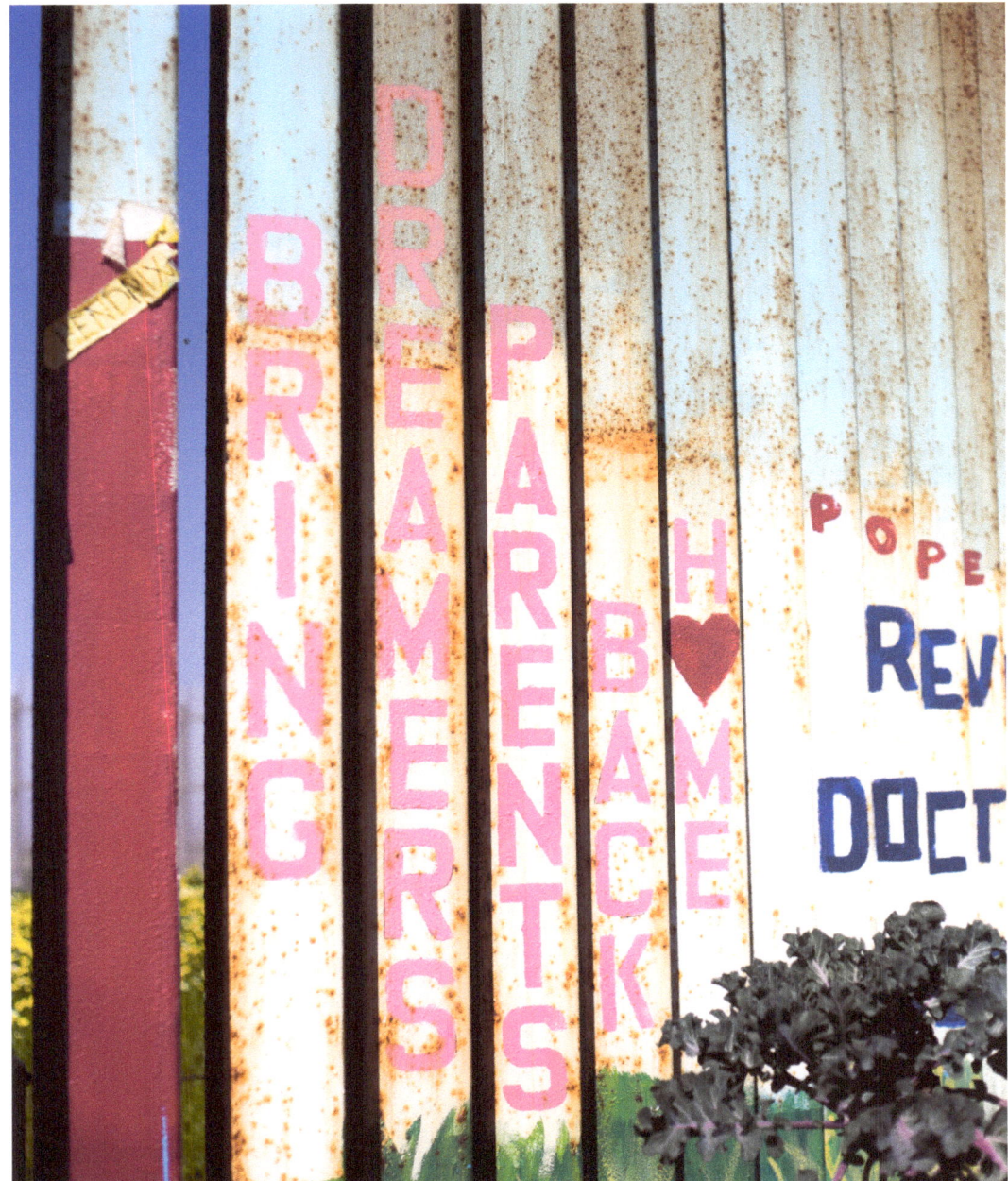

The Tijuana side of the U.S.-Mexico border artistically displays the hopes and dreams of separated families.

Photo by: Molli Kaptein

MODERN MIGRATION *to* CALIFORNIA

California is home to more immigrants than any other state – over 10 million unauthorized persons reside here.

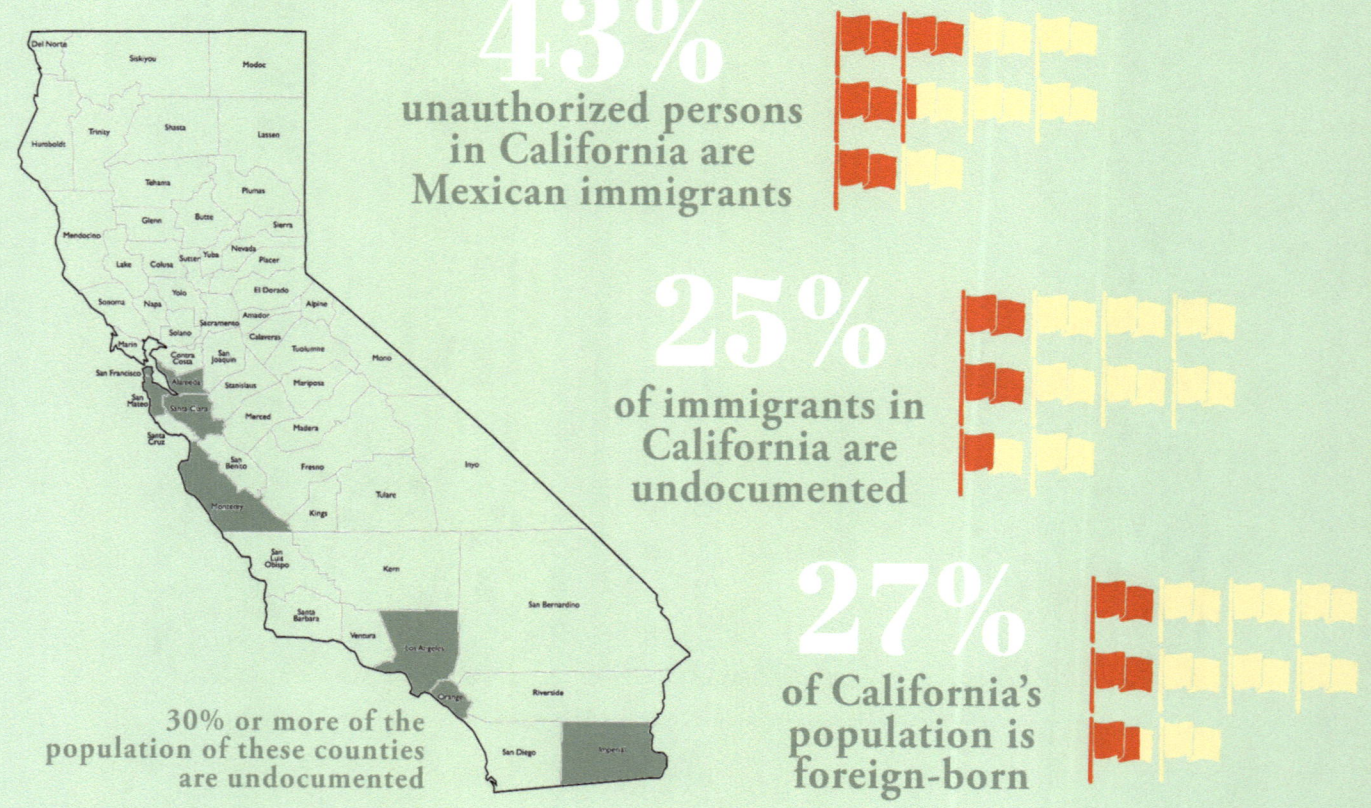

43%
unauthorized persons in California are Mexican immigrants

25%
of immigrants in California are undocumented

27%
of California's population is foreign-born

30% or more of the population of these counties are undocumented

http://www.ppic.org/main/publication_show.asp?i=258

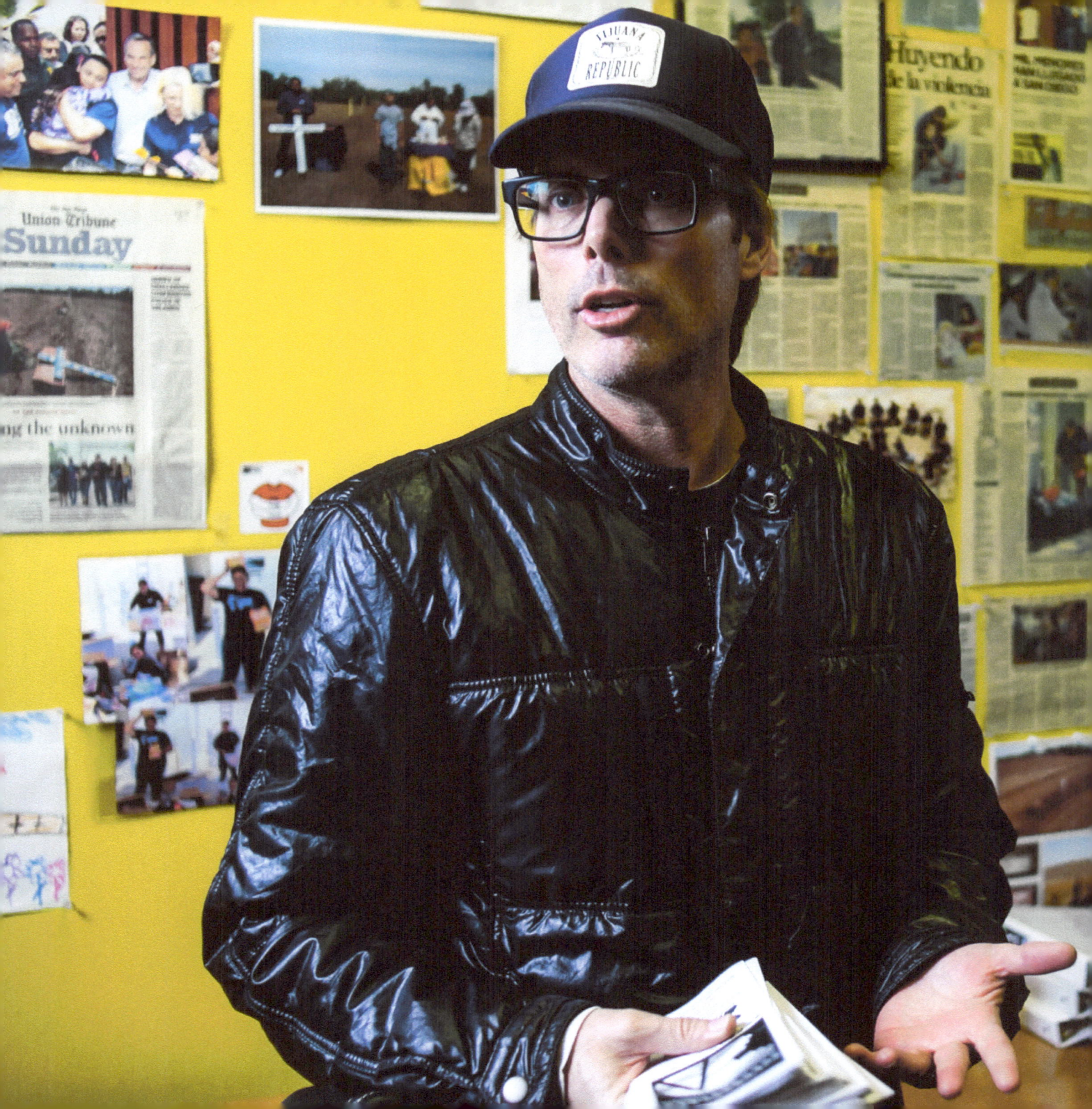

7 Border Angels

By Rebecca Mitchell

Photos by Anna Warner

"" Speak up for those who cannot speak for themselves,
for the rights of all who are destitute.
Speak up and judge fairly;
defend the rights of the poor and needy. ""

Proverbs 31:8-9

"The injustices," Enrique Morones says without hesitation or explanation as to what keeps him doing his job everyday. Every day he wakes up to the reality of injustices and works against them. He continues to serve the needs of people as they rise up and the ongoing needs of migrants and immigrants.

As CEO of Border Angels, a non-profit organization based in San Diego, California which stands for human rights, particularly those tied to the United States and Mexico border, Morones plans project after project to reach the needs of many.

The canyons—they were filled with migrants, people who worked in the strawberry fields, tomato fields and flower fields. Amongst the striking view of these canyons, Border Angels began in Carlsbad, California in 1986. And it all started by listening to a story from a friend.

This friend from El Salvador shared with Morones about the reality of migrants' living conditions. She told Morones she was helping needy people in the area she lived in. She said within the wealthy area of Carlsbad in San Diego there were migrants residing in the canyons.

Morones described how he could not believe that people lived in those situations. Even today, one can hear the raw, open hearted care for those people in his voice. He began to deliver food and water, simply for the people to survive in the canyon community.

He started with families.

The families who have traveled across the border. The ones whose children drop their once fluffy, soft, caramel brown teddy bears as they frantically bound from one country to another. The ones who put torn, worn-out, discarded cloths down on the ground to hide their footprints from being discovered in the sand by Border Patrol agents. The families who use rusted, dark chocolate-colored metal ladders to make it over the wall.

He pointed to this rusted, dark metal piece and shared how the ladder brought lives across the border. Craig Penny, a member of the board of directors at Border Angels, pointed and shared, telling story after story of the painful reality of life around the border.

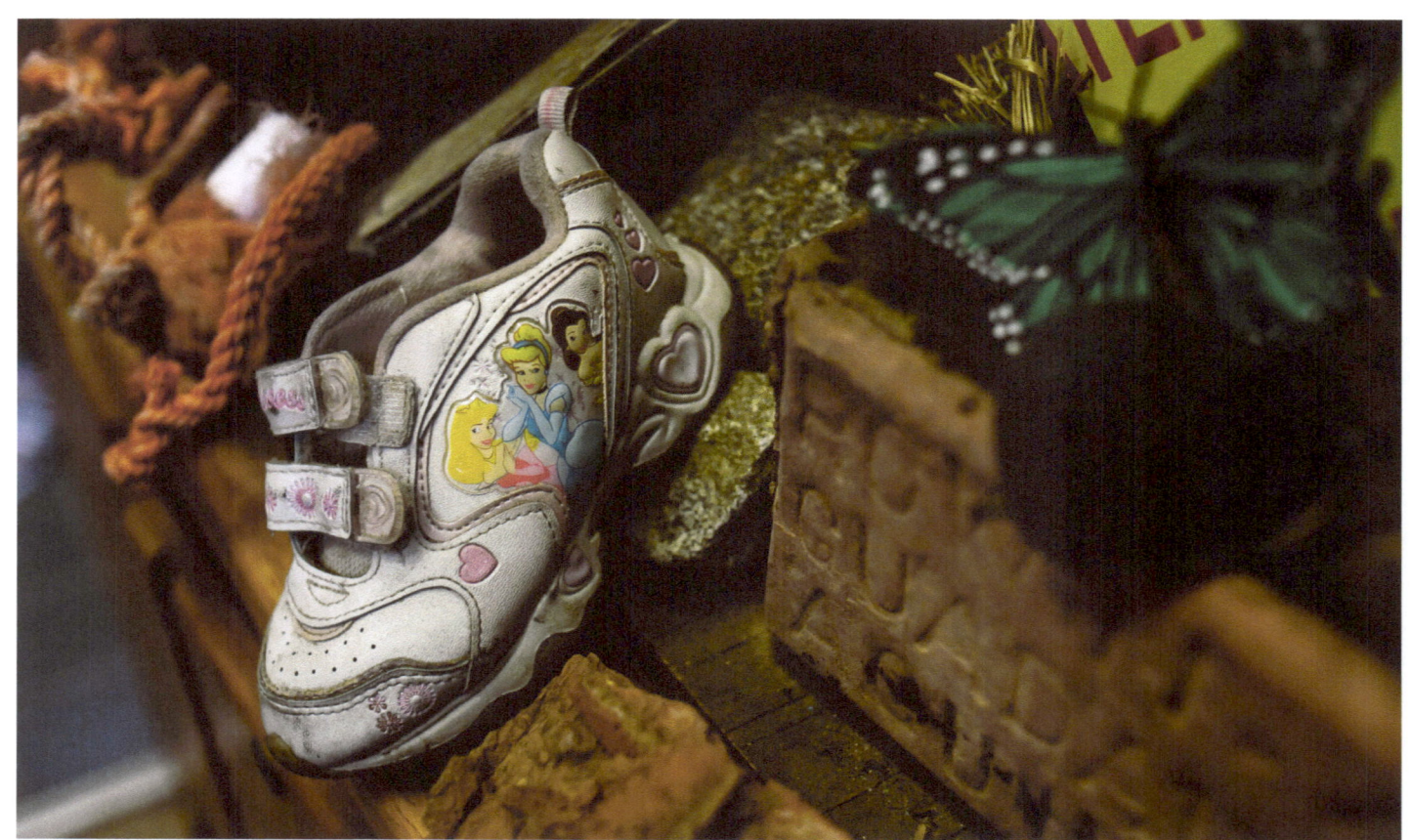

"These are things that we collect when we're out and about, so we find shoes, children's shoes, out in the desert," Penny said.

He pauses somberly, letting the reality of this ladder sink in, and then began to describe the items at the foot of the cross. The ladder precariously draped the middle of the cross, with the child-sized, white Disney princess velcro shoe and the frayed, tan, plaid embroidered work boot resting at the bottom with perfectly white and royal purple flowers gracing the top.

"It's really difficult to see what children and people have to go through," Penny said. "To see some of the conditions that other people, children have to live in and everything. It'll change your life. It'll make you want to be involved."

The office became filled with hope, not tied to the size of it or the outside looks of the gray, concrete exterior hidden in the community center, with murals covering every inch of the posts. The sunshine yellow walls softly screamed "Remember these stories!" The stories from newspaper clippings and crosses reading "no mas muertes" decorate the walls.

"No more deaths" has yet to become a reality, as over 11,000 migrants have died since the wall was built in 1994 to cover a third of the border, according to Morones.

Everything changed in 1994, Morones commented. Four events shaped immigration extending to today—the North

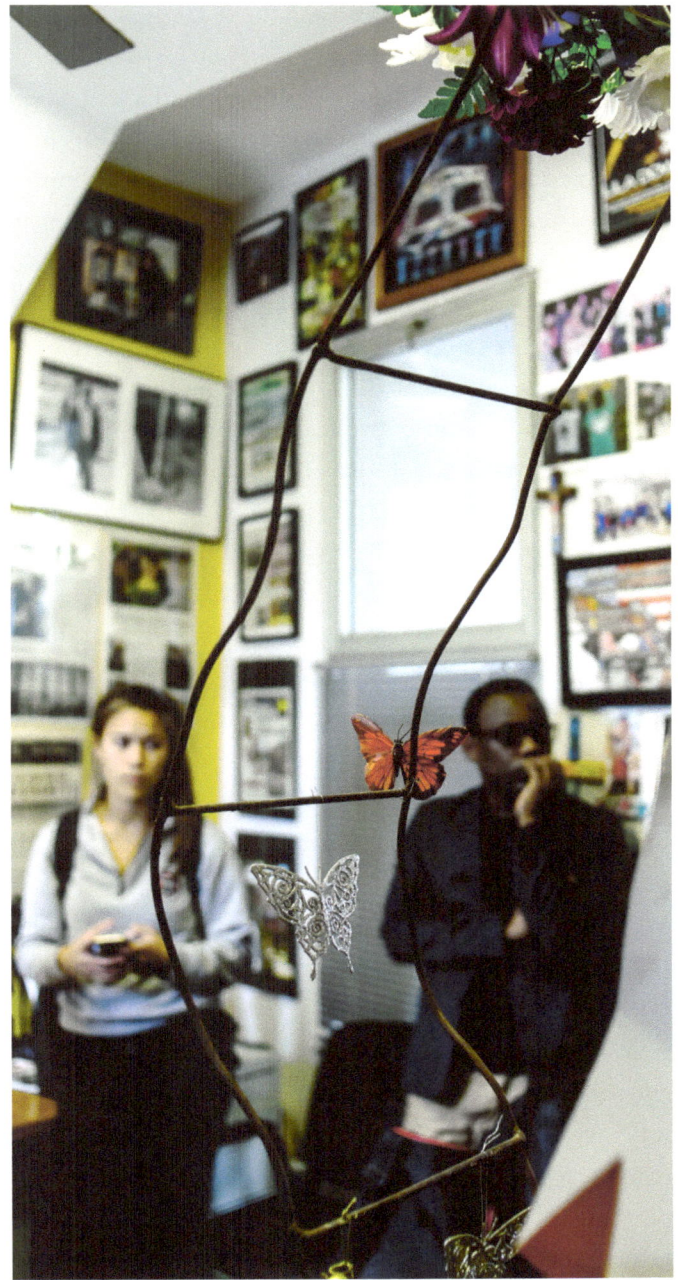

Used as part of a sculpture made of found objects, this ladder was originally made by immigrants seeking to climb over the U.S.-Mexico border wall.

American Free Trade Agreement (NAFTA), the Zapatista movement, Proposition 187 and Operation Gatekeeper.

NAFTA formed a treaty between the United States, Canada and Mexico to eliminate a majority of tariffs on agricultural products, textiles and automobile manufacturing, tripling regional trade and cross-border investment, according to the Council for Foreign Relations. Morones also explained the treaty as allowing companies to become bigger and individuals to become so small they had to move north for survival.

The Zapatista movement stood up for the rights of those people who had to move north, Morones says. The Mexican movement lasted for 12 days, according to USA Today. These group of people, from Chiapas, Mexico, proclaimed NAFTA would bring death to the natives within their land and tried to bring a power of their own rather than that of the government.

Proposition 187 would have left "illegal aliens" with no public benefits if the passed law had been enacted, according to Ballotpedia. These public benefits included the taking away of regular health care and public education. To Morones, the bill is a racist bill.

"The United States built its own wall, which is called Operation Gatekeeper, and that wall covers a third of the border," Morones said. "Today a third of the border has a wall. Wherever there's cities there's a wall, where there's no cities there's no wall. So people that were crossing the only way they can without a visa through the desert. They started dying one or two per day."

Again after hearing a story, this time about the deaths of migrants piling up every day, Morones decided to deliver gallons of fresh, life-saving water to the desert. He began alongside a team of volunteers trekking into the dust-filled desert, searching for places to leave the desperately needed water.

These water drops began in 1996, covering six migrant routes based on reported deaths in those areas and high density crossing areas, according to Morones. After 21 years of leaving water in the desert for migrants, the need is no less today. They see the white-washed, lavender stained bag and the clothes, the gray and orange striped t-shirt, once stored in a little boy's backpack. These items are commonplace, but running into people is not. As a part of the water drops, volunteers carry gallons of water into the desert and leave them along the routes.

"We're not encouraging them to cross, we're not helping them to cross. We just don't want them to die when they're crossing," Morones said.

The water drops involve a two and a half hour drive from San Diego to the Jacumba wilderness and a hike six miles into the desert, according to an AJ+ video from a water drop in spring 2016. "The isolation, the heat, the dangers," Morones said to describe only a snapshot of the days migrants spend in the desert, wishing to venture beyond the border.

"And now with Trump the situation's gotten even more desperate because people are curious. And I mean the messages of hate he's promoting, the sexism, the anti-Muslim, all that, we can't stand for that. We need to stand up and make knowledge and say this is wrong, and that's what we're doing," Morones said.

While messages of hate are swirling, Border Angels and those working on the immigration issue, such as the Global Immersion Project, bring messages of hope. They share how these immigrants have such care for their families. They share how these immigrants are fighting for their lives.

"They're threatened down there, and they're seeking mostly their lives for their kids. They know of a relative up here and they're trying to get to them to save their kids from getting killed," said Shaun Sheahan, learning lab project coordinator for the Global Immersion Project headquartered in San Diego. Sheahan presents the unique perspective of having lived in Tijuana and now in San Diego, creating in him a heart for people on both sides of the border.

In continuing to save lives, Border Angels brings hope within the water drops and beyond them, right up to the wall to wall interaction of families at Border Field State Park. Penny described touch through the wall as pinkies only. The once diamond-shaped chain link fence became a fortified, inescapable trap in 2006.

"The only way you can touch somebody on the other side of the border is with the tip of your pinky," Penny said. "The links in the fence are so tight."

The emergency door, colloquially called the Door of Hope, to Friendship Park from Tijuana.

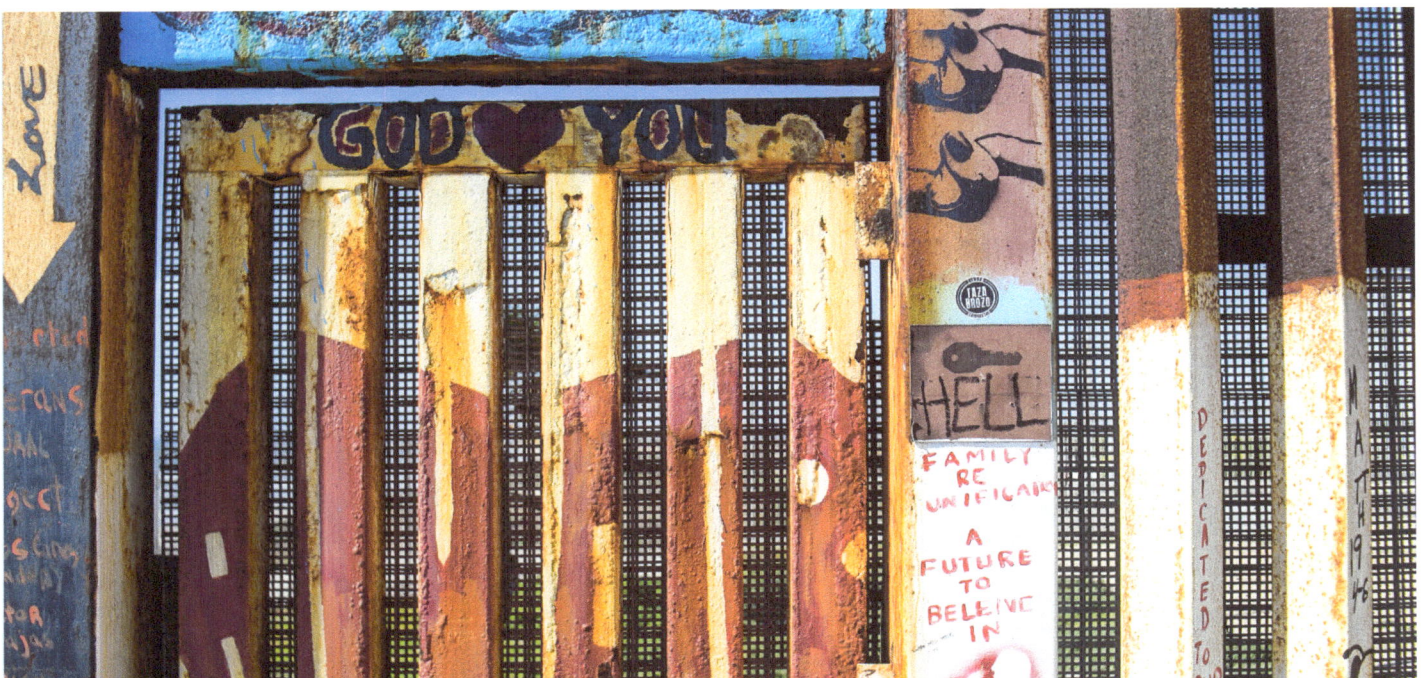

Rather than having one fence, two walls were built— one on the United States side and the other on the Mexican side. On the U.S. side, the wall opens every Saturday and Sunday from 10 a.m. to 2 p.m., according to the California Department of Parks and Recreation. On the Mexican side, the wall keeps families from touching one another.

The emergency door on the Mexican side has slowly started to creak open, with the first ever Open Door of Hope day in 2013. As the years continue, Border Angels strives to see the reunions of families, the meetings of grandchildren and grandparents and the joy of squeezing one another's hands happening every weekend.

"I've never seen anything like that before in my life, quite frankly," Penny said. "To actually see, for the first time in history, a door being opened on the border and families being able to reunite too like that, there's almost no words to describe it."

The six families who are accepted for the day are allowed to gather together for five minutes each, according to Penny. However, the number who apply for those dear five minutes is far beyond six. The desperation for this project has only increased with the Trump administration planning to build another wall.

"[The U.S.] shouldn't be building a wall, it should be building bridges, it should be having a way that people can get in line," Morones said. "We should be working with other countries as partners, not looking down on them, but looking equal to them."

New doors continue to open for Border Angels and the immigrants they work with as Morones continues to dive into the issues surrounding the border. To continue to love the immigrants in every way possible without breaking the law, as Sheahan said.

The projects Morones started with in the beginning, the providing of food to migrants, water drops and connecting immigrants with attorneys, live on today.

"My parents always instilled in me a great love for Mexico and a respect for the country that we live in and I know that we as people should be treating everybody with dignity and respect and that's not seen here," Morones said. "And so it's important that we all do our little bit. And that's what we try to do with Border Angels, we do our little bit to make this a more just world."

The life of every man, woman and child crossing the border, praying to see their family in the next year, and working every day for barely minimum wage remains at stake in the work Border Angels does.

"There's a lot of life and death involved in this," Penny said.

The stories continue to pour in. The reality of lives lived on the border festers like weeds on one's front porch. The injustices continue to occur. There seems to be no way to stop them. Morones rises for the day, Border Angels volunteers by his side, and begins to fight the day's fight.

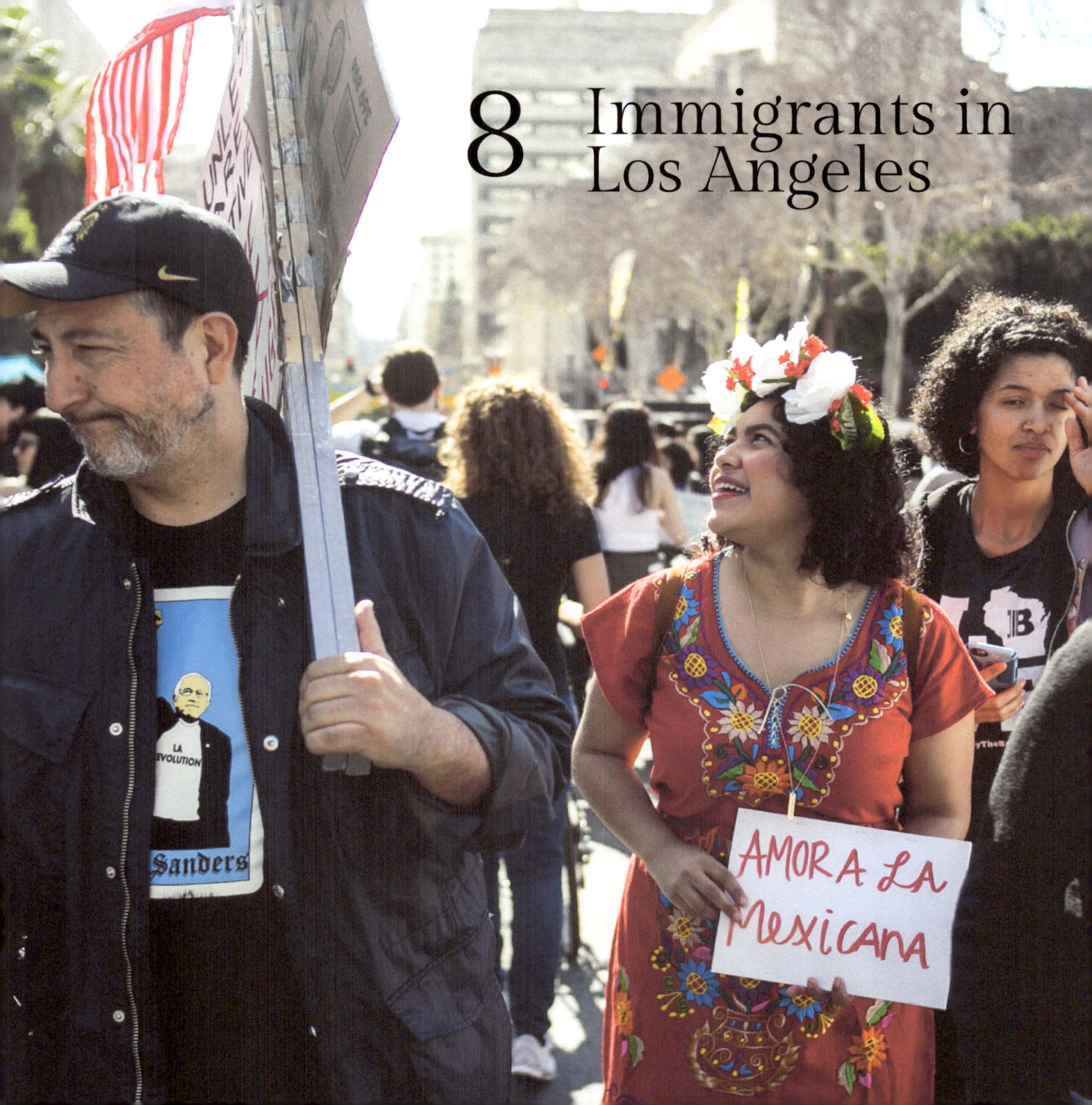

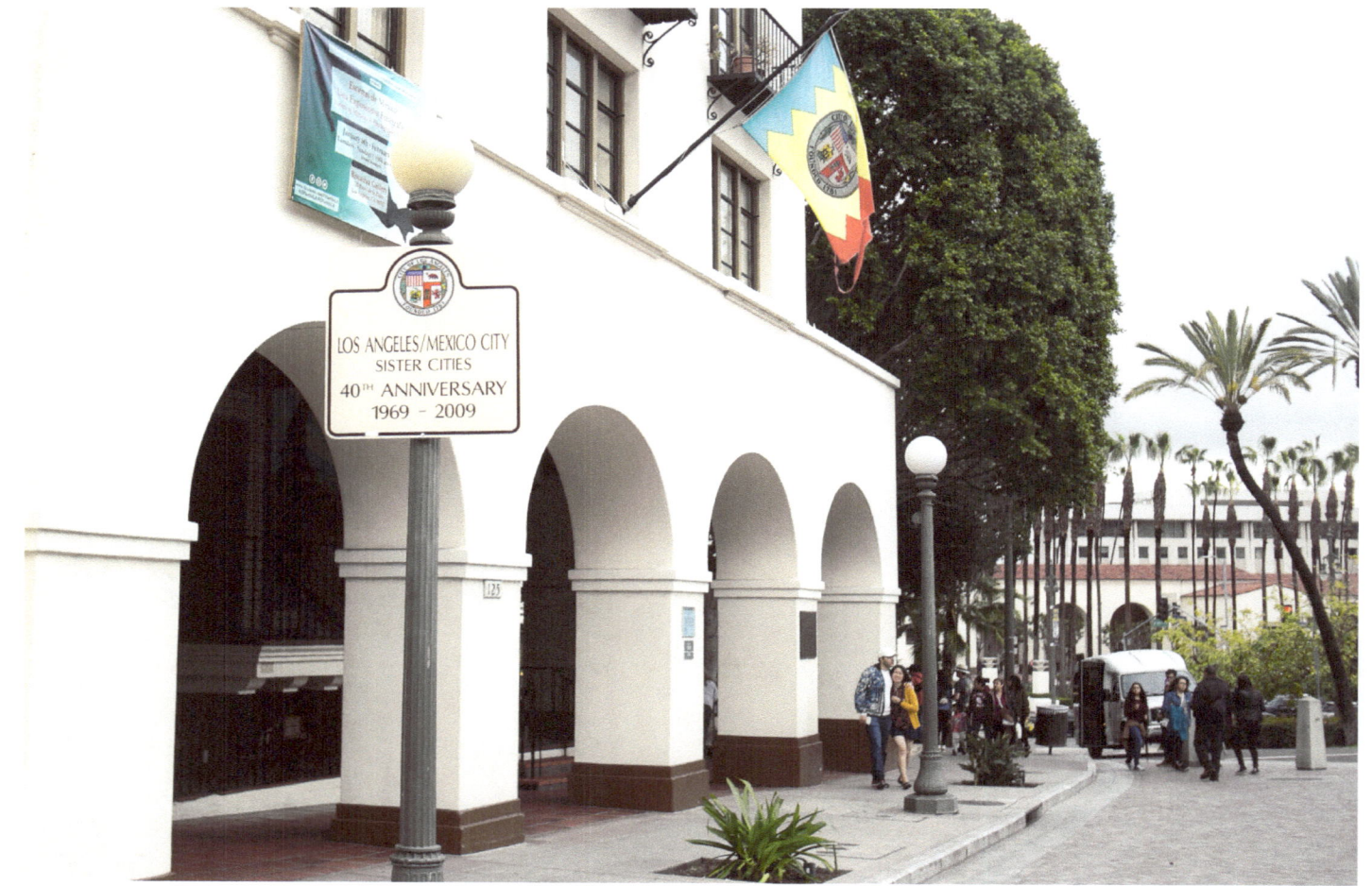

At the center of the Los Angeles Plaza Historic District is La Plaza United Methodist Church, facing the plaza housing El Pueblo de Los Angeles Historic Monument and abutting Olvera Street. Union Station pictured in back.

Cover photo and above photo by: Anna Warner

EXPRESSIONS OF CULTURE

Founded in the late 1800's, Los Angeles is home to the largest Hispanic population in the country. The heart of the city was originally titled "El Pueblo de Nuestra Señora la Reina de los Ángeles del Río de Porciúncula," centered around "La Placita" (plaza), and the founding street, Calle Olvera (Olvera Street). This area was the city center for more than a century and is now the most historic district in Los Angeles (pictured to right). Olvera Street is now a celebration of Mexican heritage, boasting many restaurants, shops and stalls, and historic buildings–including many museums and churches.

[*]pbs.org

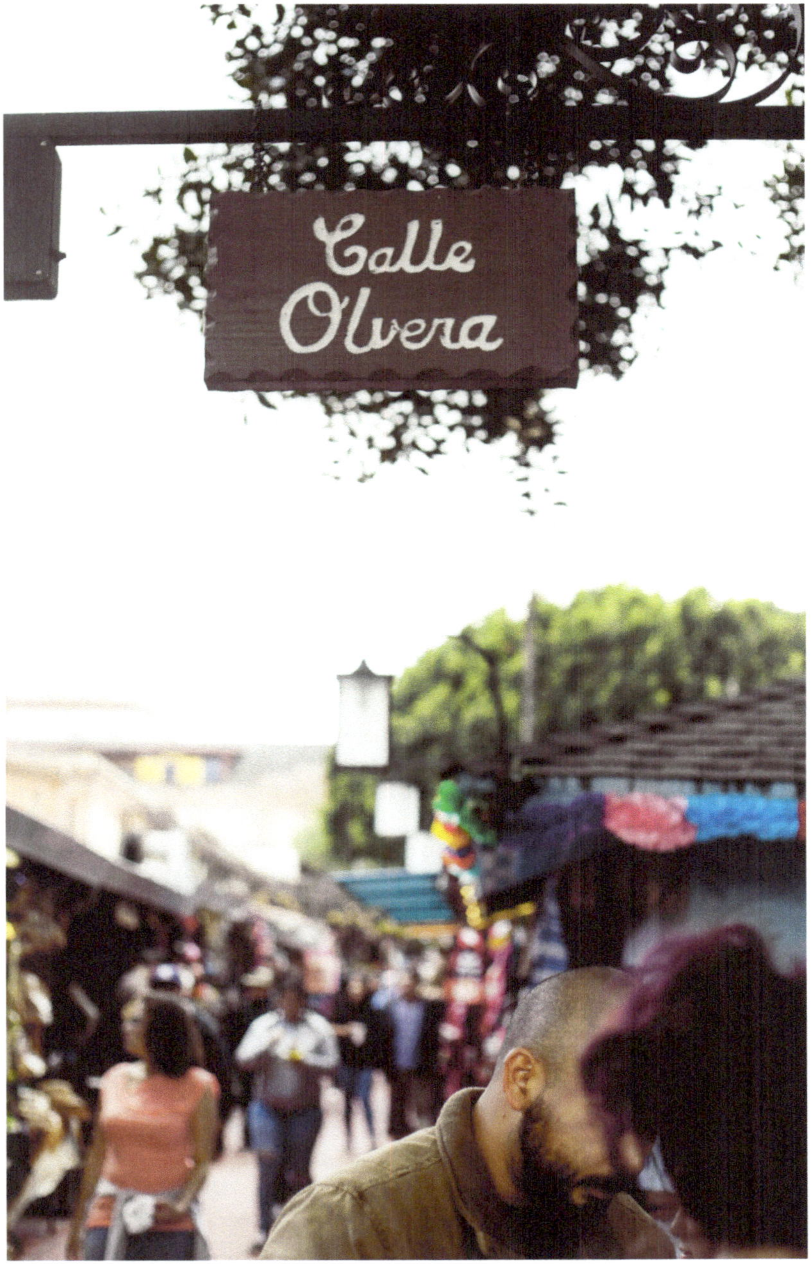

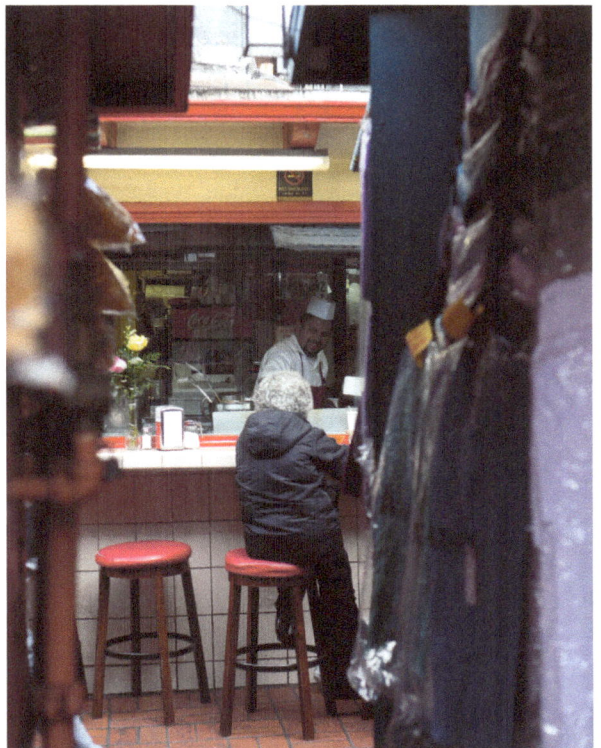

A woman buys Mexican street food on Olvera Street.

Photo by: Molli Kaptein

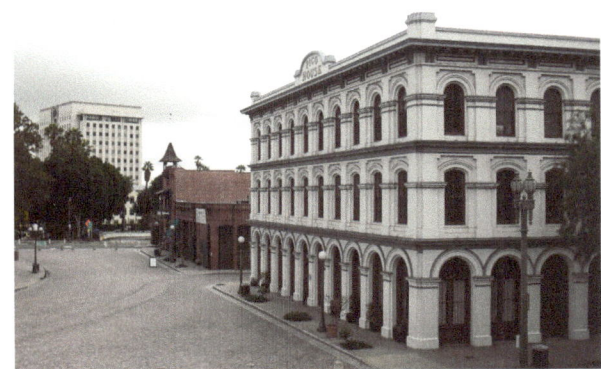

The north entrance to Olvera Street.

Photo by: Molli Kaptein

Pico House, a hotel built by Pío Pico, California's last Mexican governor.

Photo by: Anna Warner

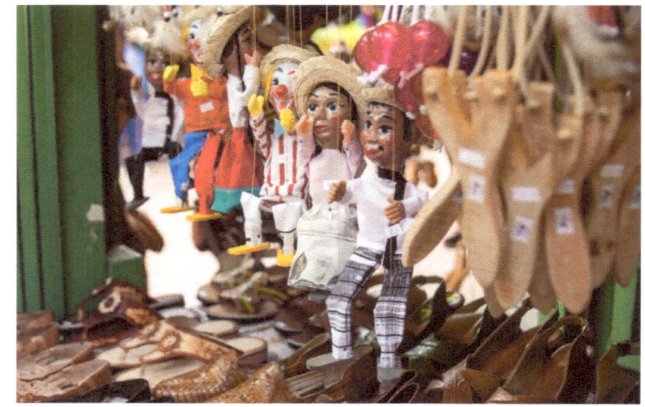

Left: Marionettes for sale in an open-air stall on Olvera Street. These stalls, as well as many restraunts, populate the street.

Below: A traditional mariachi band travels through Olvera Street playing as a celebration of their Hispanic Heritage.

Right: At the Pueblo de Los Angeles Historical Monument outside of Olvera Street and the historic Pico House, performers gather to present traditional Aztec dances in celebration of not only their Mexican heritage, but its root in Aztec culture.

Photos by: Anna Warner

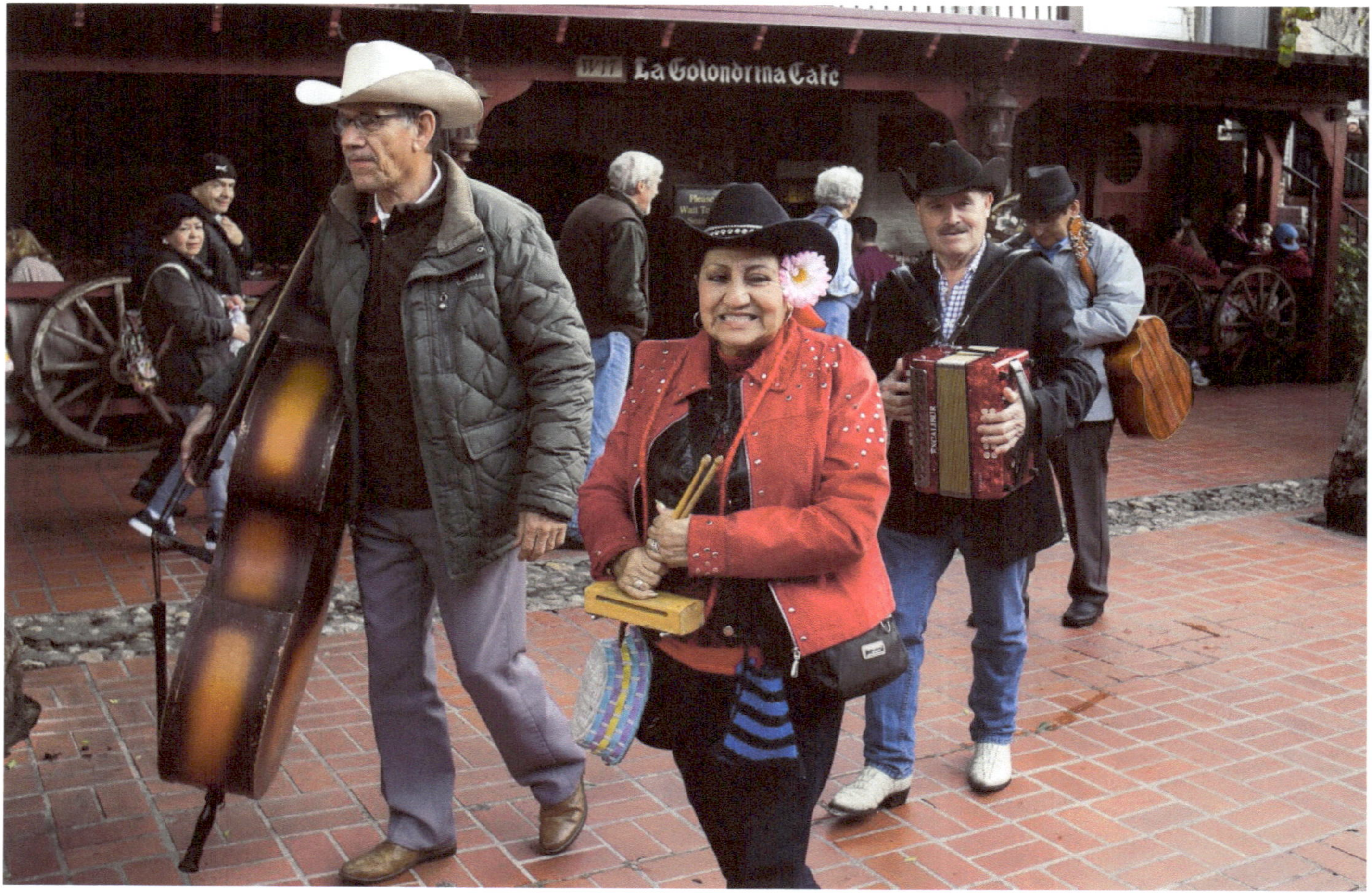

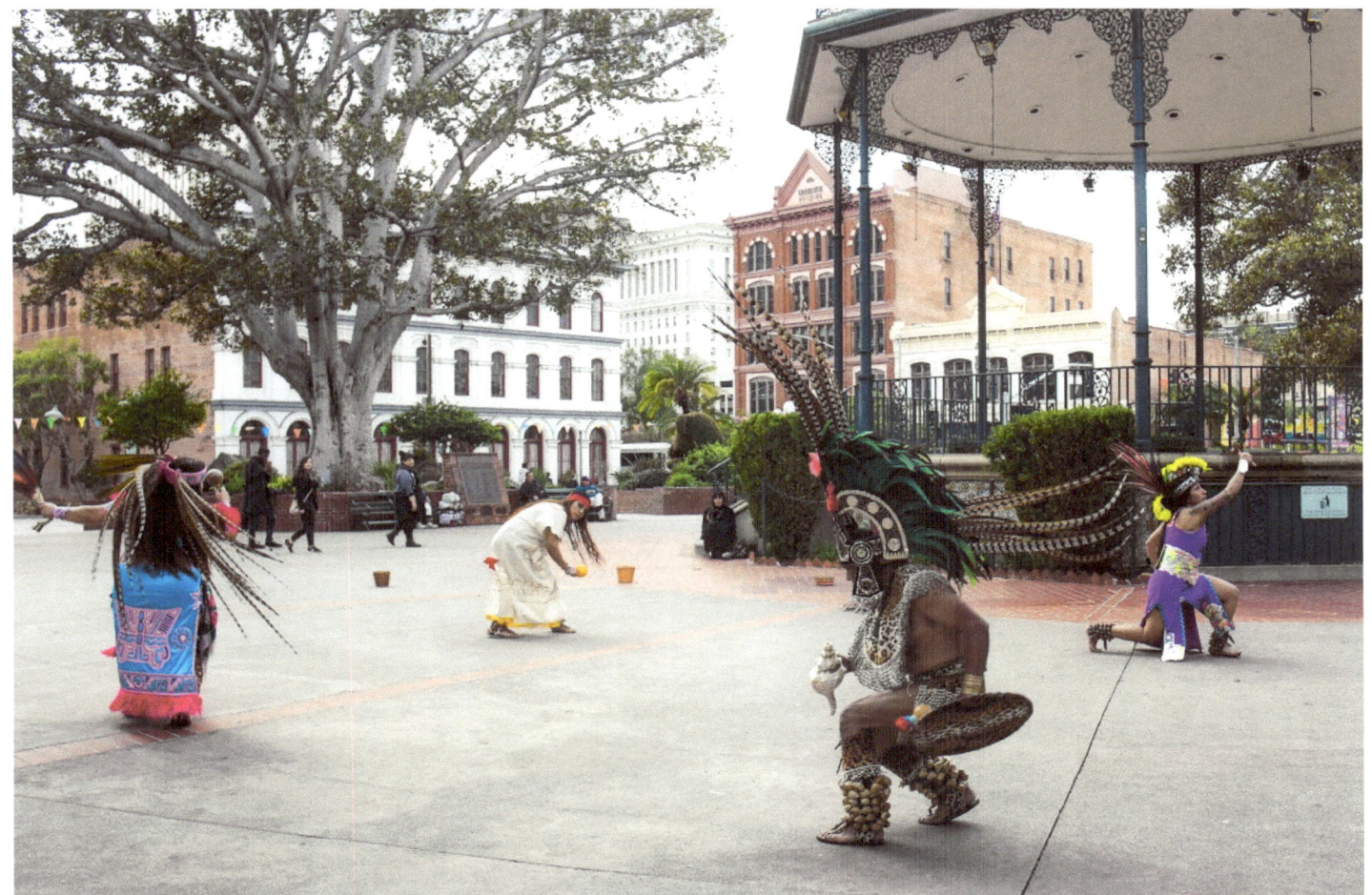

Chicano Heritage

"Chicano," believed to come from the Aztec word for "Mexicano" and later "Xicano," refers to a person whose heritage stems from Mexico's indiginous Aztec people. In the 1960's, the term became popular as a celebration of cultural and ethnic identity during the Chicano Movement, a parallel push for civil rights stemming from Southern California. Chicanos found they did not fully identify with either their Mexican or American heritage, but desired to take on the ingenuity, cultural vibrancy and advanced socio-economic development that their Aztec ancestors are often associated with. Today, to be a Chicano implies a sense of self-determinism and a desire to better the community. South Los Angeles is characterized by its Chicano presence and as of 2015, 74% of the population is Hispanic.

*vividhues.com, censusreporter.org

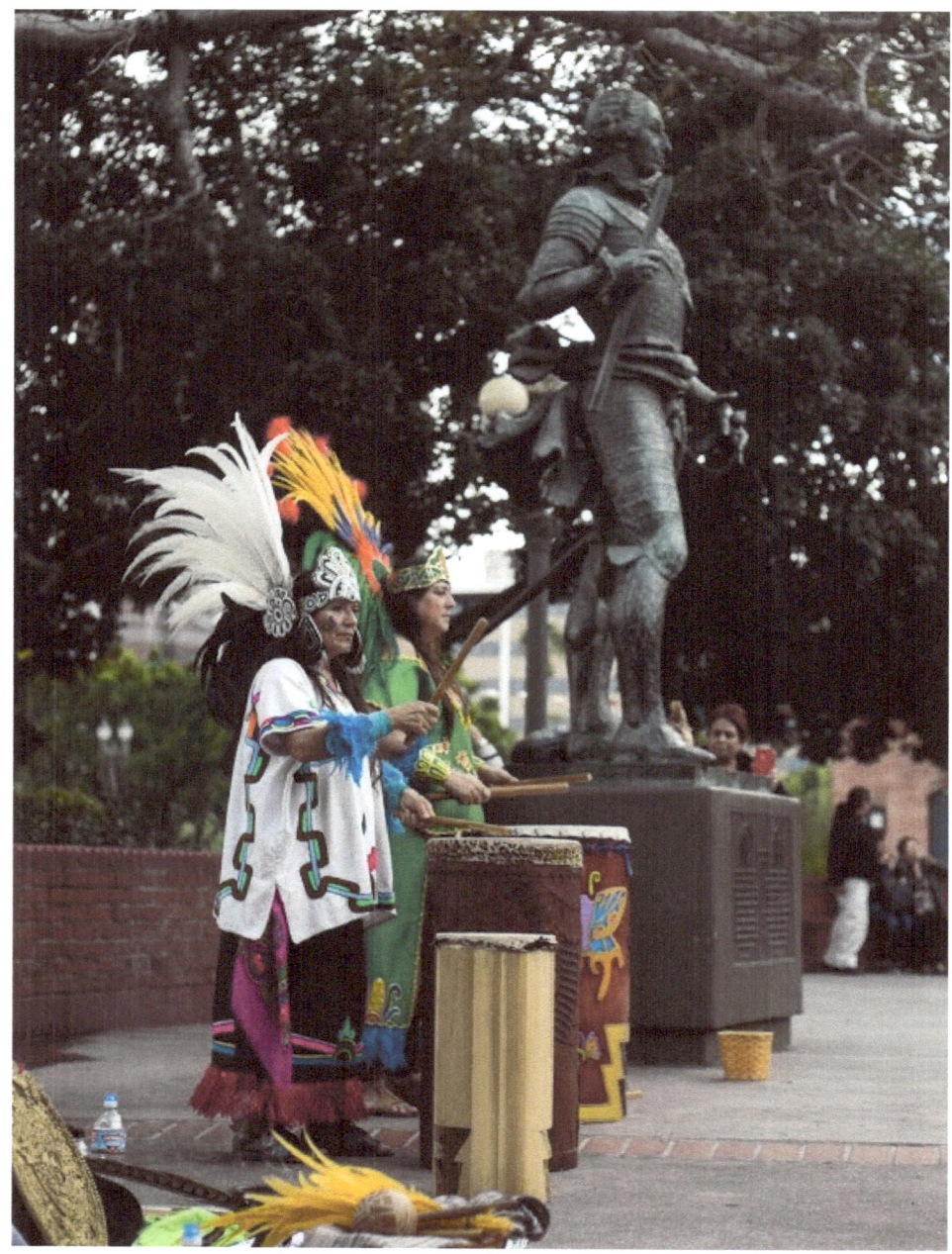

Women drum a traditional Aztec beat for the dancers performing at the Pueblo de Los Angeles Historical Monument.

Photo by: Molli Kaptein

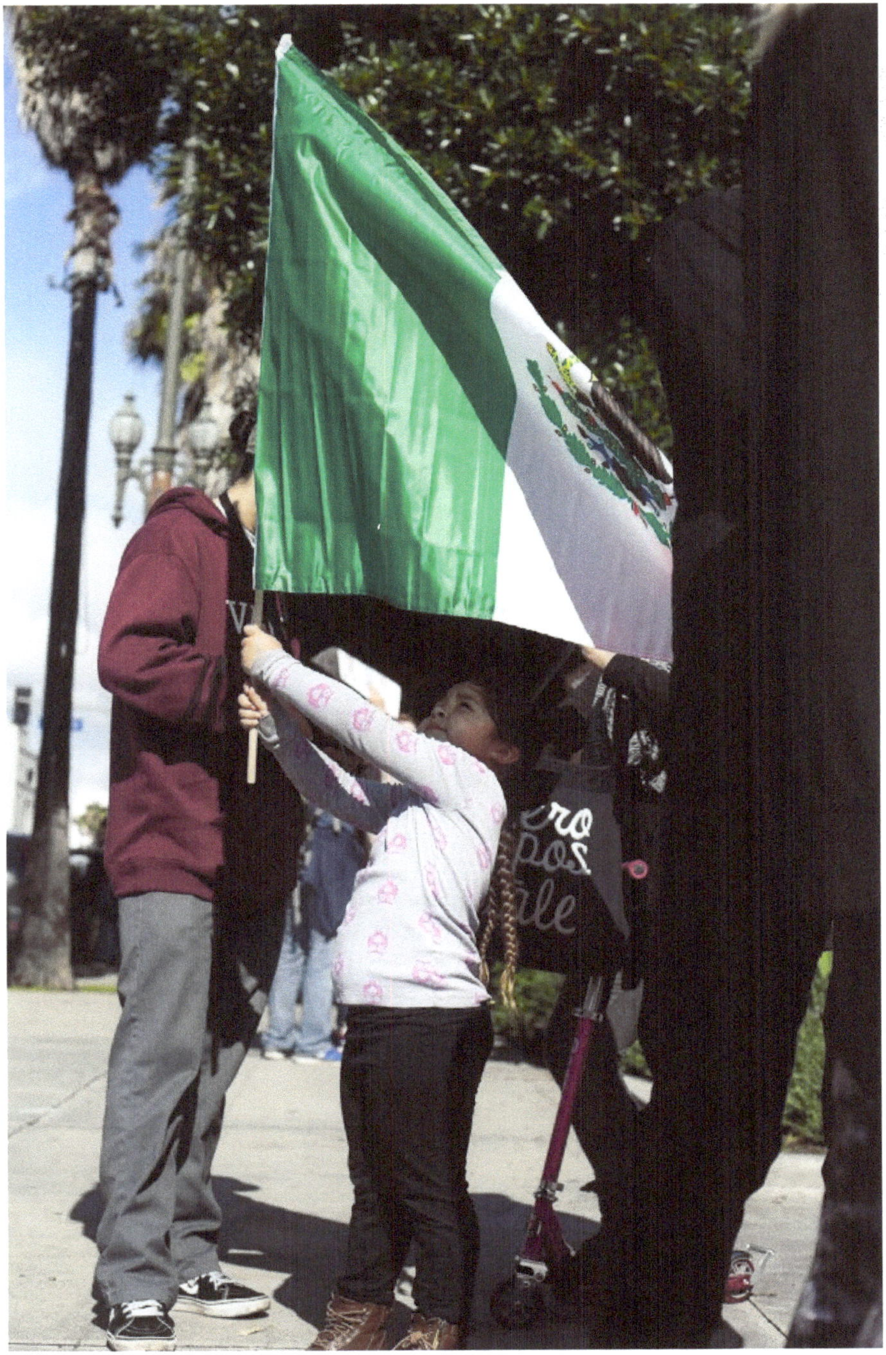

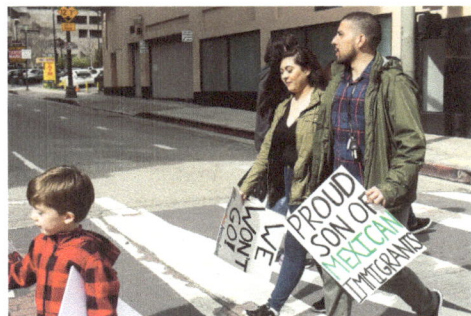

Free the People

In defense of Chicano heritage, many hispanics attended the Free the People Immigration March which occured on February 18, 2017. This march was in response to a shift in policy under the Trump administration with regards to immigrants and refugees. The goal was to raise support to keep Los Angeles' policies regarding sanctuary for immigrants and increase protection for minorities. Beginning in the famous Pershing Square, the march terminated on the steps of Los Angeles City Hall, a mere few blocks from Los Angeles Plaza Historic District.

Left: A child waves the Mexican flag on the steps of Los Angeles City Hall during the Free the People March.

Photo by: Molli Kaptein

Above: A couple attends the Free the People March bearing a sign indicating the man's heritage and personal stake in the march.

Photo by: Anna Warner

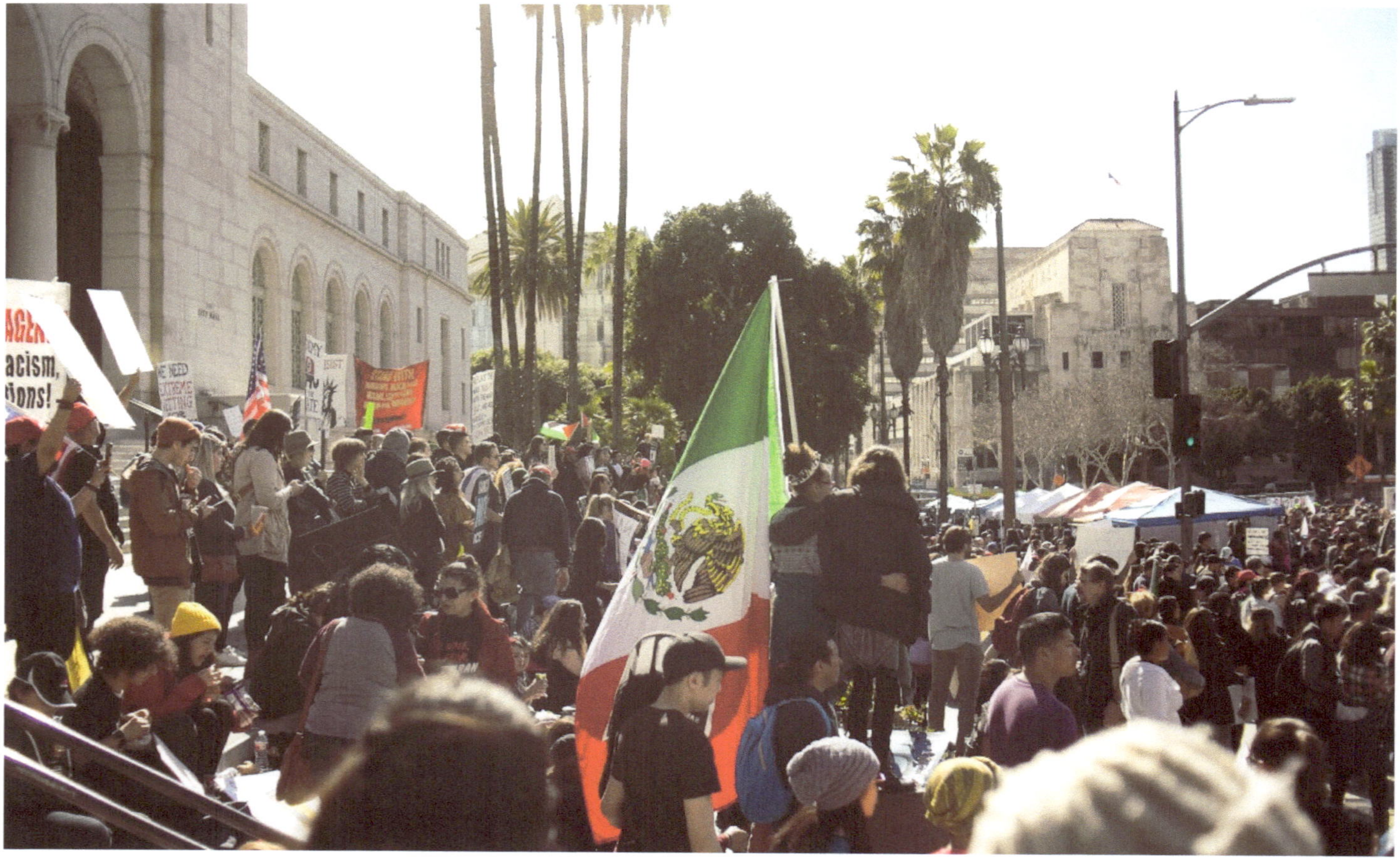

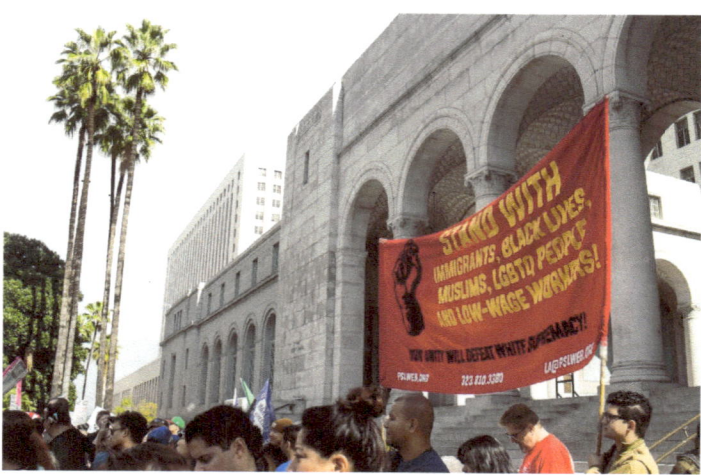
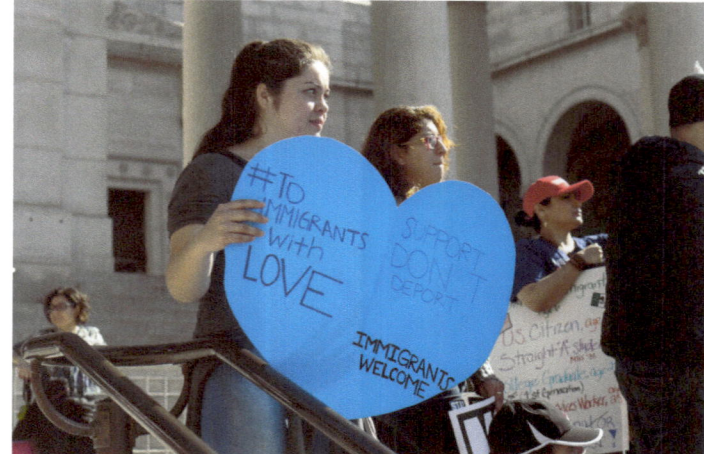

Top left: Two women hug and carry a Mexican flag on the steps of Los Angeles City Hall while various speakers engage the crowd.

Photo by: Anna Warner.

Bottom Left: Several immigrant communities come together to show support for each other during the march, as evidenced by the multitude of signs, including a young Latina bearing a sign declaring "to immigrants with love."

Left Photo by: Anna Warner.
Right Photo by: Molli Kaptein.

Top right: A man at the march proudly shows off his Frida Kahlo socks.

Photo by: Molli Kaptein

Below: Woman emphasizes the U.S.'s history as a nation of immigrants.

Photo by: Molli Kaptein

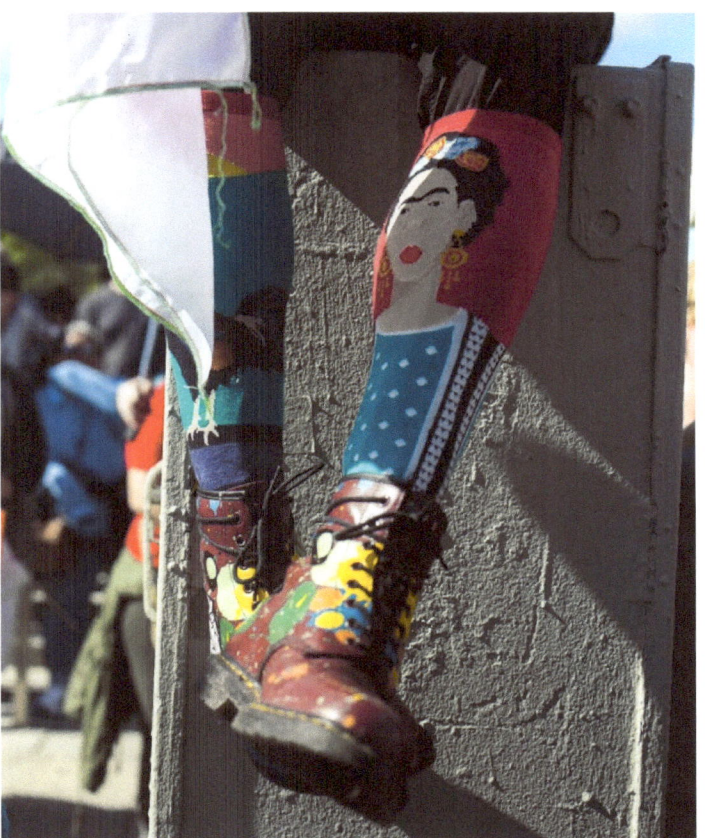

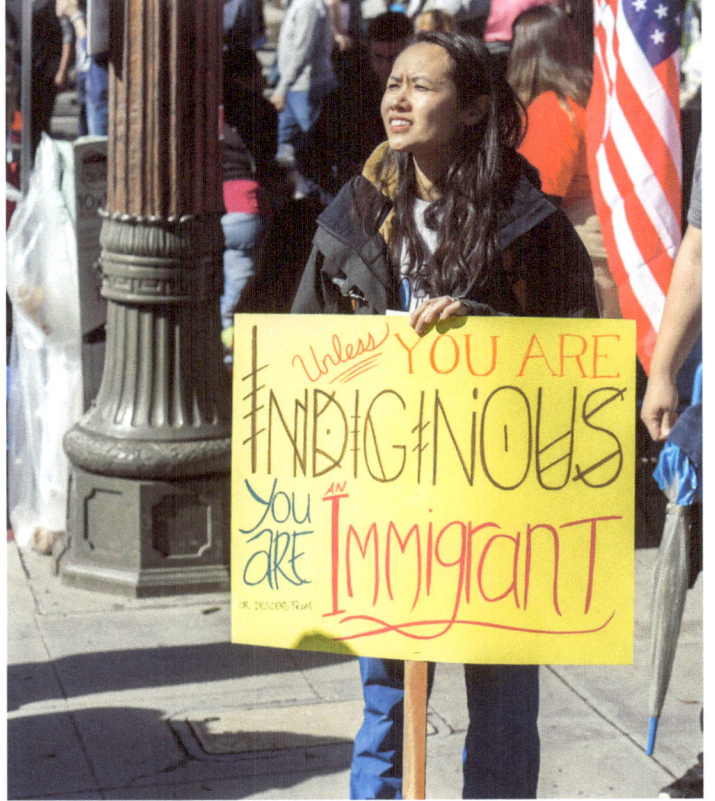

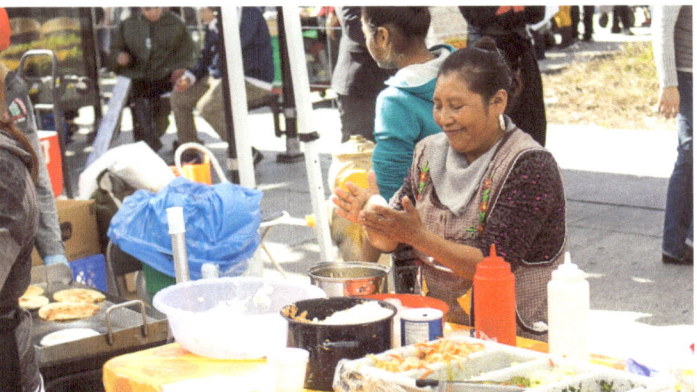

A woman happily makes tradtional Mexican street food at the march.

Photo by: Anna Warner

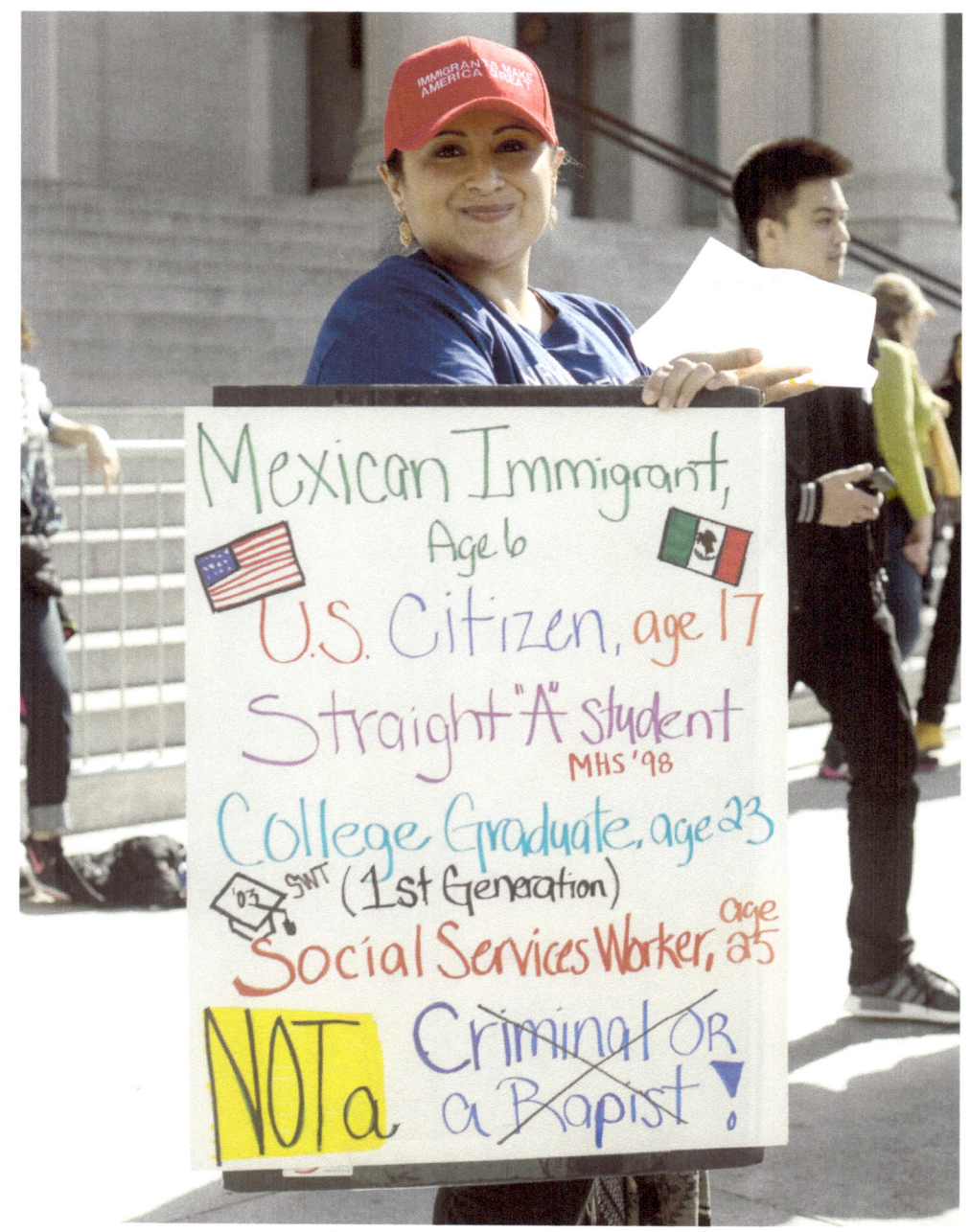

A woman proudly displays her sign on the stairs of Los Angeles City Hall.

Photo by: Molli Kaptein

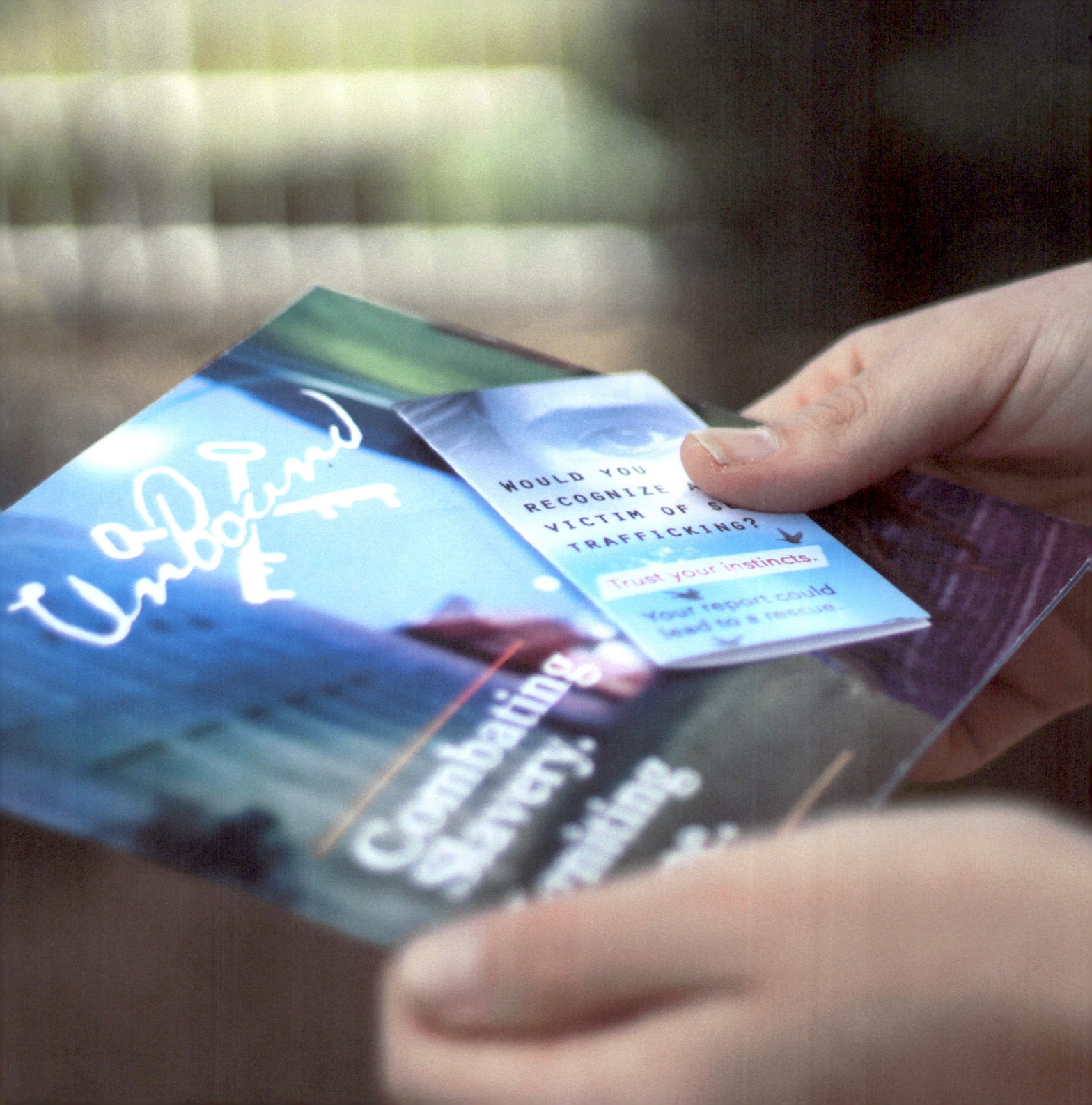

9 Human Trafficking on the Border

By Sarah Pineda

Photos by Alyssa Yee

> " Defend the weak and the fatherless; uphold the cause of the poor and the oppressed.
> Rescue the weak and the needy; deliver them from the hand of the wicked. "
>
> Psalm 82:3-4

Walking through Zona Norte—otherwise known as the red light district in Tijuana, Mexico—there are bars, gentlemen's clubs and women lined up on the sidewalks. Speakers blare with loud music fading from Spanish to English, almost drowning the catcalling whistles of the men sitting outside these businesses. For the women who are dressed in bikinis, tight short dresses and towering stilettos, this is their life. Stuck on the Mexican side of the border, these women have fallen into the world of human trafficking.

According to the International Labour Organization, human trafficking has seized the lives of over 20.9 billion people around the world, resulting in a $150 billion industry. Human trafficking is defined by the U.S. Department of Homeland Security as modern-day slavery, involving the use of force, fraud or coercion to obtain some type of labor or commercial sex act. In a joint data collection project between Polaris and Consejo Ciudadano, Mexico's first international human trafficking hotline, the organizations were able to identify 508 undocumented victims of human trafficking living in the United States in 2016. Fleeing the war-torn streets, the sounds of gunshots flying past their home and the grumbling sounds coming from their stomach, this is their motivation in taking the trek across the border into the United States. Yet, they are welcomed by people prepared to take advantage of them in their vulnerable state by stripping away their identity and their basic human rights. Victims are forced to please man after man in a grimy motel or work long hours in the beaming sun or enclosed in a house. In a country known for being the land of the free and home of the brave, people being trafficked are scared and see the United States as a prison. Luckily, there are many different ministries, outreach programs and task forces that are helping those who are trapped in human trafficking by increasing awareness and providing resources for this growing crime.

SAN DIEGO'S $810 MILLION HUMAN
TRAFFICKING BUSINESS

In California, the top three cities with the most human trafficking cases being reported are San Francisco, Los Angeles and San Diego. All three cities share a large group of undocumented individuals in their population. A Pew Research study ranked San Diego as the 13th highest for trafficking among cities in the U.S., bringing in about $810 million. PETALS, which stands for Pervasive Encounters That Agape Love Shines, is a human trafficking outreach ministry from Rock Church in San Diego County. The purpose of the ministry is to contact women with ads on Backpage.com, who may be victims of human trafficking. Backpage is an online advertising website which makes most of its revenue off adult escort ads. It contributes to the human trafficking business as it is known as an online brothel, generating millions from these ads and contributing to illegal sex trade. A press release from the Office of the Attorney General stated, "Backpage's internal revenue reports show that from January 2013 to March 2015, 99% of the site's worldwide income was directly attributable to the 'adult' section." Suyapa Ulloa and May Guerrero are co-outreach leaders of PETALS and have about 20 volunteers who meet once a month to call these women and reassure them there is someone out there who cares. PETALS begin their outreach night by logging onto Backpage and calling the numbers on the women's ad to reach out to them. They can make about 30 calls in two to three hours and engage in conversation with the women and asking if they need any help or prayer.

Ulloa explains how PETALS focuses on unconditionally loving these women, regardless of their lifestyle, and do not try to convert them, but instead show them they are a group of people who genuinely care and can help when they are ready. PETALS strives to build relationships, calling back women from previous months to check up on them and gain their trust. Ulloa believes human trafficking has reached the severity that it has due to those who work or visit San Diego with no attachment to the city. "We are a tourist city, so this is not their home, they have the mentality that I am just here to party and have a good time," said Ulloa, also stressing how San Diego is a "border town" too.

UNDOCUMENTED VICTIMS IN THE DESERT

In places more remote in Southern California, Riverside County and the East Coachella Valley struggle with high human trafficking rates too. Since 2010, Operation SafeHouse has collaborated with the Riverside County Sherriff's Department to create the Riverside County Human Trafficking Task Force. To remove the victim mentality, they call the victims "clients" instead. They have been able to assist over 400 clients of human trafficking. The organization is based throughout the Riverside County and Thousand Palms , and focuses on serving victims of any kind of human trafficking, undocumented or domestic, with no age restrictions. Anti-human trafficking director Kristen Dolan has had few cases of undocumented clients, but while they are few, she knows they exist.

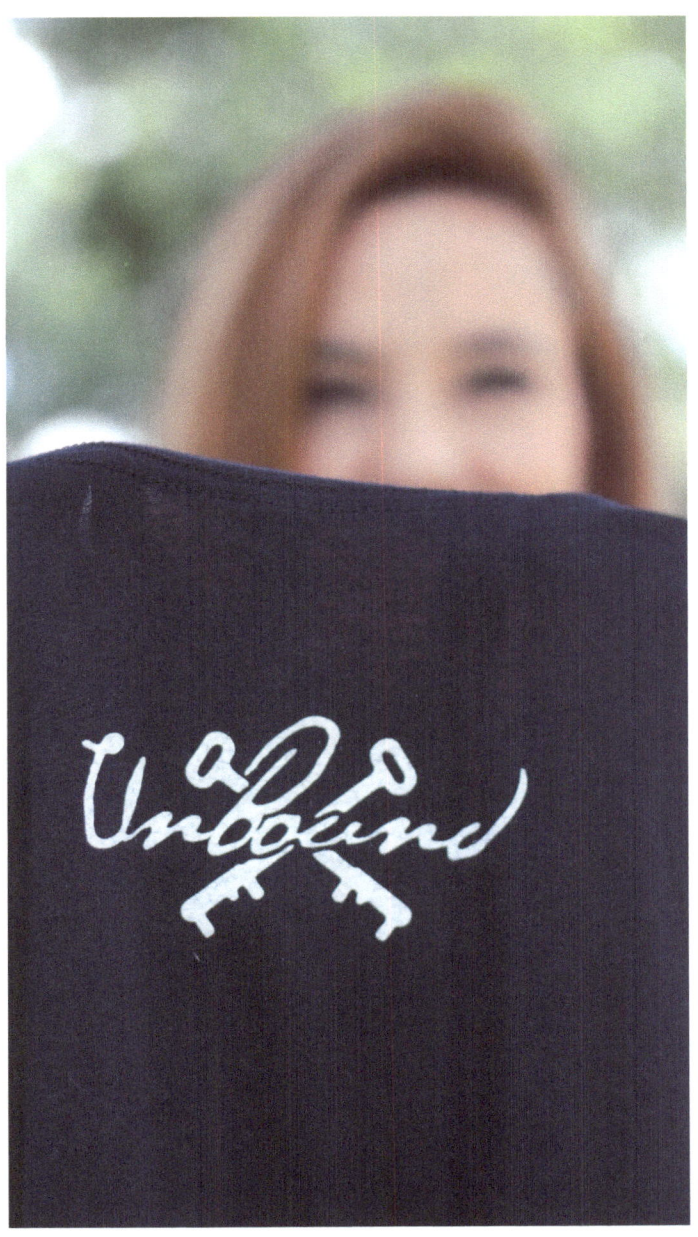

Phoenix Freeman is the Director of UnBound Orange County. The local organization has joined the fight against human trafficking. UnBound unites local churches, organizations, law enforcement, government, businesses, and individuals in pursuit of justice.

"It takes a while to build up trust and let someone know that we are there to help and not to hurt them. Especially in the times we are now, politically, it's a lot harder to gain someone's trust that they are not going to be deported if you're illegal," said Dolan.

Operation SafeHouse's outreach to those who are undocumented looks different than reaching those who are domestic. Instead of putting up flyers, they must create relationships and build credibility as a trusted organization. When working with undocumented clients, Operation SafeHouse values stabilizing the client and making sure they receive the proper documentation, despite what they have gone through. The U.S. Citizens and Immigration Services protects human trafficking victims by issuing a T nonimmigrant status or a T Visa. This allows victims the right to stay in the United States and assist law enforcement in the investigation of their human trafficking cases. These victims are living in fear, and Dolan wants to reassure them they can come forward to Operation SafeHouse. The Riverside Human Trafficking Task Force also partakes in certain protocols when dealing with undocumented victims. "Their stories are usually ones of fraud," said Dolan, as someone has manipulated them into thinking they were coming to the United States for a better life.

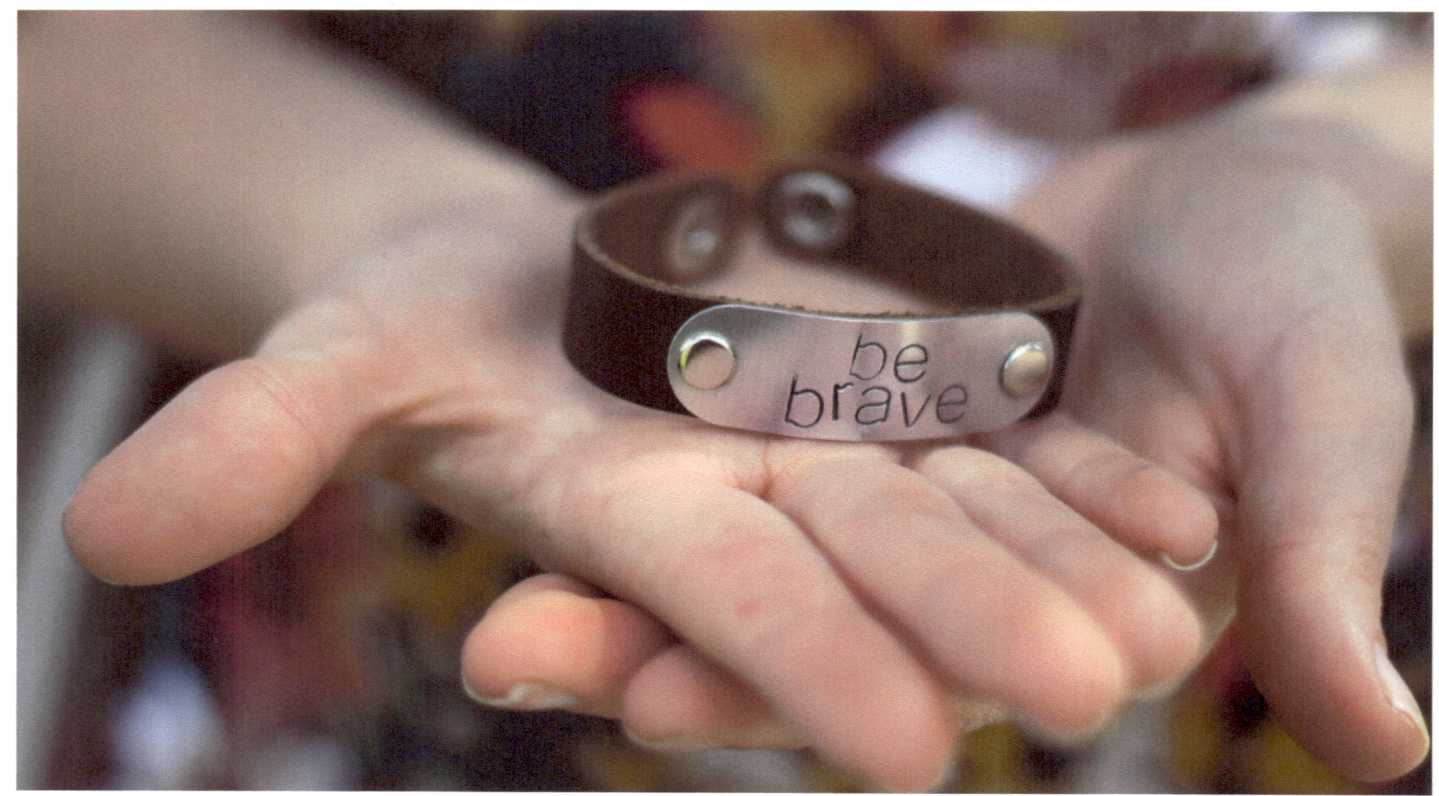

This "Be Brave" bracelet was hand-made by a rescued victim of sex-trafficking. According to Phoenix Freeman, the woman who gave her the bracelet is now married and counsels girls who have stories similar to her own. Freeman wears the bracelet as a reminder that there is hope in these seemingly hopeless situations.

UNBOUND IN ORANGE COUNTY

Affiliated with Antioch Community Church in Fullerton, UnBound has opened up a chapter this year in Orange County, to serve as a ministry to bring awareness to human trafficking. Through prevention awareness, victim advocacy and professional training, Phoenix Freeman leads the chapter towards accomplishing the goal of decreasing the demand of human trafficking. Freeman is passionate about bringing awareness to the issue of human trafficking. In addition to volunteering with the Orange County Human Trafficking Task Force or OCHTTF, she has interned with the A21 campaign and has even been approached by traffickers herself in the past.

Freeman believes it is important the church created this chapter in its location because "men will pay for more girls in Orange County because of how affluent it is compared to other places."

UnBound also strives to bring attention to labor trafficking since it is an aspect of human trafficking which is difficult to investigate. Freeman believes labor trafficking is "harder to spot and not talked about as much because it has many different forms." She provided examples such as employees at a well-known hotel and a nanny for a family, identifying the victims of human trafficking hiding within society. In her previous experience in working with the OCHTTF, she describes the evolution of what law enforcement and the task force were searching for. Though they began by solely looking for domestic, minor girls as the only victims of human trafficking, the OCHTTF has begun to shift their attention to looking for undocumented men who are being used by a trafficker.

RESEARCH ON LABOR TRAFFICKING

You see foreign words exiting the mouth, none of which make sense except the few which carry a negative connotation: harsh words, spoken with that loud tone in which you associate with how it's time to get to work. In the life of an undocumented labor trafficking victim, this is what they are faced with. As many are restricted by the language barrier, they are unaware if this is the norm in the United States or if this is slavery. The Center for Public Policy Studies share how labor trafficking of immigrants in California could be estimated at 495,000 potential victims. Since labor trafficking is harder to detect than sex trafficking, they are named potential victims until they have reached out for help.

Sheldon Zhang, a sociology professor at San Diego State University, conducted studies on human trafficking across the U.S.-Mexico border, funded by the United States Department of Justice. In his research, Zhang looked inside the sex trafficking and labor trafficking in San Diego County from immigrants. In Zhang's study, "Looking for a Hidden Population," the population targeted were Spanish-speaking migrant men in the San Diego County workforce. He found that "30% of our target population are victims of labor trafficking, and 55% are victims of abusive labor practices or gross exploitations." The top three labor industries with the most labor trafficking are in agriculture/farms, domestic work and landscaping/gardening. Similar to the women being sex trafficked, these victims are forced to work in dangerous conditions and risk their lives out of fear of being deported back to their deteriorating country.

As the women stood only a few feet apart from each other in Zona Norte, they waited for someone to pick them up. With somber faces, their youthful age could not cover their old eyes. For many, human trafficking begins before they even leave for the United States.

According to an investigation done by Fusion, 80% of women are raped while crossing the border.

Because it is well-known among immigrants this will happen, some choose to take contraceptive pills before crossing to avoid getting pregnant. This leads them into developing the idea this practice is normal during the migration across the border. They find their new life in brothels and working for pimps as something which is supposed to occur when entering the United States.

In a separate research, Zhang found that the border community of Tijuana served as a gateway into human trafficking across the border. Aware of these individual's thirst to get into the U.S., Zhang recognizes that "regardless of how and where one chooses to enter into the migration process, force and fraud can quickly compel people to engage in activities that they would otherwise not have chosen of their own free will." He notes that many of these women are uneducated and unable to speak English. Therefore, they do not have the proper requirements for a job, leaving them to sell their bodies. These women's stories of how they entered the commercial sex industry show how they were manipulated and sought after financial stability.

Why not investigate? Why are none of these victims coming forward? Why do none of the victims come forward? Fear. These victims are afraid to come forward due to the possibility of being deported. Fear is the root of the sustained business of recruiting undocumented men and women to stay stuck in the world of human trafficking.

To raise awareness for human trafficking three major initiatives focus on prevention, professional training, and survivor advocacy.

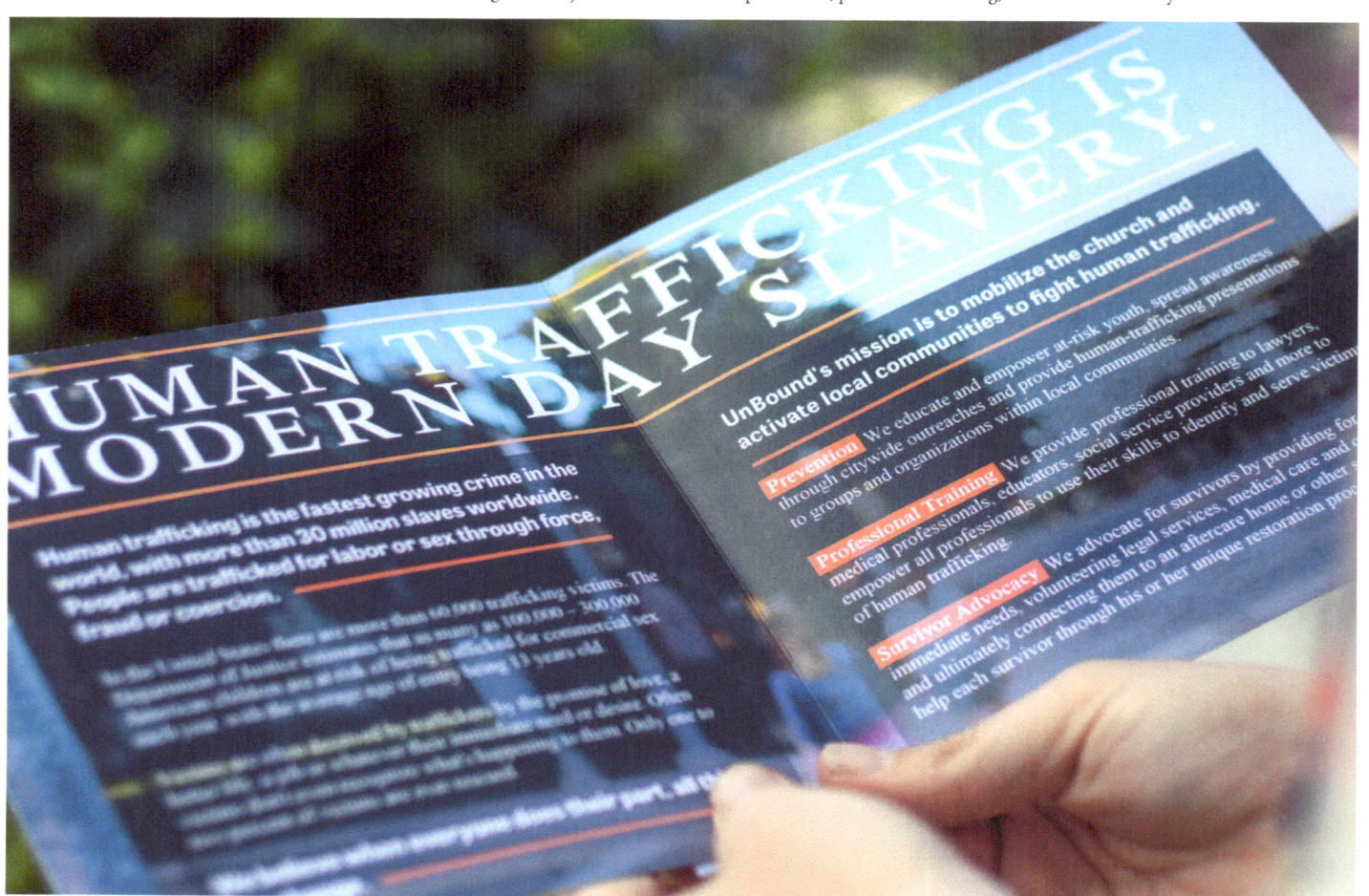

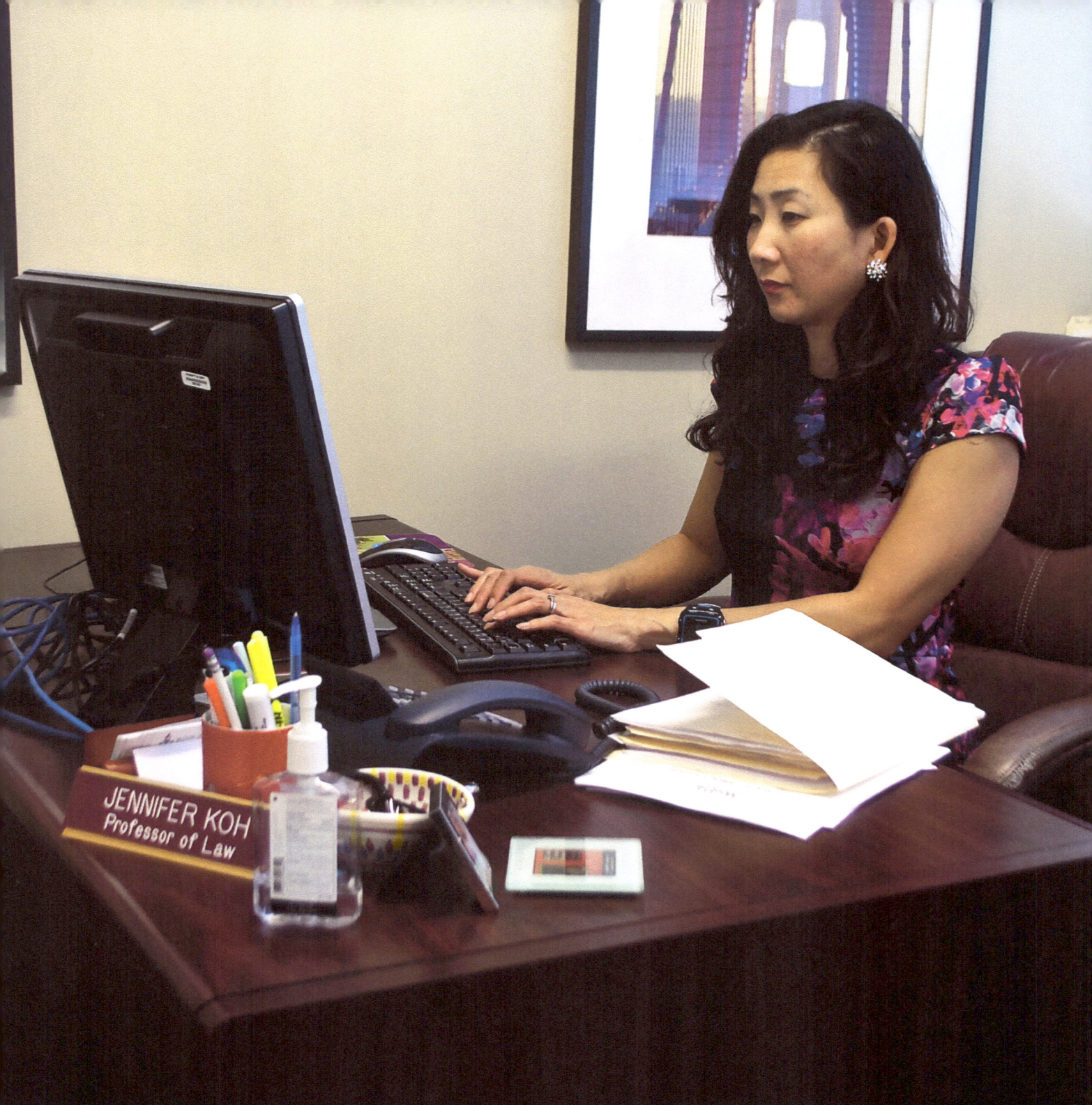

10 Legal Aid for Immigrants

By Jessica Goddard

Photos taken by Aili Acone-Chavez

> " We hold these truths to be self-evident, that all men are created equal, that they are endowed by their Creator with certain unalienable rights, that among these are life, liberty, and the pursuit of happiness. "

Preamble to the Declaration of Independence.

Jennifer Koh is an associate professor of law and the director of the immigration clinic at Western State College of Law in Irvine, California. She has lived in Southern California for over ten years, though she originally hails from the East Coast. She earned her bachelor's degree from Yale University and her J.D. from Columbia University School of Law. Koh has a passion for helping her students work for social justice and care for the marginalized in society.

DO YOU OFFER LEGAL SERVICES TO IMMIGRANTS, AND IF SO, WHAT ARE THOSE SERVICES?

"We do offer services to immigrants. My role is I'm a law professor here at Western State, but part of what I do is I run a legal clinic for low-income noncitizens. . .We provide pro bono legal representation to noncitizens in a range of matters, things like U Visas for victims of crimes, T Visas for victims of trafficking, other applications. For example: for young people or maybe people who are seeking asylum based on persecution in their home countries, for people who are facing deportation. Then we also do community based education and advocacy in Orange County around immigration issues."

We don't have a huge volume of cases because part of the clinic's mission is to be a teaching clinic, meaning that most of the cases are handled by law students who work under either my supervision or the supervision of another attorney. . . That's a way also for law students to develop their practical lawyering skills before they graduate from law school."

WHY ARE YOU PASSIONATE ABOUT HELPING IMMIGRANTS?

"Oh, so much to say. I mean for me . . . I really think that immigration issues dovetail with just basic human rights issues of the ability to seek a better life for yourself, the ability to stay together with your family. It dovetails with constitutional rights of due process, and it's an area of law in which the U.S. legal system treats immigrants so poorly, especially those who are going through the deportation process with so few options to exercise their rights. For me it's always been a really intriguing area of law. It's sort of like you have the Constitution and you have our democracy, and then you have immigration law and immigration law sort of operates in its own little black box area where a lot of the rights you would normally associate with the U.S. legal system do not exist . . . I think being a child of immigrants myself, it's an area of law that's always really interested me. The way we treat immigrants very much reflects who we are as a country. It's wrapped up in questions of race, like inequality . . .It's an area where I think there's a lot of room for improvement, where we could be doing much better. There's a huge amount of need where lawyers can make a huge difference in what we do."

HOW, IF AT ALL, DO YOU HELP DETAINEES IN DETENTION CENTERS?

"Because of our teaching mission, we don't take a huge number of cases on, but we do some representation in the area of bond hearings. So, the way it works is if someone is detained by immigration, then sometimes—not always—sometimes, they're eligible to ask an immigration judge to consider releasing them on bond. It requires showing a couple of things: showing that you're not a flake, like you're not a danger to the community, showing that you're willing to appear for your future court hearings. But that's often something where . . . you need something more than just your word. You need evidence, arguments. You need proof, and it helps to have a lawyer to develop those arguments and evidence for you. So that's part of what we do with bond hearings. So there are a couple of detention facilities in Orange County, and one is the James Musick Facility in Irvine. . . There is a nonprofit that once a month goes and holds free legal consultations with the detainees there. So we'll participate in that, and we'll meet with people and do the best that we can in a pretty short amount of time. There are a lot of asylum seekers at that facility right now. A lot from Haiti, a lot from Africa, who have just literally traveled around the world to try to come to the United States, and they find themselves jailed. Then, also, there are a number of Orange County residents there as well. We try to meet with them, provide advice, point them in the right direction in terms of what their legal options are and go ahead and go from there, but it's usually limited to the one time consultation."

WHAT LEGAL RIGHTS TO REPRESENTATION DO UNDOCUMENTED IMMIGRANTS HAVE?

"There's no right to government appointed counsel. So, if a person is facing deportation, they have a right to a lawyer only if it comes at no expense to the government. That's literally

had bad experiences in the past. Like their families have, or they know people who have essentially paid thousands of dollars to attorneys who have only done more harm to their cases. So, I'd say that's probably one of the areas. You know, I think for us because we're pro bono and because we don't charge, often times our clients are immediately more trusting. They can see that we're not in it for the money. If we're giving people good advice or bad advice, there's no financial benefit to do that."

WHAT ARE SOME OF THE STORIES YOU'VE HEARD ABOUT SCAM LAWYERS?

"It's really common. There are a lot of lawyers out there who either, like they're just bad. They don't provide quality service . . . They know there's no relief. They know people will pay them a lot of money and that ultimately what they're doing is going to land the person in a deportation facility.

FROM WHAT I'VE ALREADY, PRISONERS HAVE MORE RIGHT TO REPRESENTATION THAT IMMIGRANTS DO, WHAT IS YOUR PERSONAL OPINION ABOUT THAT?

"Oh no, that's true. It's not an opinion. If you're a criminal defendant, in a criminal case, you have a right to government appointed counsel. You have all kinds of constant--I mean I'm not saying the system is great because there's all kinds of ways in which criminal defendants in the criminal justice system are not really given meaningful representation and there's a huge racial disparity in that area--but technically speaking, criminal defendants in the criminal justice system have far more access to counsel and to legal rights and protections than people in the immigration system. So it's not just for the right for counsel, it's for example, the right to double jeopardy or the right to not have an ex post facto or retroactive law, a law that changes the terms after the thing happens, a right to a jury trial, a right to unlawful searches and seizures . . . It's actually the way that the law has developed."

AND WHAT DO YOU THINK ABOUT THAT?

"I think it's terrible. . . One illustration of this is that for many people the consequences of deportation are far more serious than the consequences of their criminal case. In a criminal case, you could be prosecuted for a pretty relatively minor crime, let's say something like shoplifting and serve no jail time at all. We've had various clients who've served no jail time for their underlying criminal case, and then when they got to the immigration part of the case, that's where it really mattered. That's where they had lived here since they were children, lived here for decades, don't want to be separated from their family, and yet, [they're] facing permanent deportation.

Many clients have also spent time in detention. We had a client who was still nursing her four month old when she was detained and this was after a shoplifting incident for which she served no jail time, and she had originally entered the country when she was just a couple months old. I think that whole experience was far more traumatic for her than the underlying incident.

We've had other clients, who've yet again, no jail time. We had a client who almost died in immigration detention. It's really just this black hole in American legal system where we're kind of taking people away from their families, we're

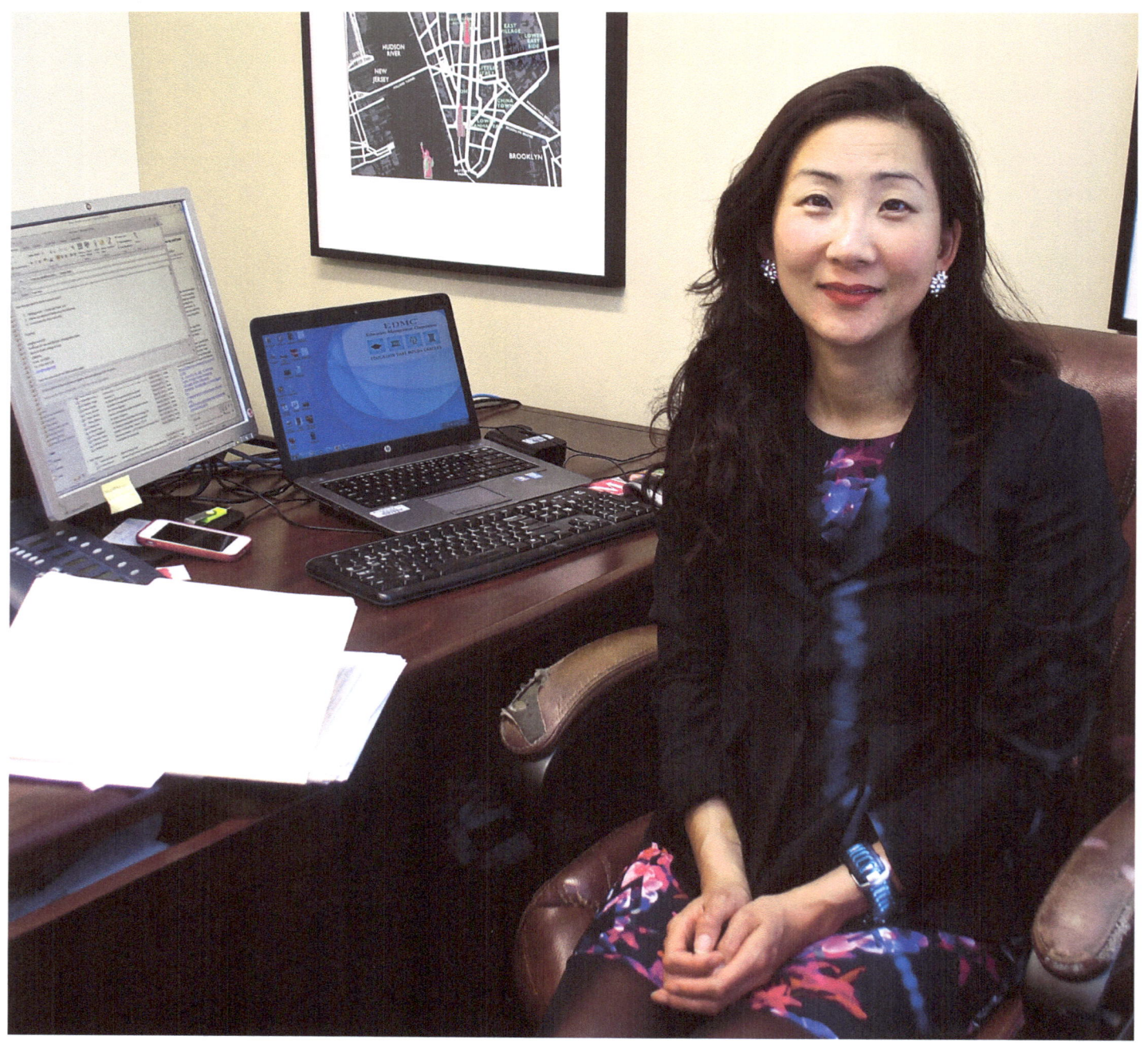

Jennifer Koh at her desk in her office at Wester State College of Law in Irvine, California. Koh acts as a Professor of Law and the Director of the Immigration Clinic.

plucking people out of their communities and then we're just throwing them into jails with very little process."

How would the law go about requiring that immigrants have legal representation in court?

"The most direct way to do it would be for Congress to amend the law. So Congress is the source of the immigration laws. I don't think that's likely to happen anytime soon at all. That's the federal government Congress, the legislative branch, but the other way that it is happening these days is for local jurisdiction, so for example, like cities or states, to set aside funding so that people get a lawyer in immigration court. That's happening in New York right now. There's a bill in California that would provide some funding. . . In Los Angeles there's been a commitment [of] $10,000,000 towards that. That's the more likely route because I don't think with this Congress that will happen. Certainly that would be something the President, the current President would veto."

How do you ensure that clients aren't afraid when they come to you?

"Generally our clients are not. Some things that I emphasize with my students are really developing a rapport with the clients before just asking them a whole bunch of questions about their past. It's maybe partly about fear and partly about trust. It's a lot to ask someone to tell one's whole life history to a complete stranger or to share details of one's past, even if those details can be helpful.

I do in my clinic, in preparing students to meet with clients, emphasize ways my students can create a welcoming atmosphere, ways that they can build rapport, even just simple things, like making eye contact, listening to the clients, the way they converse with clients. We assure clients that when they're speaking with us as attorneys, everything is confidential, and it means that we would get in trouble if we shared any information about their case with anyone else. The confidentiality helps. A lot of it is how people relate to another person treating them with respect, treating them with dignity, showing them that their stories are valuable and that we appreciate what they're telling us and that we are committed to caring for them and being their advocate."

How do you feel about how little people know about actual immigration laws?

"It's very challenging. It's always been challenging. Immigrants don't have a huge political voice. They're not particularly politically popular. That's been the case throughout the history of the United States from Irish immigrants to Chinese immigrants, to now Mexicans. So, it can be frustrating at times. While there has always been misinformation, it has not been spread actively by the leadership of the country in ways that it currently is now. Now we have a President who is just actively spreading lies and shaping people's minds around immigrants in ways that are dangerous and do very little to make us safer. To me, I think [they] are creating a very dangerous path for us in the future in a way that is just going to devastate a lot of families, devastate children and have really lasting effects on like communities and families."

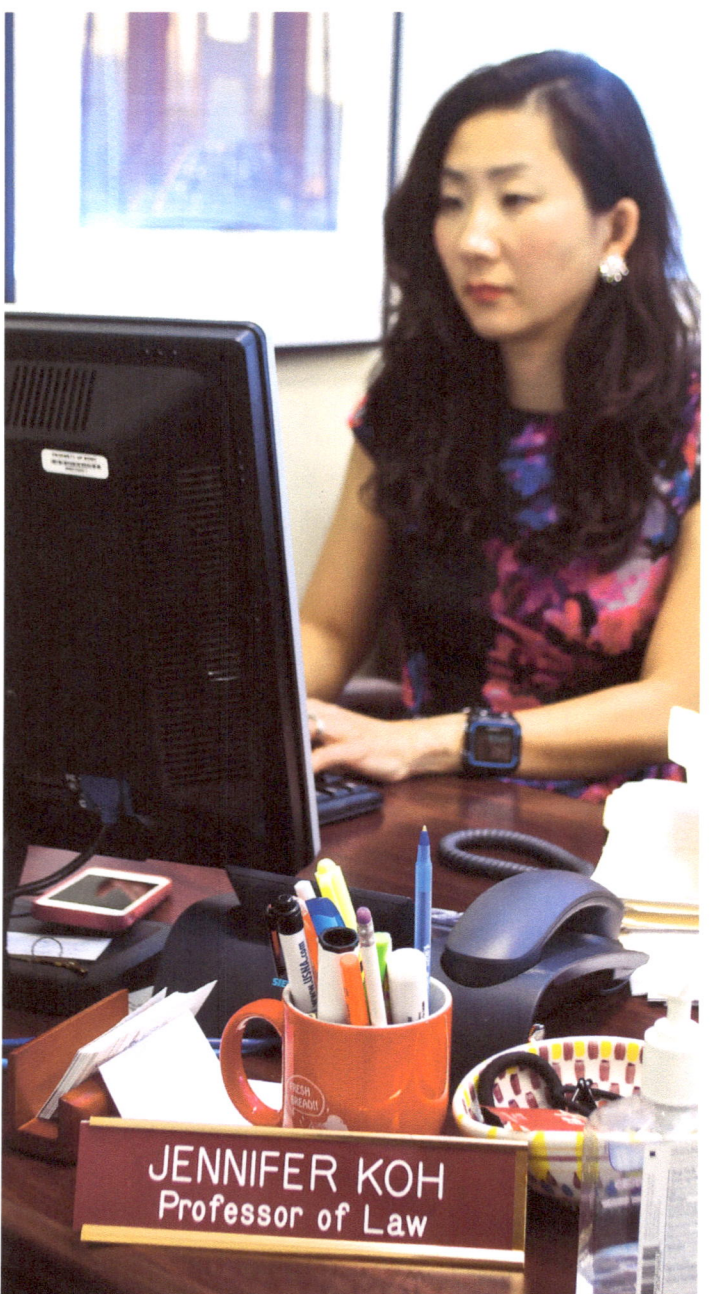

Professor of Law and Immigration Attorney, Jennifr Koh, works at her desk in between teaching classes on 22 March 2017.

WHAT ARE THE DIFFERENT REACTIONS BETWEEN OLDER IMMIGRANTS AND YOUNGER IMMIGRANTS THAT YOU HELP?

"For a lot of younger immigrants, especially people who essentially came here as children, they really are American. I mean, you can imagine coming here when you were two, right? In some ways there's more political engagement amongst the younger generation. There's a huge movement among immigrant youth right now that is really heading up a lot of the resistance to current policies. I think they speak with some moral authority.

It's very hard to think of another example in American law where we hold people accountable . . . Basically with immigration law, we are holding people accountable for their actions from when they were babies and toddlers, essentially marking them for life. There is no way for people to get around that unless the laws change, and there's complete resistance to the law. . . Amongst younger immigrants, there's more of a righteous anger and energy, and ultimately, I think there's a belief that they have that America's meant to be something different, and they're actively shaping it.

Amongst older generations, that's true too, but I think part of it's when you're older you've lived life and maybe are a little more tired or cynical and maybe have your hopes more with your children and in the younger generation. . .

I think in terms of the younger generation, there's that activism that's going on. . . When we think back to the civil rights movement that Martin Luther King Jr. led, there's a very similar commitment, and they're essentially fighting for their lives. For the immigrants who came here as children, they have to be part of this fight."

126

DO WOMEN GET TREATED EQUALLY IN THE LAW OR BY OFFICIALS, OR ARE THEY OFTEN TAKEN ADVANTAGE OF?

"There's definitely reports of sexual abuse in the detention centers. One thing that women have to contend with is there's the violence caused by deportations and detention and whatnot, and then there's also the privatized violence in the form of especially domestic violence. . .Someone who's an undocumented immigrant already has a lot to contend with, but if they have been abused by their spouse and maybe rejected by their family, it's another layer of difficulty."

LASTLY, WHAT CHANGES IN IMMIGRATION LAW DO YOU HOPE TO SEE IN THE NEXT TEN YEARS IF ANY OR HOW DO YOU SEE THE LAW IN THE NEXT TEN YEARS?

"The government has basically declared war on immigrants, and so what I'd like to see under this current administration are as few casualties as possible. I think we're going to be looking at a lot of casualties, a lot of families broken up, a lot of childhoods pretty much devastated. In the long term, we need to provide some kind of pathways to citizenship or status to people who are here who are undocumented. That's probably the biggest one and then some way to ease up on how we treat immigrants who have made mistakes and to allow for maybe some more mercy and forgiveness in the system. There are so many ways in which we could reform the system, but those are just two of them."

"There are literally cases where you have toddlers sitting in court, and there is no right to a government appointed lawyer. I have colleagues who work a lot with children in this area, and they tell stories about seeing a three year old sitting in court and the immigration judge is giving like these legal advisals. Then the government is represented 100% of the time by a government attorney. . . It's the nature of this work."

FIFTY YEARS
of IMMIGRATION REFORM

 1965

Immigration and Nationality Act: abolished the quota system based on national origins that had been American immigration policy since the 1920s. The new law maintained the per-country limits, but it also created preference visa categories that focused on immigrants' skills and family relationships with citizens or U.S. residents.

 1980

Refugee Act: raised the annual ceiling for refugees from to 50,000, created a process for reviewing and adjusting the refugee ceiling to meet emergencies, and required annual consultation between Congress and the President.

 1986

Immigration Reform and Control Act: Legalized undocumented aliens who had been continuously unlawfully present since 1982 and certain agricultural workers, sanctions for employers who knowingly hire undocumented workers, and increased enforcement at U.S. borders.

 **1990**

Immigration Act: instituted the Diversity Visa Lottery Program. Starting in 1991, every year the Attorney General, decides from information gathered over the most recent five year period the regions or country that are considered High Admission or Low Admission States.

 **1996**

Illegal Immigration Reform and Immigrant Responsibility Act: the Act was designed to improve border control by imposing criminal penalties for racketeering, alien smuggling and the use or creation of fraudulent immigration-related documents and increasing interior enforcement by agencies charged with monitoring visa applications and visa abusers.

 **2002**

Homeland Security Act: to prevent terrorist attacks within the United States, reduce the vulnerability of the United States to terrorism, and minimize damage and assist in recovery for terrorist attacks that occur in the United States. It also established the US Department of Homeland Security.

 2006

Secure Fence Act: to help secure America's borders to decrease illegal entry, drug trafficking, and security threats by building 700 miles of wall along the Mexico-United States border. It also authorizes more vehicle barriers, checkpoints, and lighting as well as the increased use of advanced technology like cameras, satellites, and unmanned aerial vehicles to reinforce the border.

 2007

Comprehensive Immigration Reform Act: a bill discussed in the 110th United States Congress that would have provided legal status and a path to citizenship for the approximately 12 million undocumented immigrants residing in the United States. The bill was a compromise between providing a path to citizenship for undocumented immigrants and increased border enforcement. It failed 34-61.

 2012

Deferred Action for Childhood Arrivals (DACA): certain people who came to the United States as children and meet several guidelines may request consideration of deferred action for a period of two years, subject to renewal. They are also eligible for work authorization.

 **2014**

Deferred Action for Parents of Americans and Lawful Permanent Residents (DAPA): would offer a legal reprieve to the undocumented parents of U.S. citizens and permanent residents who've resided in the country for at least five years. Many could also receive work permits. It would expand DACA . Immigrants older than 30 now qualify, as do more recent arrivals.

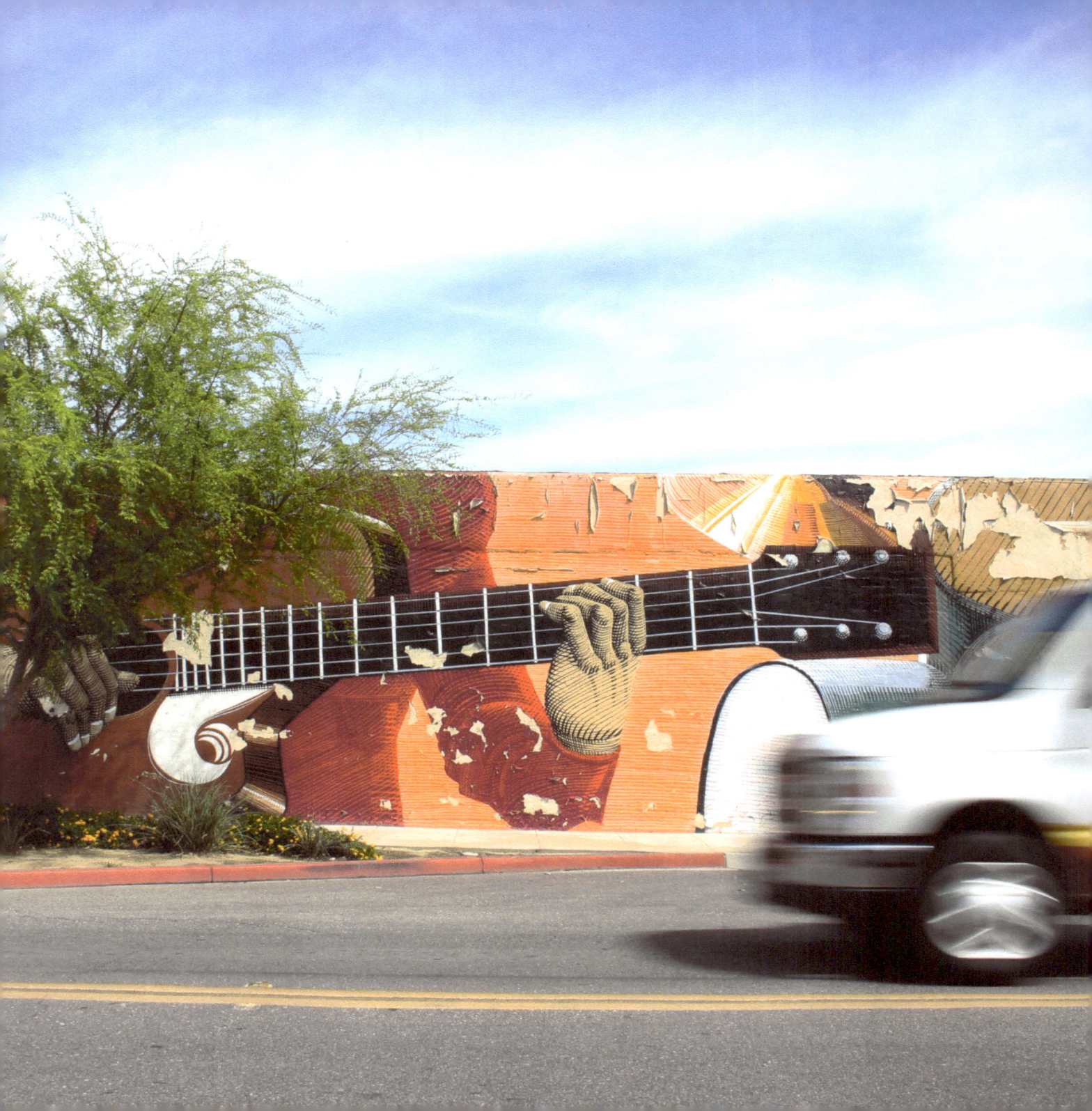

11 Music, Minorities, and Migrants

By Max Heilman

Photos by Alyssa Yee

" It should never be censored. This is part of history being written, and whether you want to look at it as music, a book, a movie... it's all the same thing. All they're doing is telling very accurate stories about what life was like. "

Craig Penny

The present time of uncertainty for migrant communities on either side of the border has given rise to vibrant music scenes everywhere from Coachella Valley, California to Tijuana, Mexico. Bands of unique styles, cultural perspectives and sociopolitical voices have emerged from the cross-pollinated environment. Regardless of how they embraced this emotional catharsis, each member of the scene becomes an equally vital piece to a multifaceted puzzle, allowing it to breathe both as a means of cultural export and as a source of positivity within a dismal financial and sociopolitical situation.

The power of music as a means of amplifying the voice of the voiceless is elaborated upon by the Library of Congress in an article called "Songs of Immigration and Migration," citing the African slaves forced into emigration from their country to America as one of the prime examples of people using music to preserve their culture and persevere through horrible circumstances. Ultimately, this forms camaraderie in spite of being unbelievably far removed from their own culture of origin. This desire for unity through common interest has defined generations of countercultural and civilly disobedient generations throughout history.

While some musicians adapted more westernized genres and fit it into their purposes, others bring Mexican tradition to the public with nothing held back. The latter breed of musicians operate under the umbrella term corridos, translating to "ballad" in English. This genre has remained based around storytelling since America first became aware of it during the early 18th century.

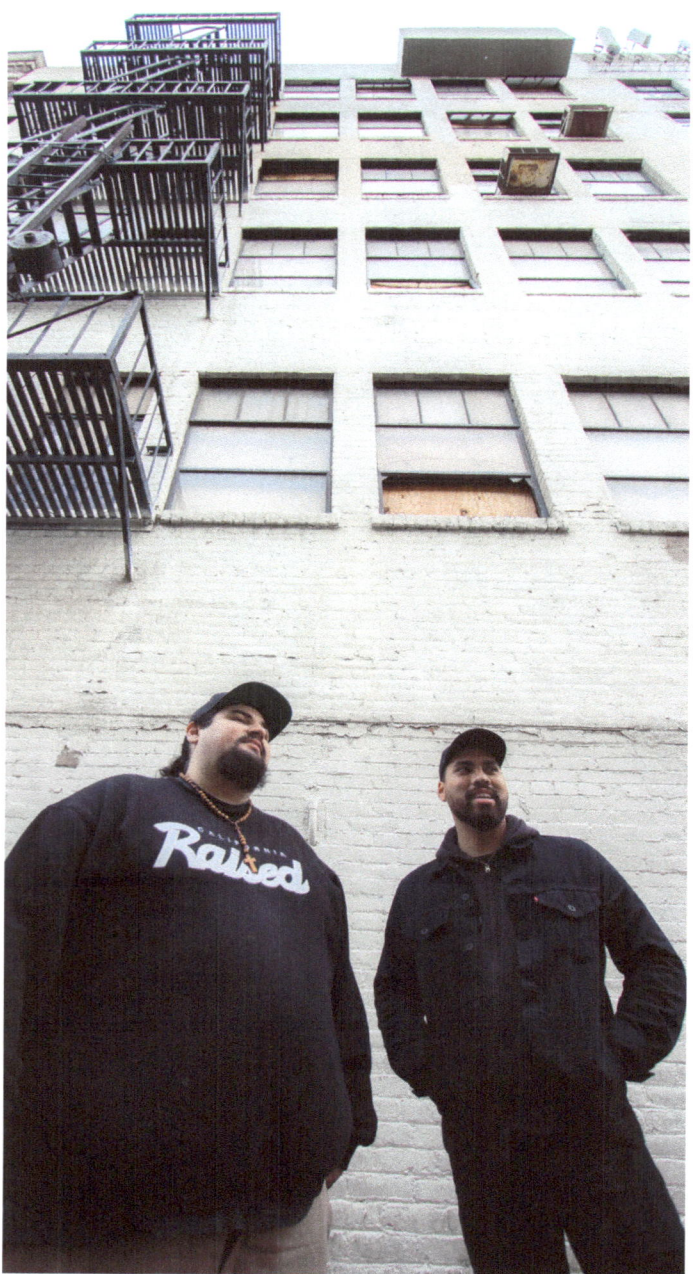

Xibalba members, Brian Ortiz and Jason Brunes, represent Pomona hardcore through their unique imagery and confrontational approach.

These songs traveled with those who sang them wherever they went, essentially providing a slice of their culture wherever and whenever it is needed.

In their article called "Introduction: Music and Migration," John Bailey and Dr. Michael Collyer argue that music allows migrants to take their culture with them when they leave their home country behind. "It is clear that music offers a possible insight into migrants' own interpretations of their migrations and visions of their new societies," they claim. "As such it is worthy of much greater interest." Underground music's history alongside the disenfranchised and unaccepted people within a culture has become so deep that one can hardly find a fringe community without a style of music helping it gain traction. Anything from the Washington, D.C. hardcore punk Rastafarians Bad Brains to the hyper-controversial Compton rap coalition known as N.W.A. have found a place in the struggle of minorities to tell true stories about their experiences within a society they feel ostracization and maltreatment from.

"I grew up going to punk shows, and I would go to a lot of skinhead shows," said Brian Ortiz, founding guitar player of the Pomona-based hardcore death metal band Xibalba. "The closest thing to racism I ever saw was some bonehead 'seig heiling' before traditional skinheads beat him up and ran him out of the venue."

American hardcore punk had major problems with neo-Nazi crews during the 1980s, with kids going to the shows having to put up with skinheads spreading their hateful message. With that in mind, the importance of people of color now feeling safe and welcome in the crowd is self-explanatory.

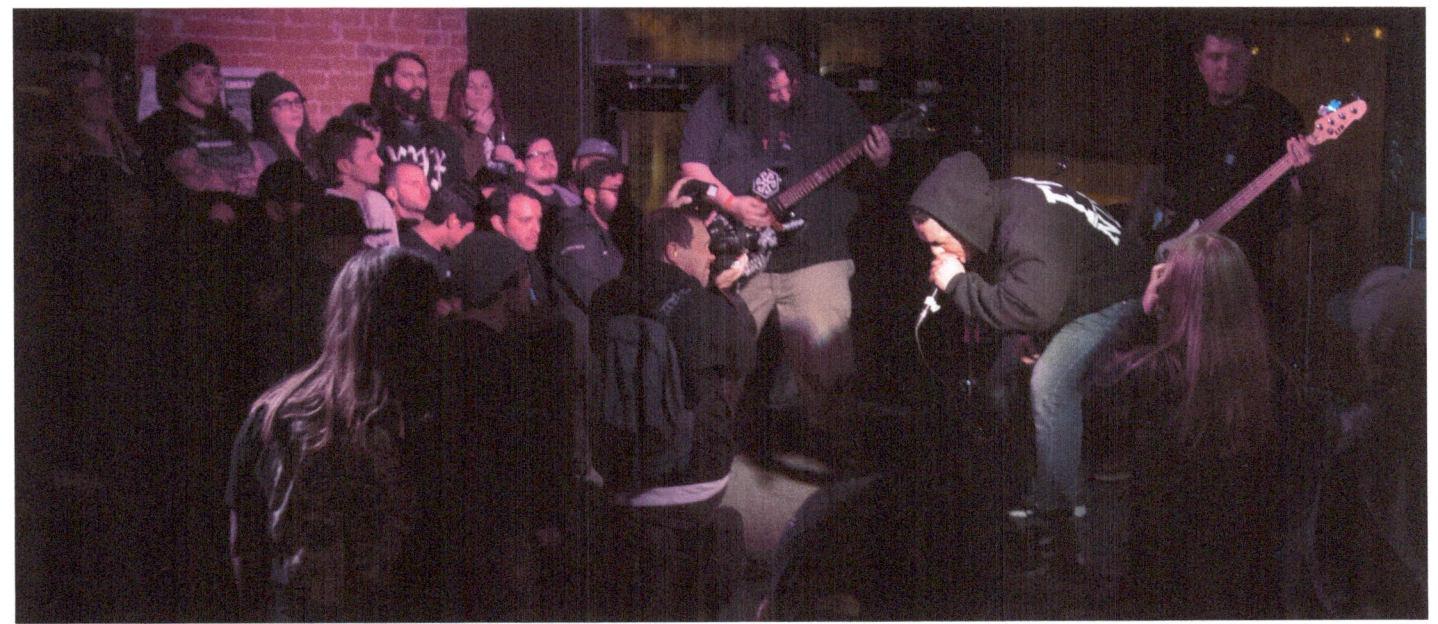

Nate, lead singer of Xibalba, sings the last song of the evening at a concert in Pomona, the band's hometown. Nearly 70 of the groups fans came out to Pizza Beer & Wings to hear these headliners play their 10th-year, anniversary show.

"Accept people for who they are," drummer Jason Brunes implores. "It's America, man. We're supposed to accept people's ethnicities, creeds and religions. But that's not always the case."

Named after the underworld of Mayan mythology, Xibalba has gained recognition for their brutal sound and their pride in their Hispanic heritage. Bilingual lyrics in both Spanish and English about Mexican history and social issues facing their people accentuate their ethnic pride, along with the pre-colonial Aztec architecture present in their visuals.

While Brunes and Ortiz claim that their musical, lyrical and aesthetic choices come naturally from who they are as people, they also acknowledge that their presentation has created a more diverse community as they inspire more people

of color to look to the hardcore scene as a way to escape from the hardships and uncertainty of the world.

Their shows might resemble a riot more than a love fest, but the tightly knit community they have fostered through a common interest in crushing riffs and guttural vocals has carried them through over a decade of making music they love. The unabashed emphasis on their ethnic and cultural history coupled with their no-holds-barred aggression has allowed them to become a beacon of light in a scene in a continuous push towards diversity and open-mindedness.

Xibalba's tenacious underground rumblings exemplify the power music has to give the minorities and misfits of society a sanctuary to say, feel and do what they want without fear. With that being said, the amount this artform has played into the social and cultural developments surrounding the border, minorities and migrants cannot be overstated. In spite of any odds stacked against them, music provides marginalized demographics a means of preserving ethnic history, forming circles of like -minded people and ultimately allowing cultural diversity to flourish in the most unlikely circumstances.

Pomona's hardcore scene just scratches the surface of communities sprouting from the passion in minority groups, especially in migrant communities like Coachella Valley. According to Coachella Unincorporated's exposé called "The Most Popular East Valley Music Venue isn't Coachella Fest, it's a Backyard," locals favor DIY shows over any nationally famous counterparts. Anything from the destructive crust punk of Terror Cult to the surf punk of Los Mumblers finds a home in this community of musicians using their art to escape and find a sense of community.

"Surf punk, especially in California... was about bands that came out of The Smell," said Jorge Gomez, the guitar player and frontman of Los Mumblers, sighting the development of Los Angeles DIY venues during the early 2000's as a key element to the style gaining traction in East Coachella. However, they see Mexican-American surf music as more traditional than their westernized counterparts.

"It has more traditional styles of surf, more in line with Link Wray and instrumental stuff like Dick Dale," Gomez said. "It's more traditional, but in Mexico City, where a lot of bands I'm influenced by are from, the have a gimmick like luchadores and just Hispanic culture overall."

While punk rock has gained a reputation for extreme political views, Los Mumblers actually do their best to avoid injecting controversy into their sons. They see their music as something to bring people together instead of driving people apart.

"It wasn't until recently that I started to get into more politics," Gomez said. "But I don't want to include that in my music. I feel that would shorten our demographic. Politics has nothing to do with the fun you have at a show." The effect this positive attitude has had on the Coachella Valley scene has, as people have come together for the love of music in spite of tensions building on the outside.

"There's a new generation of bands right now, one of our favorites is The Cathys," Gomez elaborates. His time as a promoter and a musician within this scene has given him a lot of hope for the continuation of underground music within migrant communities. In fact, giving people a place to escape from their problems for a short time is the center of what Los Mumblers espouses as a band.

"There's already enough bad news going on," said Sal Novoa, who plays drums in the band. "Just hang out and calm down." Getting rich and famous does not cross their minds, so the people forming this musical network operate entirely without record labels and corporations controlling what they do as young people with a message they want to spread.

Just like disgruntled kids in the suburbs originally gravitated towards punk rock to vent their adolescent frustrations and African-American youth turned to hip-hop to shed light on the untold stories of life in gang-infested cities, Mexican people have used corridos to tell their day-to-day lives, whether that amounts to romantic misadventures or precariously lawless behavior. After 300 years of development, the modern corridos artists have gained a reputation similar to the hip-hop MCs that originally gained traction in the United

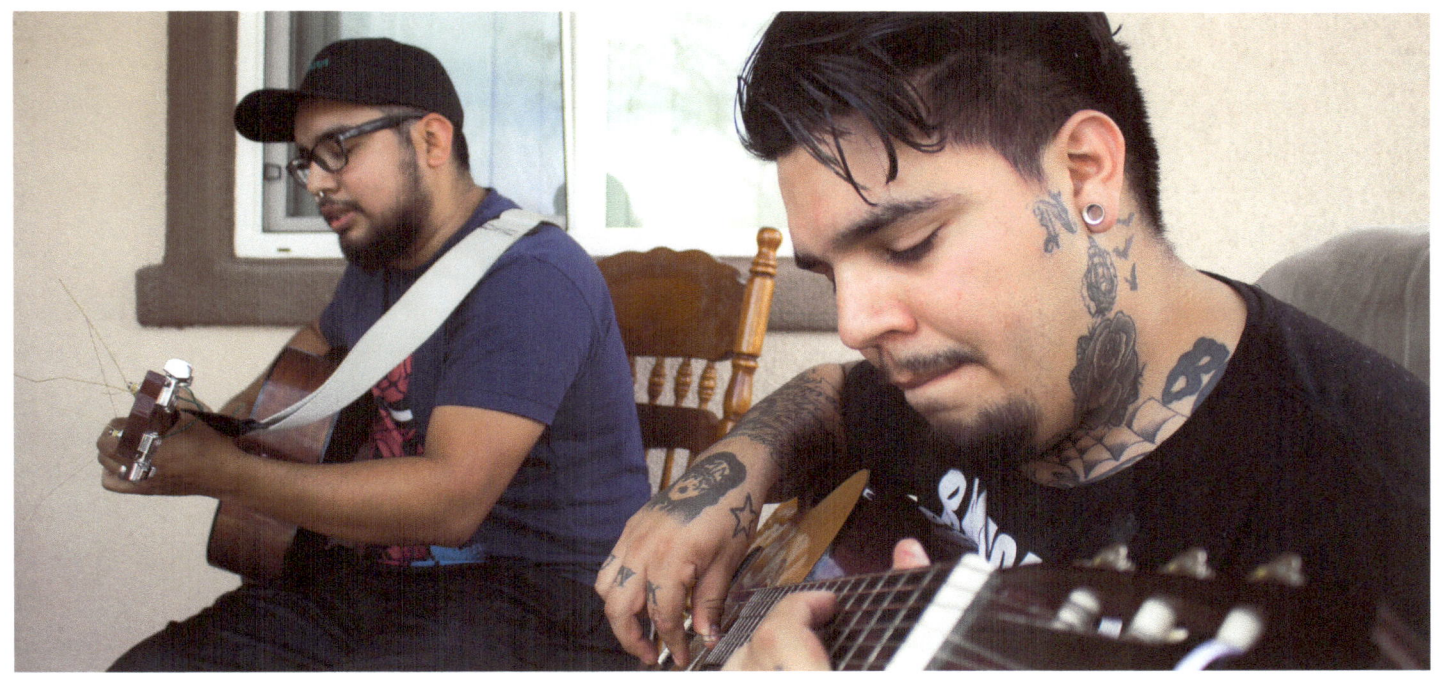

Los Mumblers' Jorge Gomez (left) and Sal Novoa (right) jam on a patio in their hometown, East Coachella Valley.

States, telling the gritty and sometimes frightening stories of life in the Mexican underground to a degree that transcends the border dividing two nations and keeps the history and lives of Mexican-Americans. With a style remaining distinct from any other style of music, corridos provides a cultural export for Mexico to a degree no one can ignore.

Several subgenres have have risen from the development of corridos, including the edgy approach of narcocorrido which translates to "drug ballad" and the more recent ultra-violent category called movimiento alterado. These categories sport parallels in lyrical content, imagery, and lifestyles with gangsta rappers like ICE T and Ghetto Boys, telling stories concerned with and sometimes mythologizing the exploits of the drug cartels that have risen in recent Mexican history. However violent and negative this might seem, longtime listeners see this music as a way to retain the edgier aspects of their community in a display of solidarity from the society they immigrated to. In his book, entitled El NARCOTRAFICANTE: Narcocorridos and the Construction of a Cultural Persona on the mexican US border, Mark Cameron Edberg found the all-too-real subject matter of narcocorridos actually strengthens a sense of community and power through its use of drug lord lingo.

The more edgy forms of corridos shed light on aspects of Mexican culture that people do not want to acknowledge, sometimes with good reason, especially when considering this sub genre's main international export — a man named Alfredo Rios, otherwise known as El Komander. All Music makes the source of El Komander's notoriety all too clear, he writes ballads about Mexican drug lords with amounts of detail that have caused many media outlets to criticize them in a way similar to the violent rappers that gained traction in the early '90s. However, these artists provide a level of realism in their cultural exports that cannot be found anywhere else. No other music examines the dark reality of living in the seedier parts of Mexico.

"Not all life is pretty," said Craig Penny, board member of the non-profit humanitarian organizations BorderAngels and BorderLife. "These guys aren't singing about pretty things, but at least they're singing about facts of life."

Providing vocals for several bands on both sides of the San Diego Tijuana border, Penny has experienced the unifying nature of music first hand. He cut no corners as he tried to integrate himself into the music scene in Tijuana, learning Spanish and extensively networking to establish himself as a musician in the country next door.

"No one has a problem with me playing down here," he said. "I'm one of the first 'gringos' to break into the rock scene down here... it's gone really well for me so far."

Penny's involvement with the aforementioned non-profit organizations has allowed him to witness truly incredible events of multinational coexistence, including an unique event centered around the famed Friendship Park—a plot of land at the border next to Pacific shore where separated families can reunite as a sign of good will and nonviolence. According to Penny, two bands on both sides of the border play sets for each other as a means of connecting divided communities through the universal language of music.

"Believe me. Historians will revert back to this music to listen to just like they will rap music in our community," said Penny. "It's a piece of history that will help serve people in the future to look back and see what life was like."

Whether one looks to the historically conscious metallic hardcore upstarts in Xibalba, the militant cultural tribalism of corridos, or the cross-country harmony Craig Penny discovered and now utilizes, music's continual effect on issues regarding the border, migrants, and minorities will continue to grow as more people discover its potential. One element all of these musicians and movements share is a sense of confidence and empowerment. Los Mumblers encapsulate the long-term effect music can have on oppressed demographics — showing them they do not have to live in misery, and look within themselves to preserve joy in the midst of their suffering. Music ultimately transcends its status as a cultural language as it gives minorities and migrants inexorable jubilation.

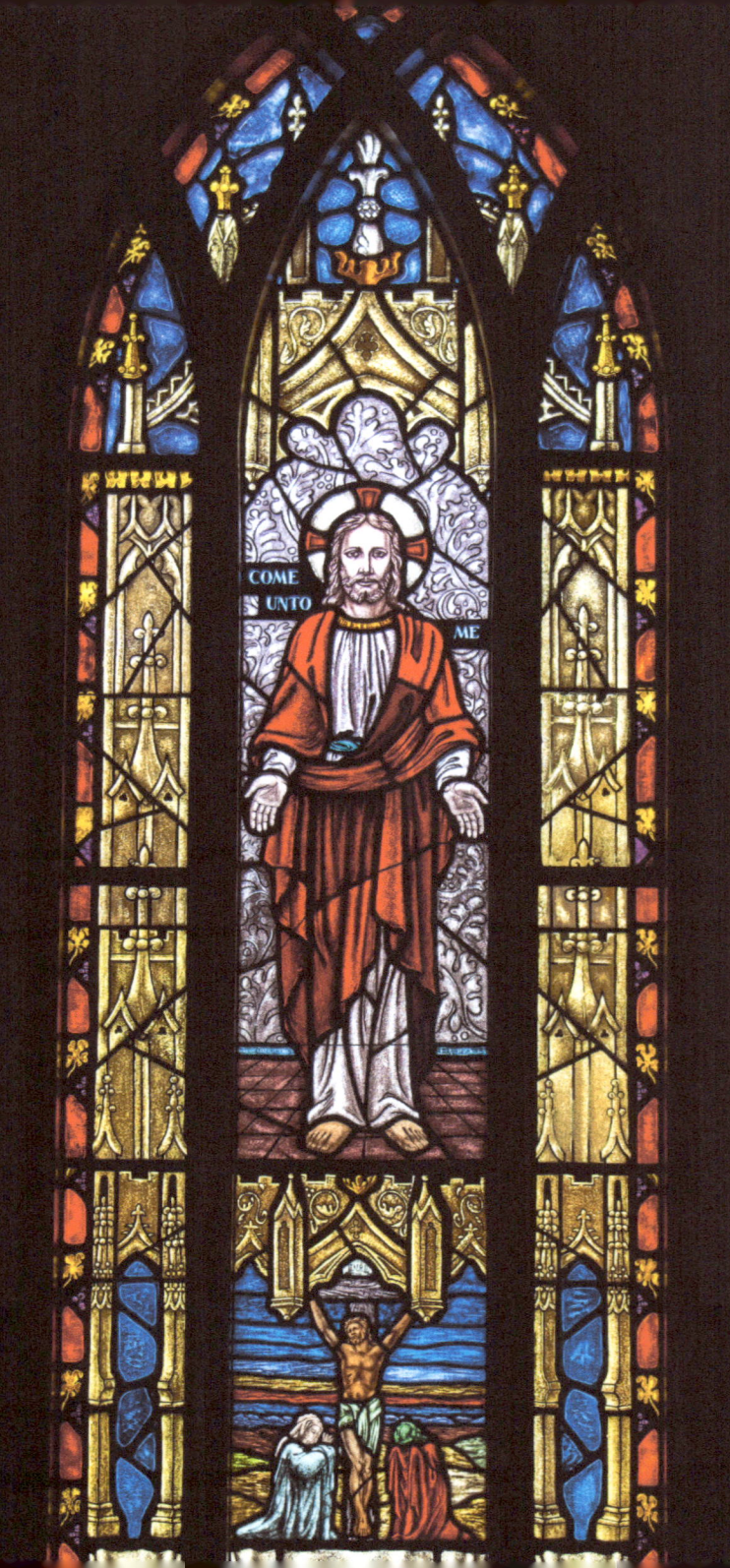

12 Ministry for Migrants in LA and Orange County

By Jessica Goddard and Rebecca Mitchell

Photos by Jenny Oetzell

> " For I was hungry and you gave me food, I was thirsty and you gave me drink, I was a stranger and you welcomed me ...'Truly, I say to you, as you did it to one of the least of these my brothers, you did it to me.' "

Matthew 25:35, 40

The mandate to shelter displaced people groups presents itself prominently in the Bible, from Israel's exile from Egypt to Jesus' teachings in Matthew 25. The Bible calls believers to act with compassion as Jesus and the Good Samaritan did. Jesus disregarded social stigmas in order to gain friendships with the marginalized, such as when he talked to the Samaritan woman at the well. The Good Samaritan noticed and took time to help the outcast man who lay beaten on the side of the road. This precedent still applies to the church today as much as it did back then, and the mandate remains the same even when cultures shift. The church must now seek to follow this mandate and fulfill its call to love in today's society.

The religious community in Los Angeles and Orange County have actively strived to protect and welcome displaced people groups and have participated as members in the immigration issue for over two decades. Ministry for immigrants has spread vibrantly through Southern California as needs have arisen. Welcoming the stranger, as Jesus encouraged his followers to do, continues to compel church leaders today.

As a response to the edict of compassion, church leaders began the first Sanctuary Movement, which physically hosted refugees in churches in the 1980s. These refugees came from Central America as they fled the disaster of a civil war crisis.

"The original sanctuary movement was a Jesus-centered movement and that was it's power," said Robert Romero, a prominent church leader and co-director of the Matthew 25/Mateo 25 SoCal Movement.

The second movement of sanctuary churches began in 2007 with Lutheran pastor Alexia Salvatierra shining a light onto the path for all to see. This movement reached beyond the breadth of physically hosting immigrants into comprehensive immigration reform.

Those who participated in this movement compared the plight of immigrants to Mary and Joseph in the Bible. As the parents of Jesus, they too sought refuge in a land not their own, just as immigrants from Central America have searched in America for a place to call home. For many, the only place willing to say "we have room for you" came in the form of church hostesses.

While the movement's goal has always included the humane treatment of individuals, the third wave of the Sanctuary Movement highlights the dignity every human deserves. This dignity comes independent of their status as documented or undocumented and includes standing with hurting communities.

"We seek humane immigration reform in the sense that it lifts up the dignity of every human being—without any prejudice, without any racism, without demonizing this community that politicians and the news have demonized," said Guillermo Torres, senior organizer for Clergy and Laity United for Economic Justice (CLUE) located in Los Angeles.

This current sanctuary movement has shifted away from the housing of families in churches, and instead focuses on becoming a network to be with individuals in the deportation court, to pray for those living in the pain of living without a mother or father and to stand up for the rights of fellow neighbors. The movement stresses standing in solidarity with those suffering and loving them and walking with them, Torres described.

The previous church definition of sanctuary continues to expand to include these motivations, to open the door beyond the walls of the church. It includes reaching out to the vulnerable and being willing to house them, according to Brad Christerson, Matthew 25/Mateo 25 SoCal movement leader and sociology professor at Biola University. They hope to slowly have fellow neighbors become aware of the sanctuary situation.

"A sanctuary church also, through its actions, seeks to promote broader awareness as to the brokenness of our immigration...as well as to bring a Biblical awareness to this issue," Romero said.

As churches have more than one response to this issue, organizations such as CLUE counter the inhumane treatment of individuals by bringing together different faith communities. They work for advocacy, for protection and for resources, with their work rooted in a love for Christ.

"We seek humane immigration reform in the sense that it lifts up the dignity of every human being—without any prejudice, without any racism, without demonizing this community that politicians and the news have demonized," said Guillermo Torres, senior organizer for Clergy and Laity United for Economic Justice (CLUE) located in Los Angeles.

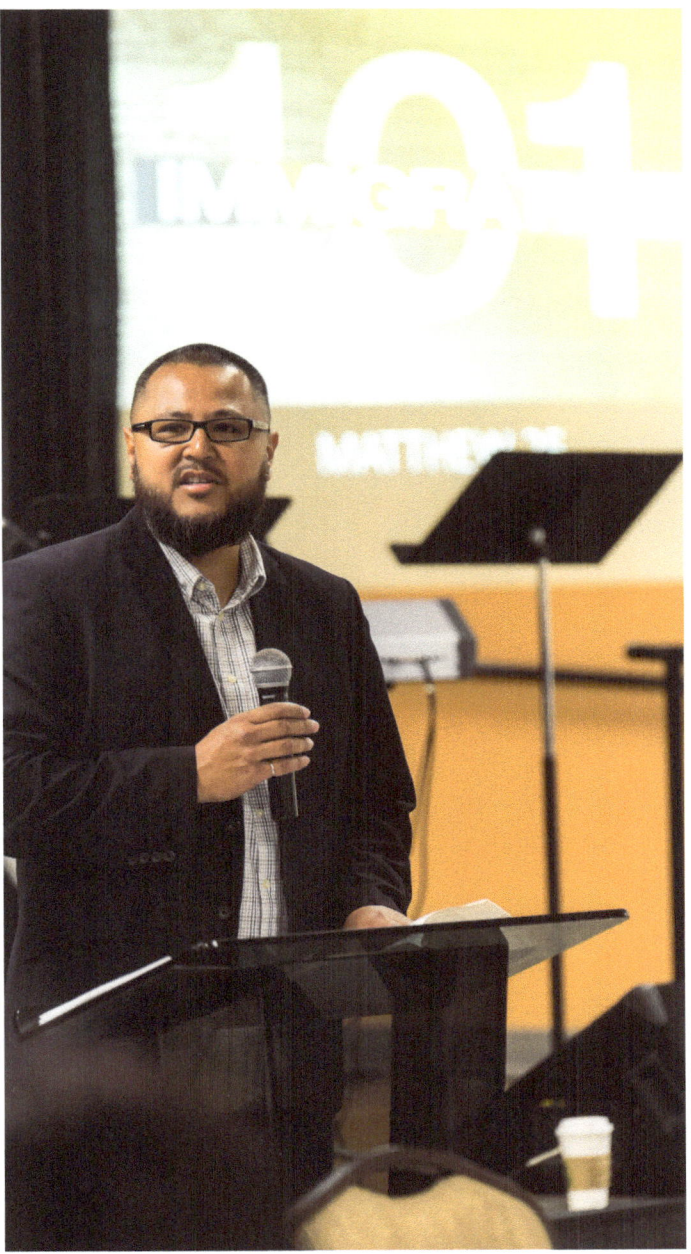

Robert Romero, Matthew 25/Mateo 25 SoCal co-leader, opens up the "Immigration 101" meeting. The meeting discussed methods for uniting Christians with the issue of immigration.

"Love is the one that moves us into that place, nothing else but love," Torres said. "Everything I have to do is love, and love is connected to the suffering of others."

With connecting to the pain of others as the starting point, CLUE reaches into the lives of impacted community members: those who do not have people to stand by their side, ones who cannot pay the bills because their only financial support has been deported, those who search day after day for jobs but do not achieve their goal because of their appearance. CLUE does not let the pain go unnoticed.

"My faith says that when children suffer, when mothers suffer, it's almost like if God is suffering," Torres said.

Taking that first step along with God into the pain and suffering of others requires welcoming people, seeing people as created in the image of God and creating a playing field where everyone is equal.

"Love requires to see people, to think of others before we think of ourselves. That's what the definition of love is. But our country, our government sometimes has taken, and people in our government, have taken a very self-centered, selfish view of America that makes us 'look at us we're here' and the immigrants are over there, they are of a different status, they are not equal to us. I don't like that narrative because God doesn't see people like that," Torres said.

With the pace the new administration has set, organizations like CLUE will find themselves drowning in the overwhelming number of requests. The coordination

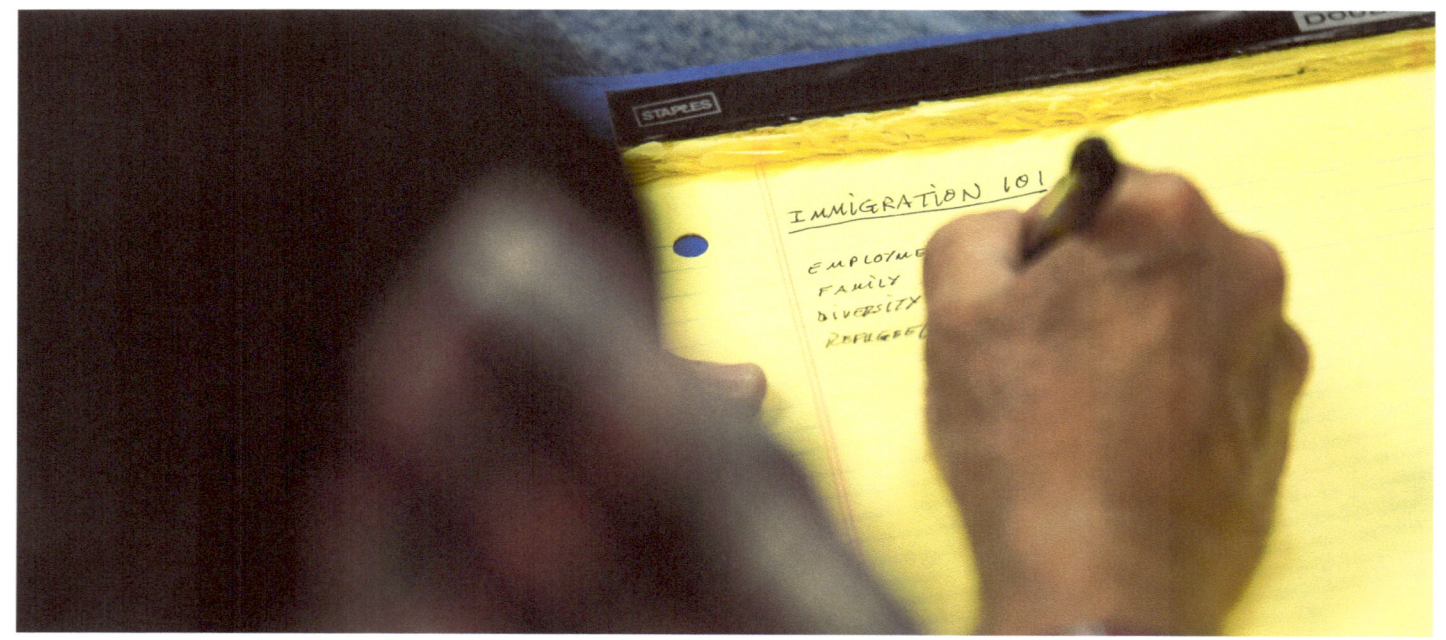

An attendee at the "Immigration 101" meeting at First Baptist Church of Maywood takes notes as a speaker defines the terms related to immigration.

and collaboration between the faith communities will have everything to fight against but nothing left to fight with.

They strive to serve as a ray of hope among the difficulties immigrants face in daily life. While fear looms over immigrants' heads with changing orders on deportation, the ministry of those who care will continue to rise.

Following the 2016 presidential election, a group of close to 40 Christian leaders from around the country met at the Highland Research and Education Center in Tennessee to discuss how they could contribute to the safety of vulnerable people groups in the uncertain political climate ahead. The Highland Center, at which many social justice movements and civil rights meetings have occurred, also served as the birthplace of the national Matthew 25 Movement, a movement of evangelical communities around America

committed to providing sanctuary and aid to immigrants and other endangered people groups. From that national movement, Matthew 25/Mateo 25 SoCal commenced on December 18, 2016.

The Southern California movement particularly specializes in ministering to Mexican immigrants, although they do serve other immigrant communities as well. It acts as a figurative sanctuary for immigrants by providing for their needs, whether those be legal aid or monetary assistance.

"We want Christ to be the center of what we're doing. We want the Scripture to be our foundation," Romero said. "We're doing this because we're followers of Jesus."

The organization focuses on the aspect in Matthew 25 of "welcoming the stranger" by committing to three specific ways to help immigrants: 1. educate, 2. show compassion and 3. advocate. For education, they host workshops where church members and immigrants can learn about the current policies regarding immigration, the legal rights immigrants have and the actions immigrants should take if they feel threatened.

The movement leaders seek to honor Scripture by emphasizing the act of showing compassion to immigrants and recognizing the 90 plus references of displaced people mentioned in the Bible. They advocate for immigrants by offering them free legal aid, helping them fill out legal papers and speaking up for them in the public forum as well as in correspondence with government representatives.

> "Jesus articulates an important principle that when we love the vulnerable and care for the vulnerable, whether they're a stranger or whether they're the poor or the imprisoned, we're caring for Jesus himself," Romero said.

Matthew 25/Mateo 25 is another vital building block in the larger scope of the Sanctuary Movement. The organization is committed to protecting immigrants in their three practical ways and by enabling the church communities to welcome and protect immigrants.

"We feel that in obedience to Jesus, we need to step in and do what we can to prevent unjust deportations and the separation of families in light of this current political climate," Romero said.

The leaders of the Matthew 25 Movement have seen many instances in which the church's work in immigration has yielded rewarding relationships between immigrant

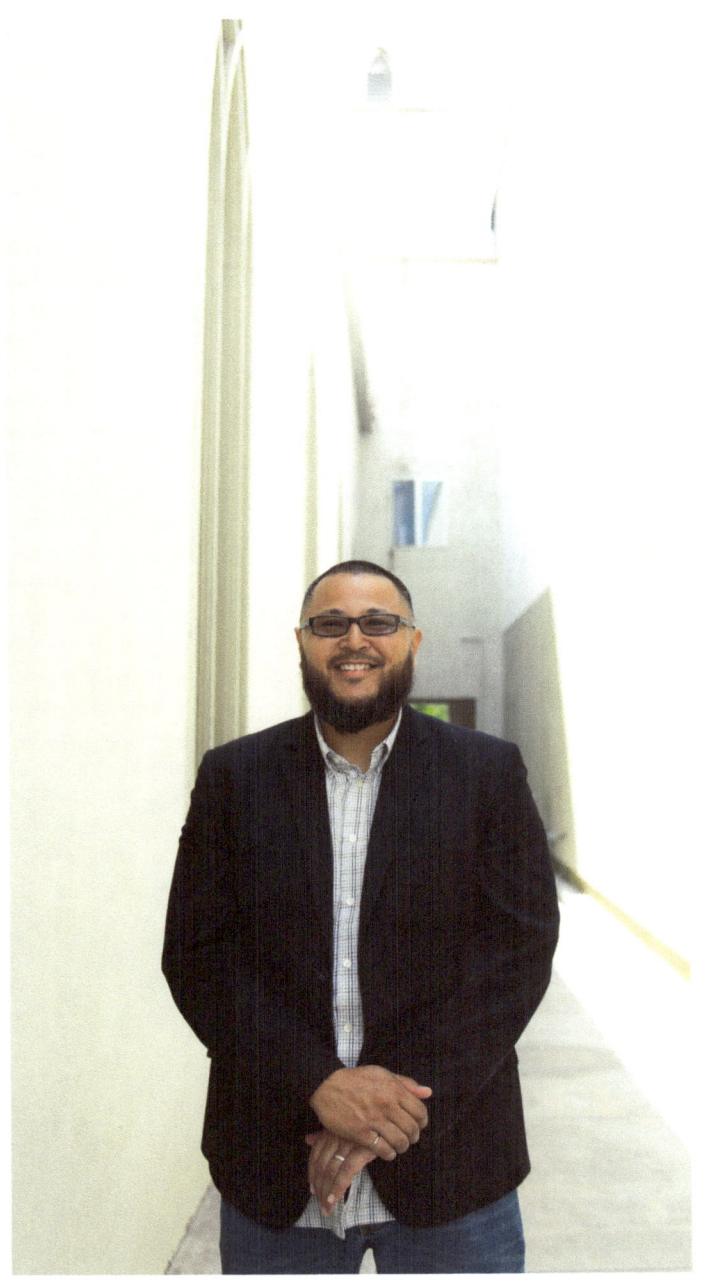

Romero believes that the church needs to step into the command of "welcoming the stranger" if they are to obey the call of Jesus.

groups and the church, encouraging them in the work they do.

When a Syrian refugee family arrived in the United States, World Relief, a refugee organization, contacted Mariners Church in Mission Viejo to see if someone could host the family, and the church gladly agreed. The pastor welcomed and hosted the family, and the church provided the basic necessities, such as bedding and clothing. When the local Syrian community heard this, they were moved. The Muslim leader teared up as he described that this church was setting an example of loving immigrants. After that instance, the leader of the local mosque told the pastor he trusted him enough that he wished to send the mosque's youth group to one service at Mariners Church. 130 Muslim children attended the youth group service that week.

"That story to me encapsulates what it means to love your neighbor in this current political climate," Romero said.

"'When a foreigner resides among you in your land, do not mistreat them. The foreigner residing among you must be treated as your native-born. Love them as yourself, for you were foreigners in Egypt. I am the Lord your God."
Leviticus 19:33-34

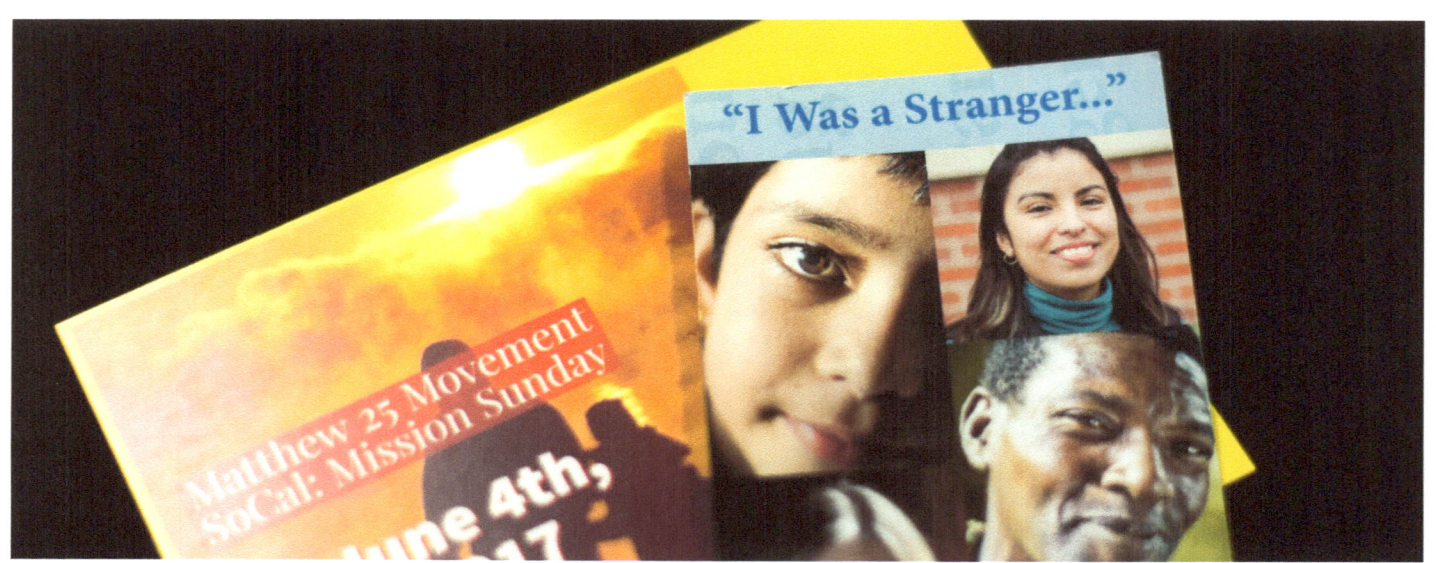

Brochures distributed by the Matthew 25 Movement in Southern California feautres Matthew 25:35: "For I was hungry and you gave me food, I was thirsty and you gave me drink, I was a stranger and you welcomed me."

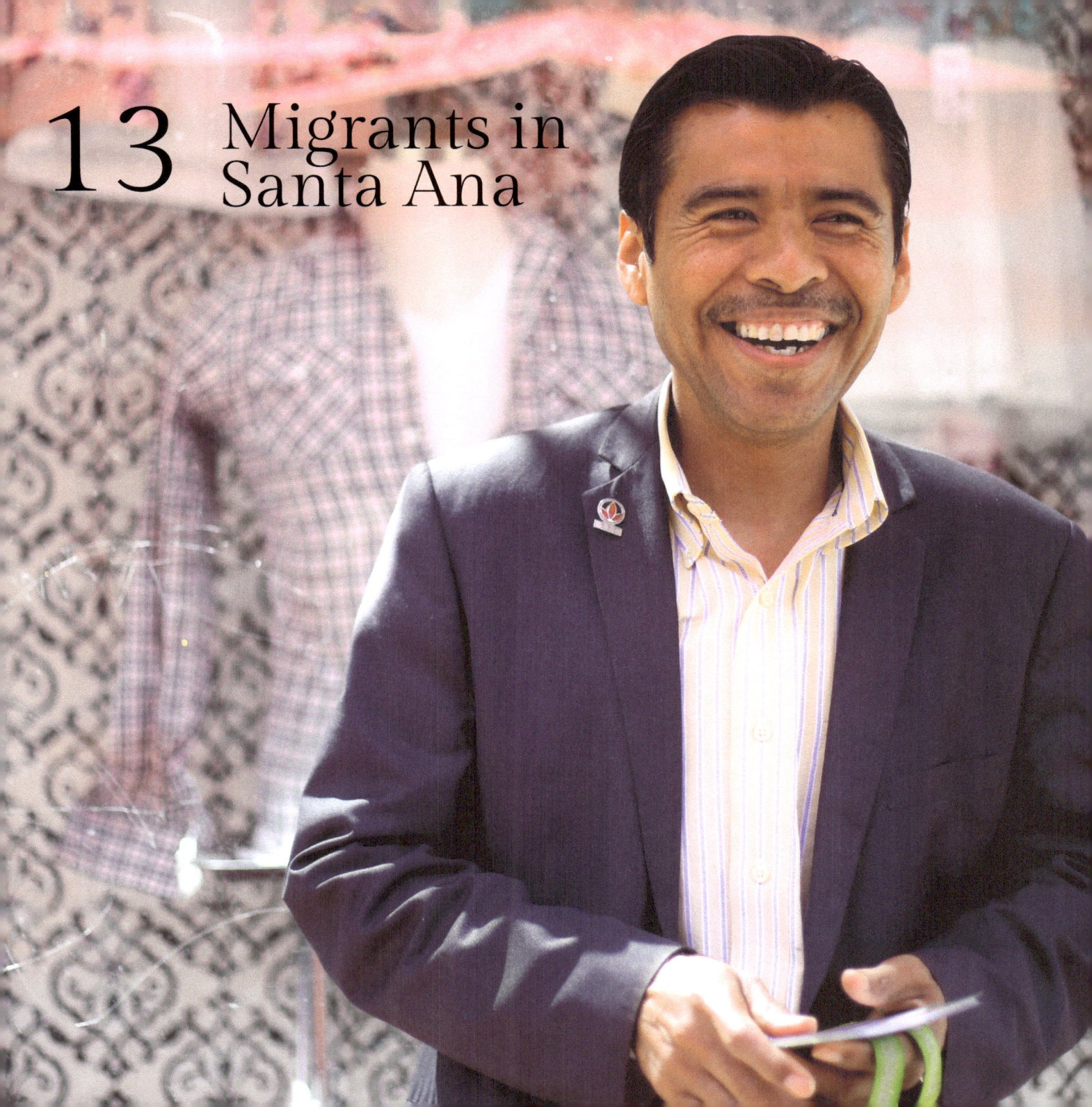

13 Migrants in Santa Ana

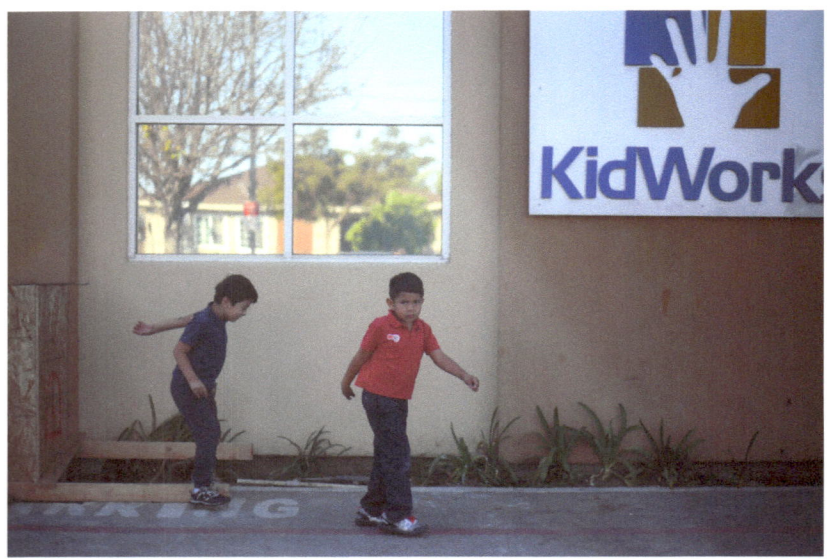

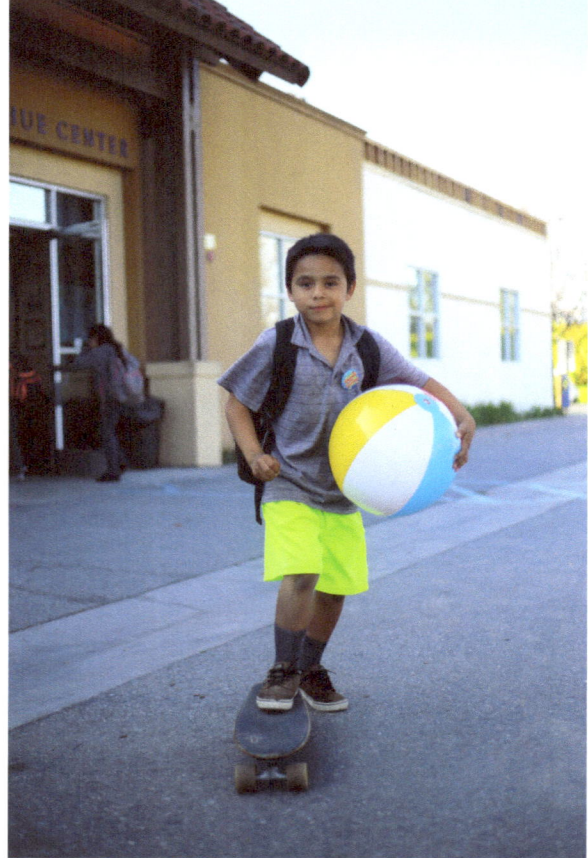

Santa Ana is largely considered the heart of Orange County, yet home to some of the most challenging neighborhoods. KidWorks, an after school program in central Santa Ana, is dedicated to restoring at-risk neighborhoods through education programs offered to these neighborhoods' children and their parents. Pictured: students outside the Don Donahue center, one of the four KidWorks community centers in central Santa Ana.

Photos by: Anastasia Waltschew

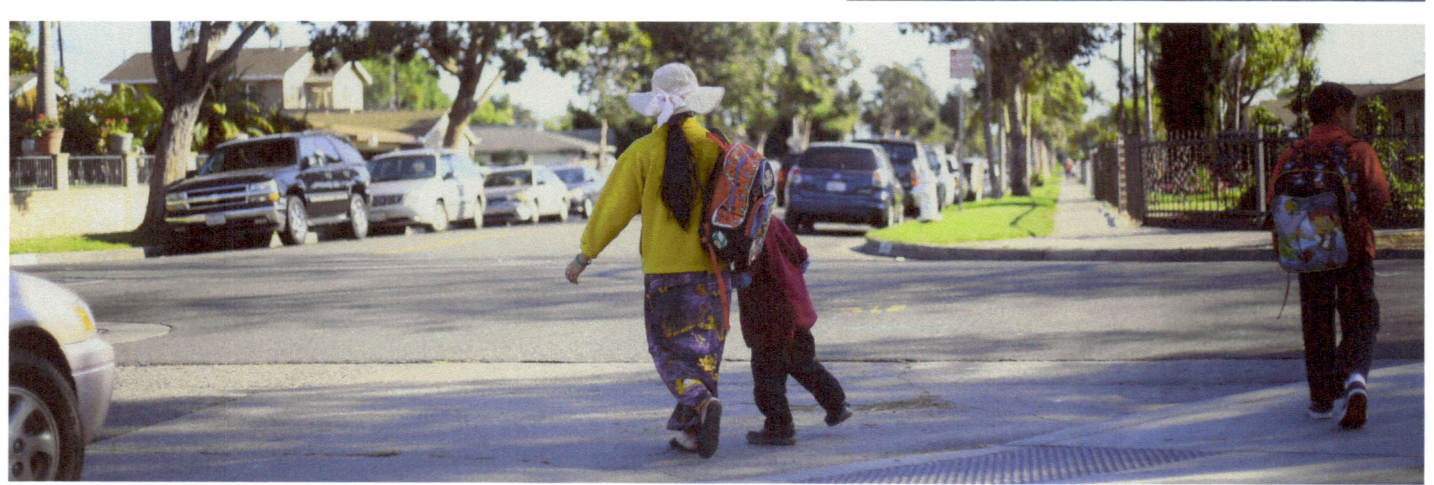

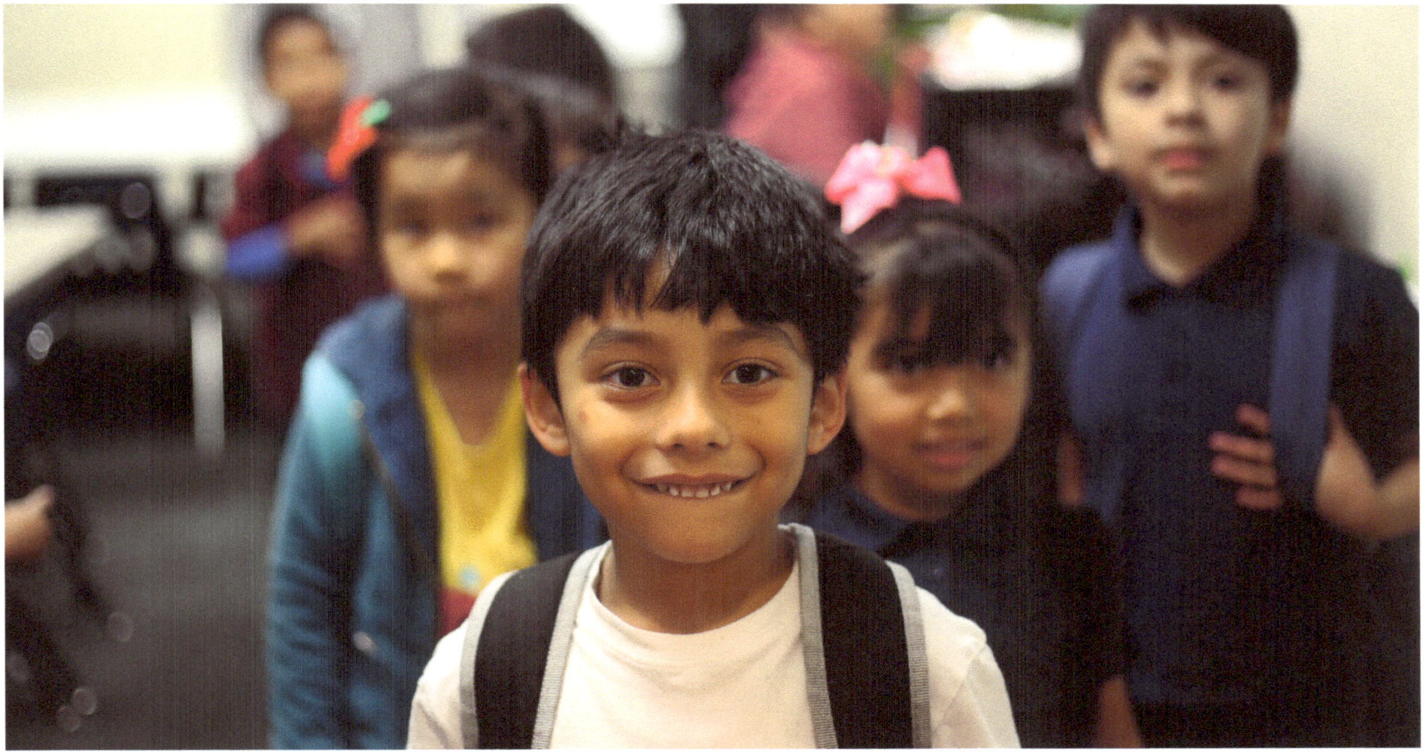

Students packed up and ready to go home after receiving turoring at KidWorks.
Below: David Benavides, city councilman of Santa Ana and director
of KidWorks in a classroom at the Don Donahue Center.

Photos by: Anastasia Waltschew

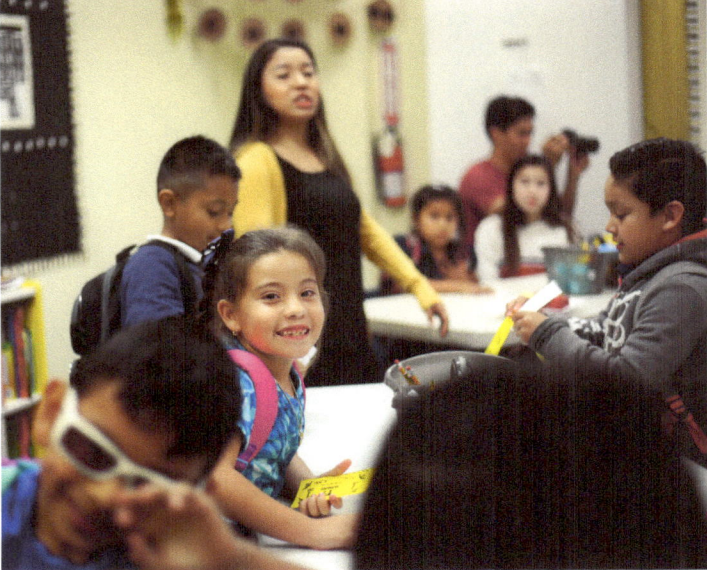

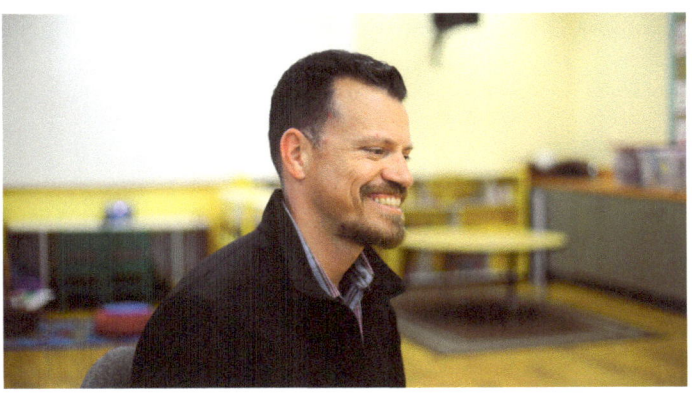

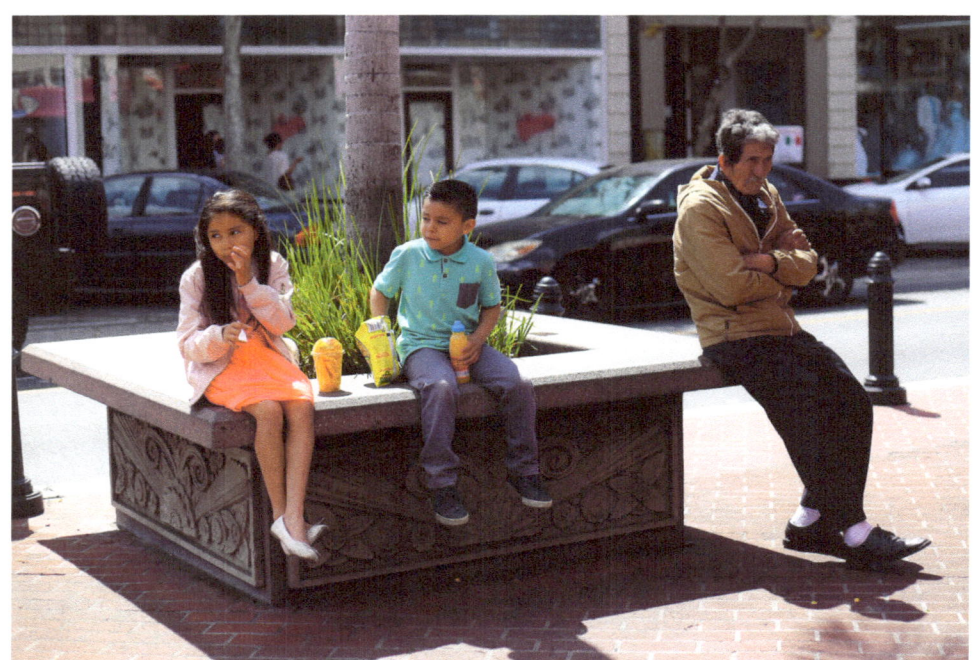

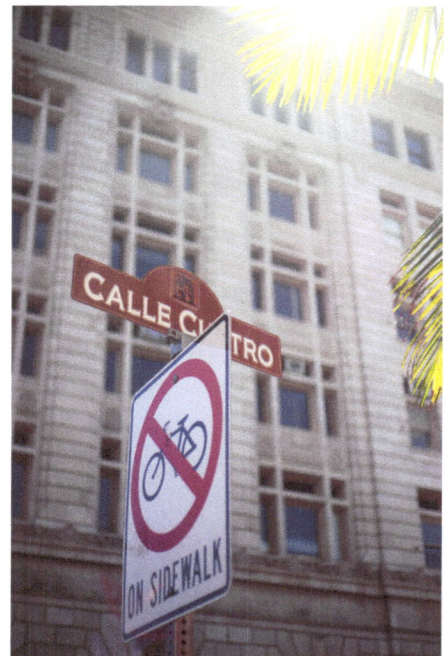

In 1889, Santa Ana was declared the County Seat of Orange County, emanating from its epicenter, Downtown Santa Ana. Today, the home to the historic "Calle Cuatro" (Fourth Street) is lined with clothing stores, bridal shops, restaurants, and fruit stands—like the one pictured to the right—and continues to act as one of the community's major centers. Above: Siblings Ivan and Daisy enjoy snacks with their family on a Sunday afternoon on Calle Cuatro.

Photos by: Anastasia Waltschew

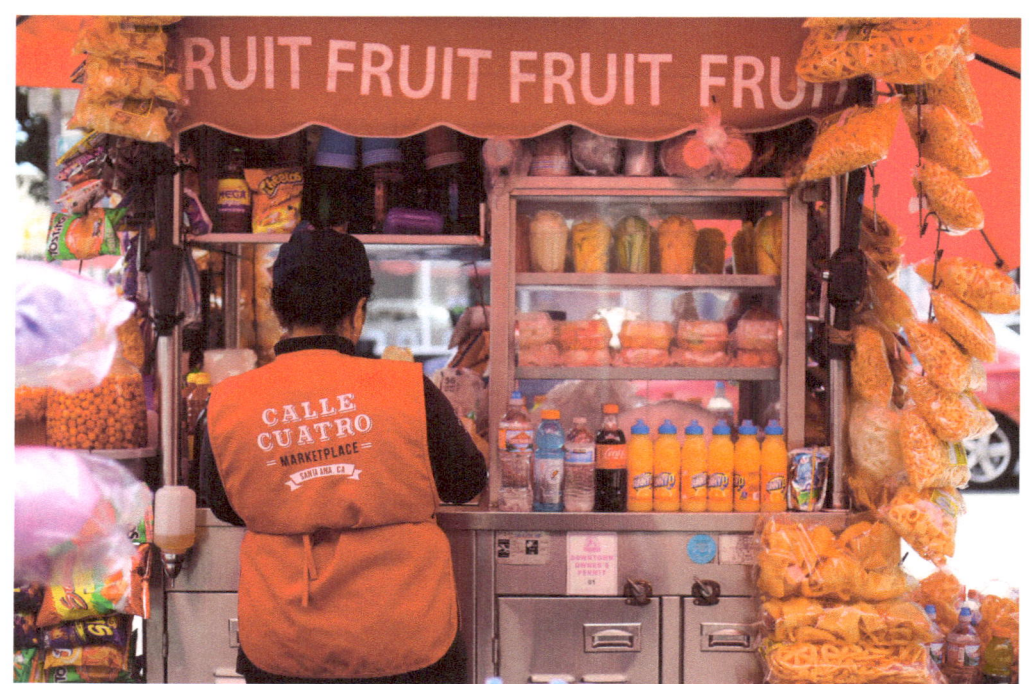

Hermon immigrated from Mexico eight years ago
and now lives and works in Santa Ana.

Photo by: Anastasia Waltschew

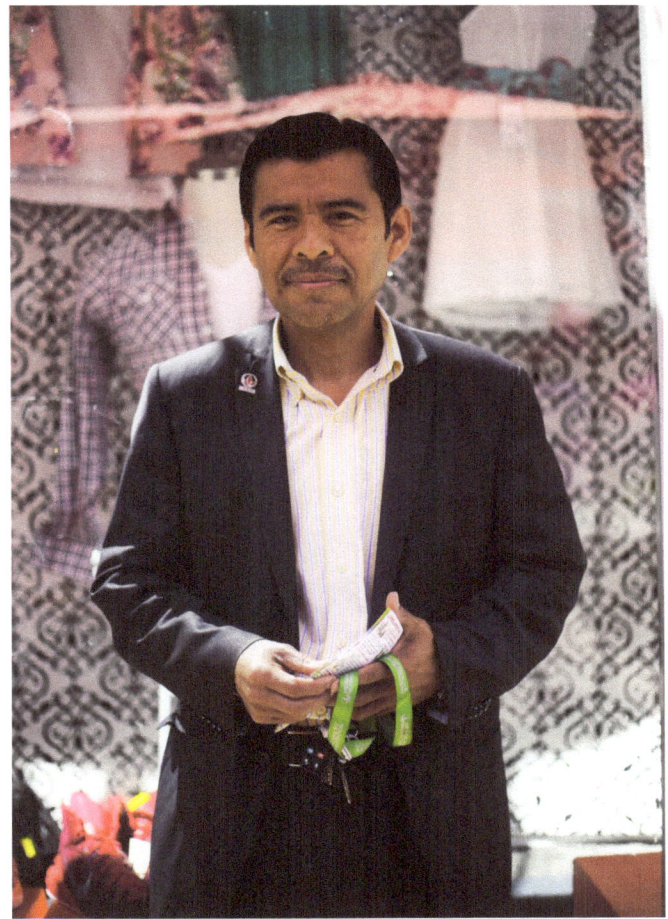

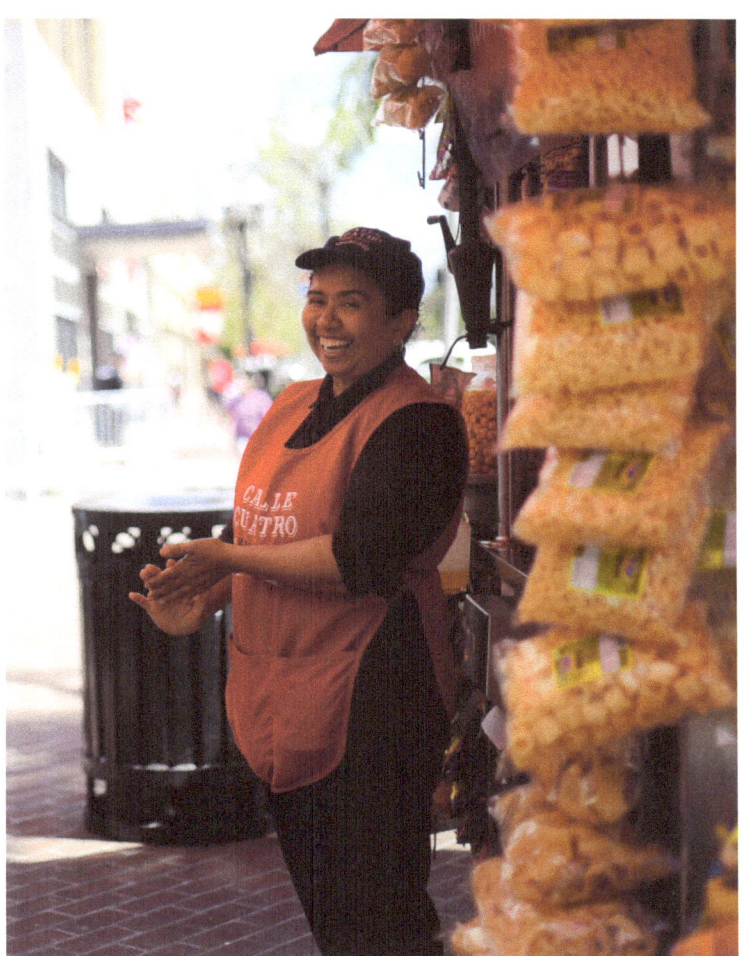

Aurora "Sixta" owns and operates a raspado stand on Main and 5th
street in the historic district of downtown Santa Ana. An Evangelical
Christian, Aurora holds weekly prayer meetings at her home in Santa
Ana. Here, she lightheardedly jokes about the linguistic barrier she
experieces as a native Spanish speaker but says she is not able to take
English classes because she spends her days running her business.

Photo by: Anastasia Waltschew

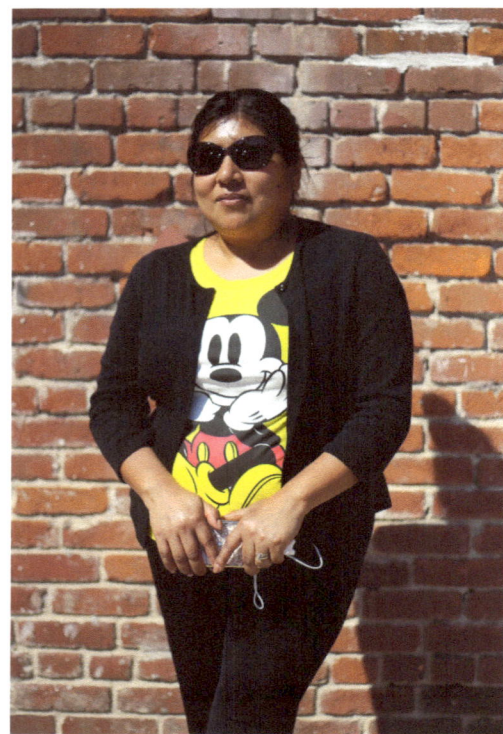

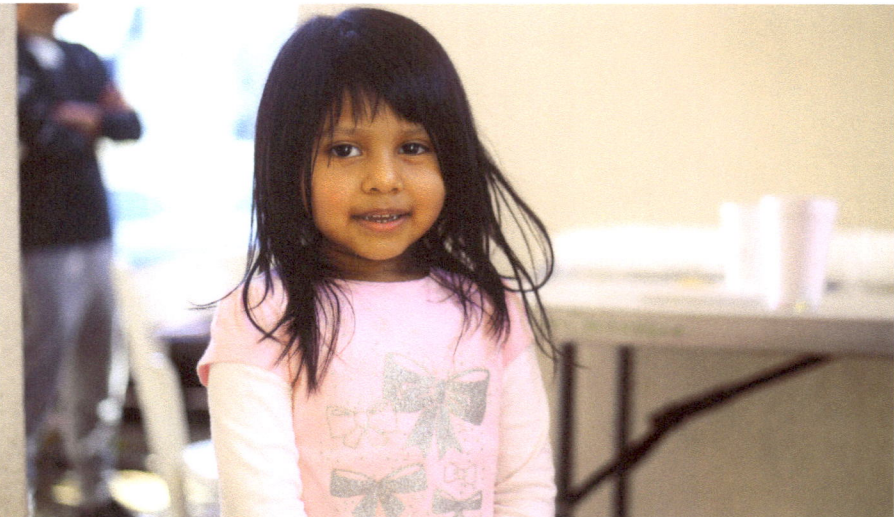

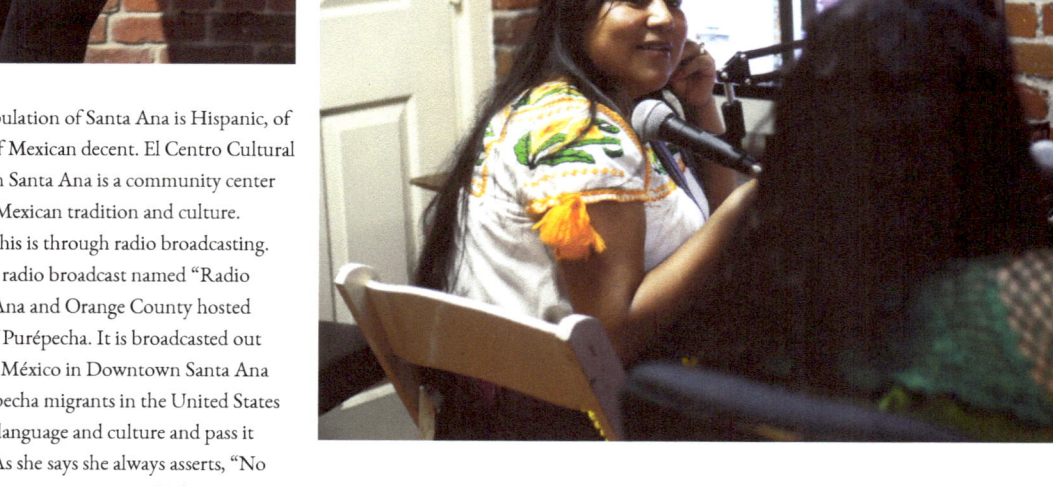

Right: 78.6% of the population of Santa Ana is Hispanic, of which the majority are of Mexican decent. El Centro Cultural de México in Downtown Santa Ana is a community center dedicated to upholding Mexican tradition and culture. One of the ways it does this is through radio broadcasting. Aguanita Zamora runs a radio broadcast named "Radio Sin Fronteras" to Santa Ana and Orange County hosted in her native language of Purépecha. It is broadcasted out of El Centro Cultural de México in Downtown Santa Ana with the hope that Purépecha migrants in the United States can celebrate Purépecha language and culture and pass it down to thier children. As she says she always asserts, "No crucé la frontera. La frontera me cruzó a mi." This translates to, "I didn't cross the border. The border crossed me."

Photos by: Anastasia Waltschew

Top Left: Santa Ana is home to a population of immigrants from the Purépecha tribe in the southern state of Michoacan, Mexico. "Aguanita" Zamora is a member of the Purépecha tribe.

Above: Aguanita's daughter sings a traditional Purépecha lullaby.

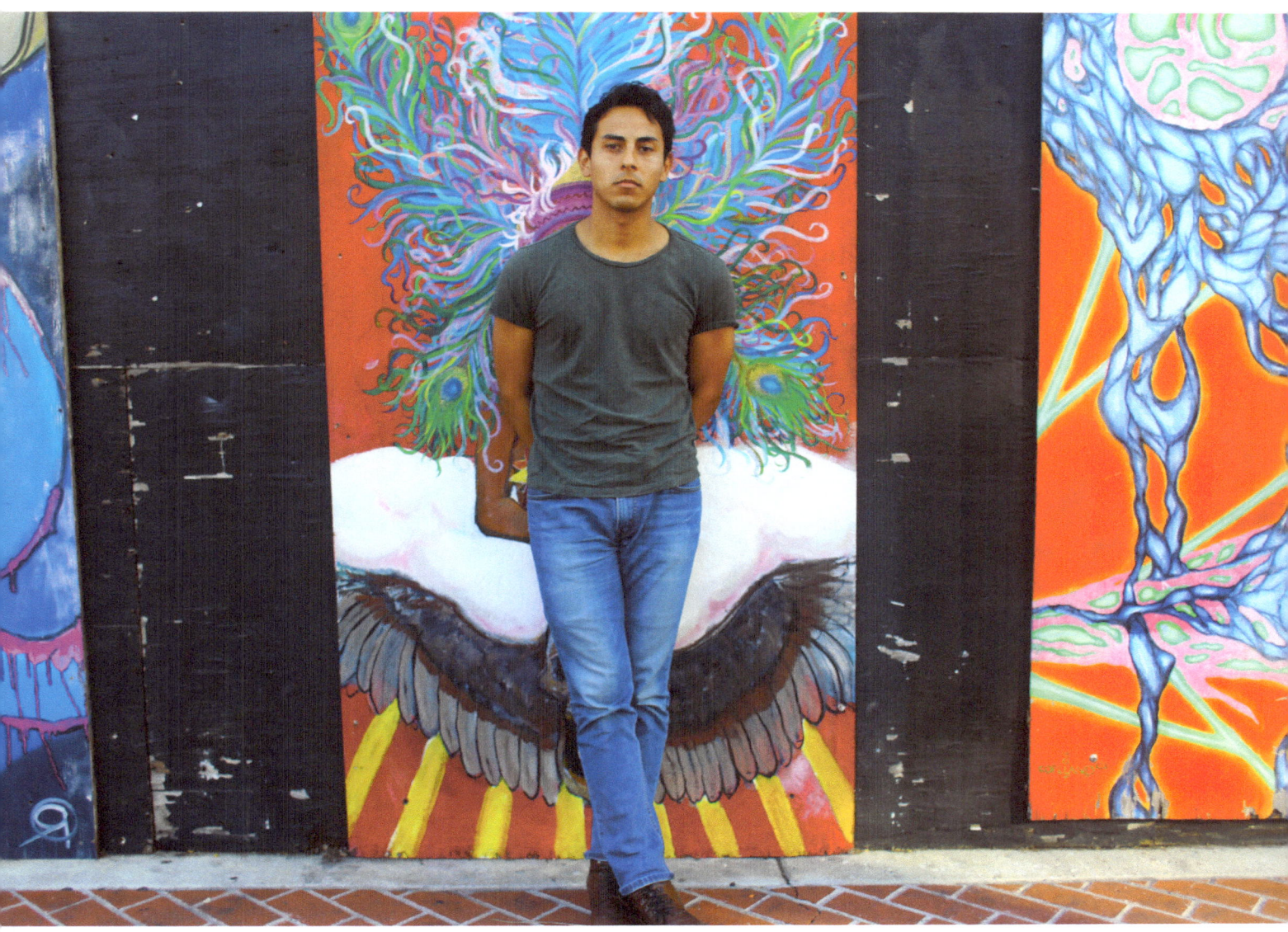

Leo Contreras immigrated from Mexico with his family at the age of three and has
been living in Santa Ana since. He proudly calls himself a "Santanero."

Photo by: Anastasia Waltschew

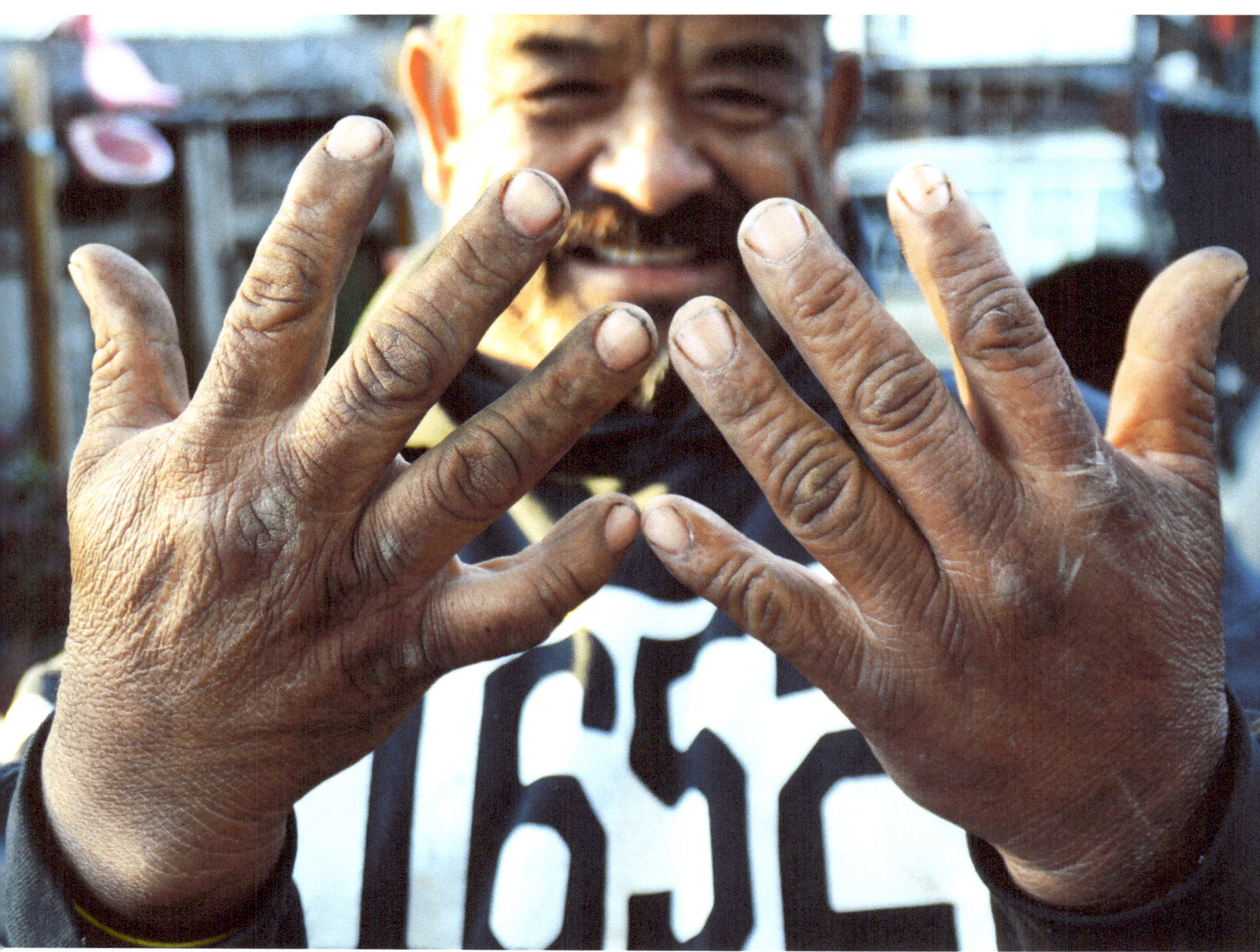

Dario shows his hands, callous from a lifetime of work.

Photo by: David Oh

A closeup of Dario's hands.

Photo by: David Oh

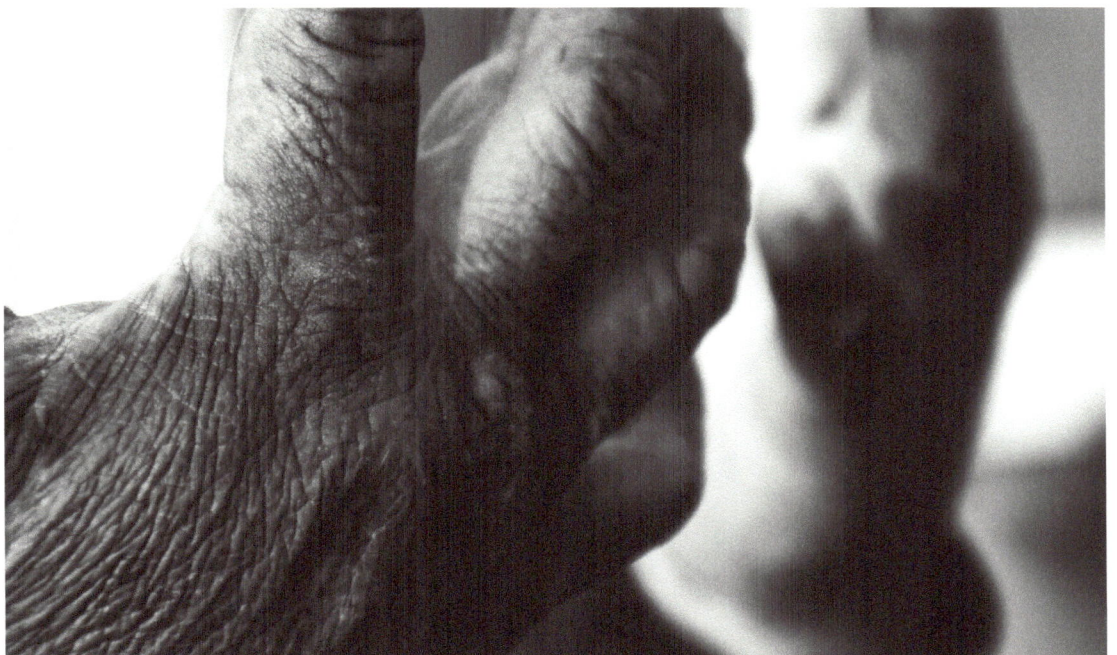

Dario fixes his family's lawn
mower on a cool afternoon.

Photo by: David Oh

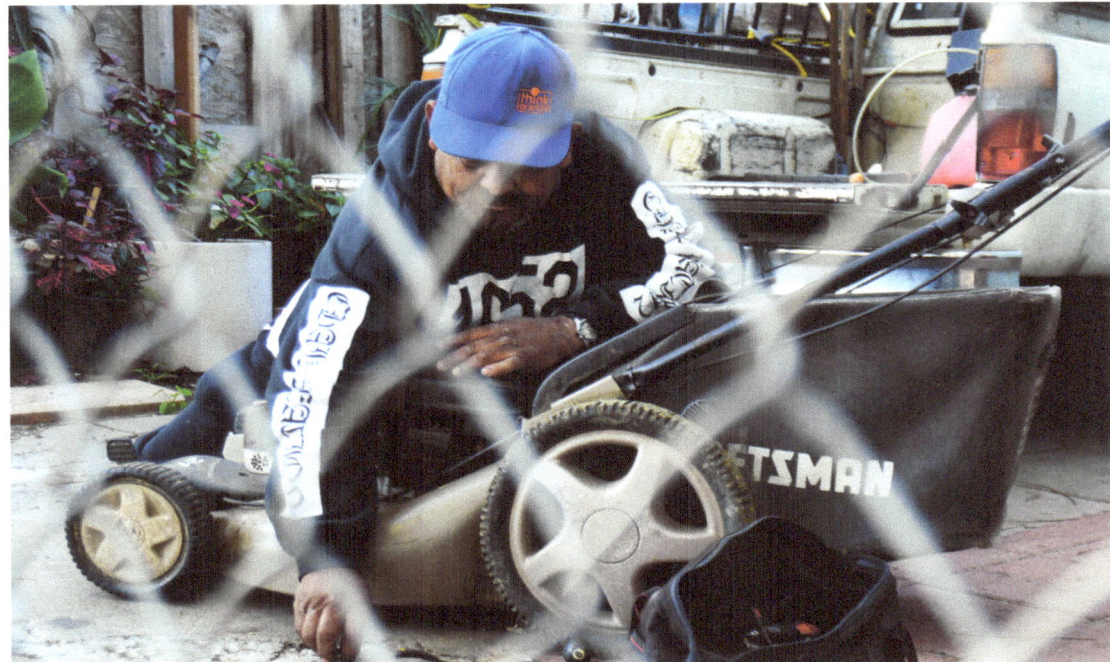

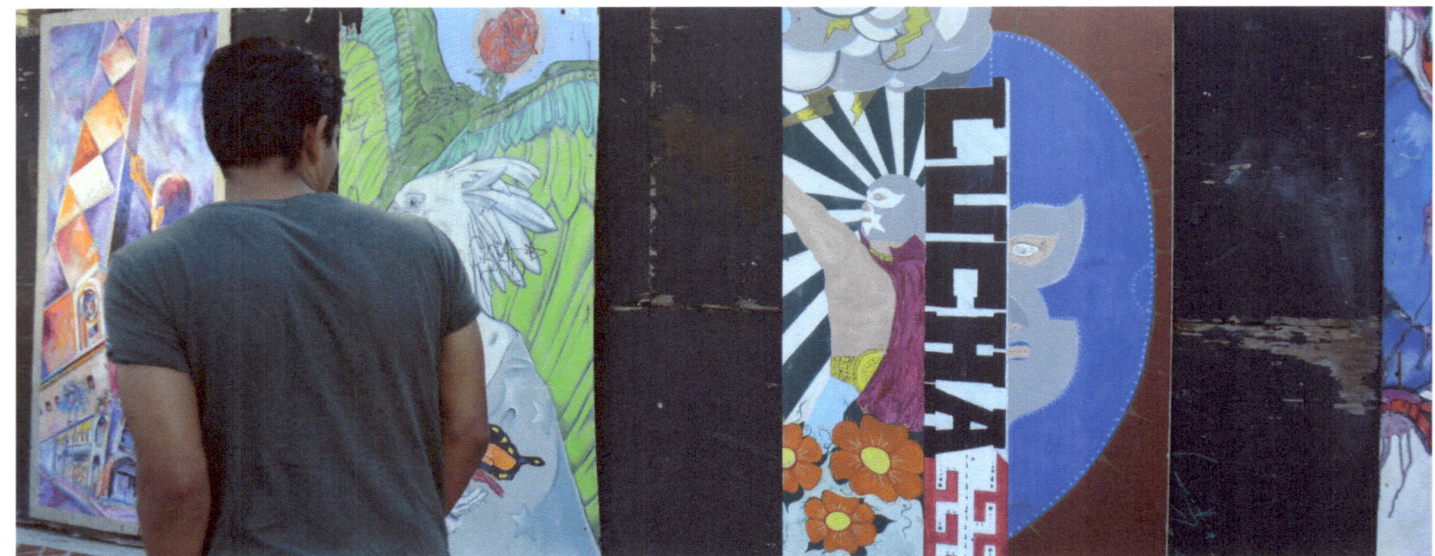

Top: Leo admires the street art in Santa Ana.

Photo by: David Oh

Bottom: Man rests on a busy sidewalk in Downtown Santa Ana.

Photo by: David Oh

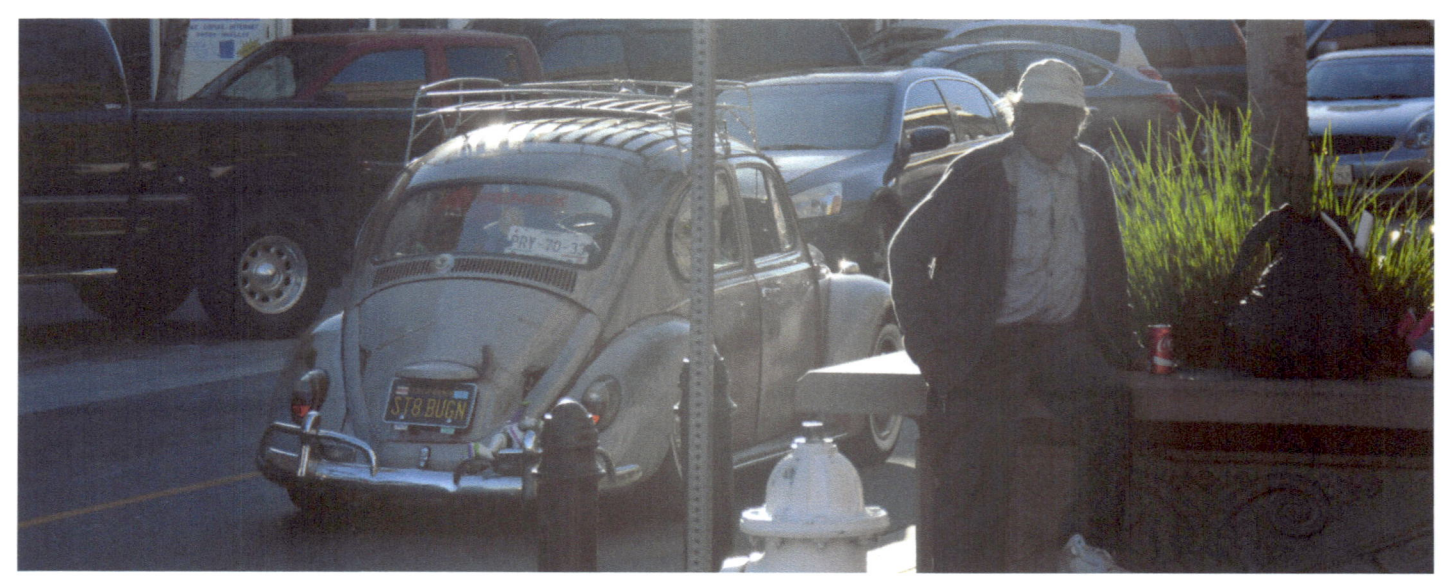

An elderly man rests alongside his dog.

Photo by: David Oh

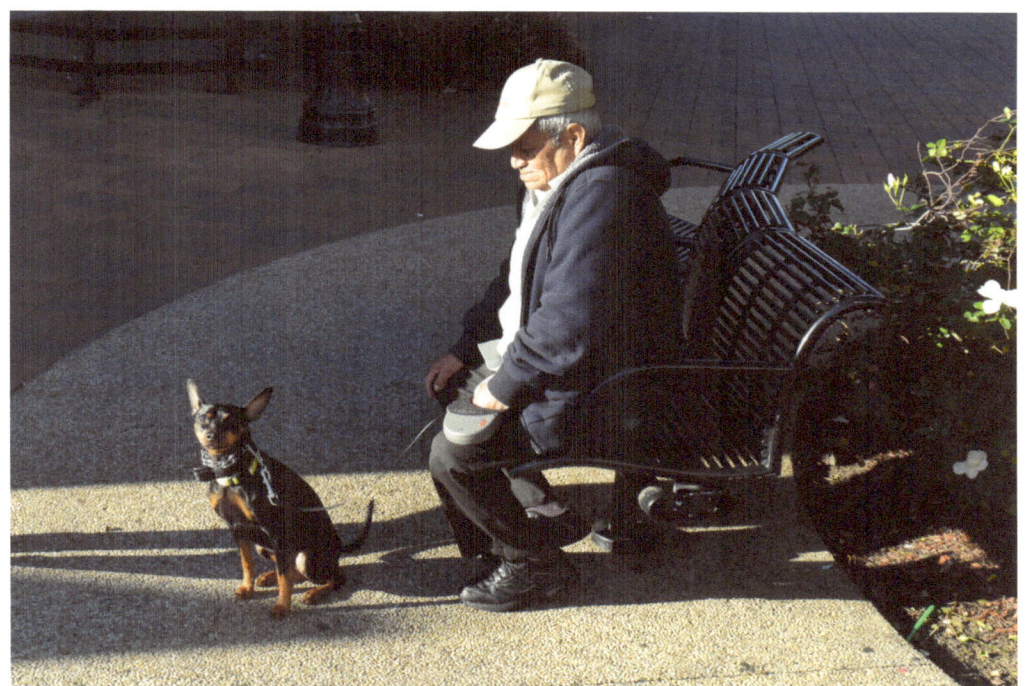

A father and his son waiting for the green light.

Photo by: David Oh

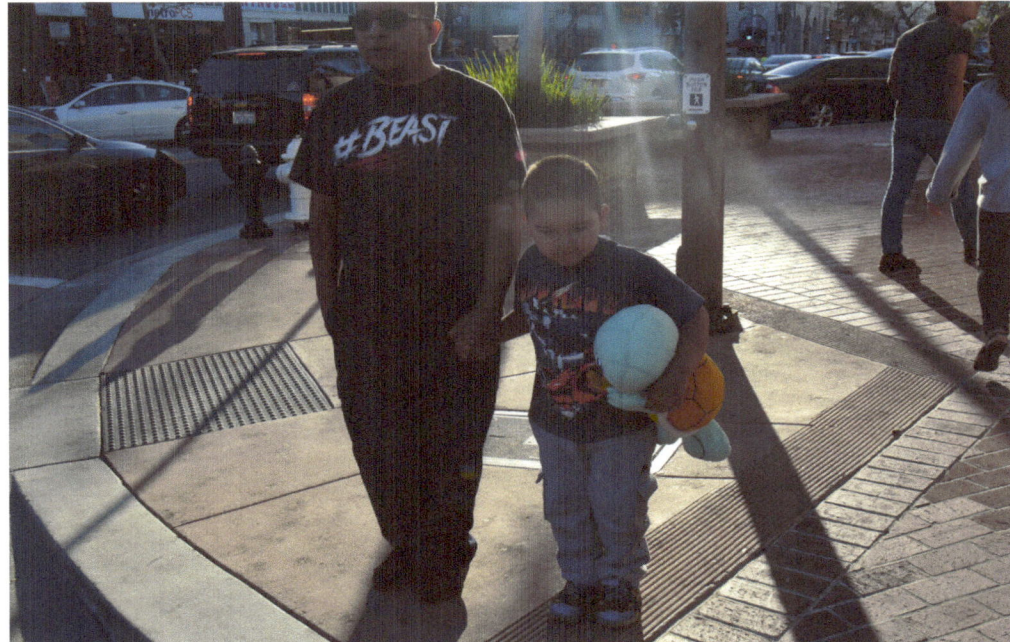

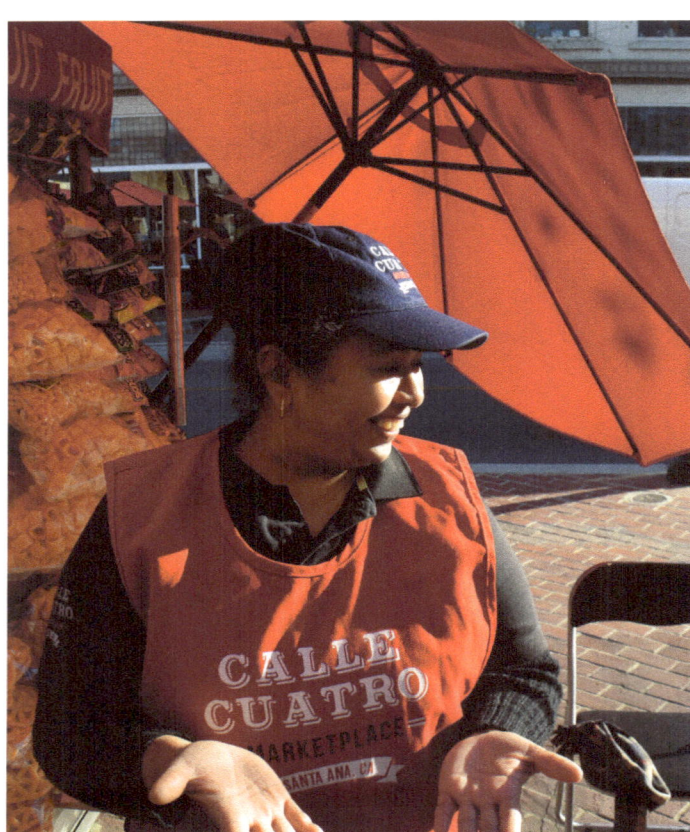

Aurora is caught laughing.

Photo by: David Oh

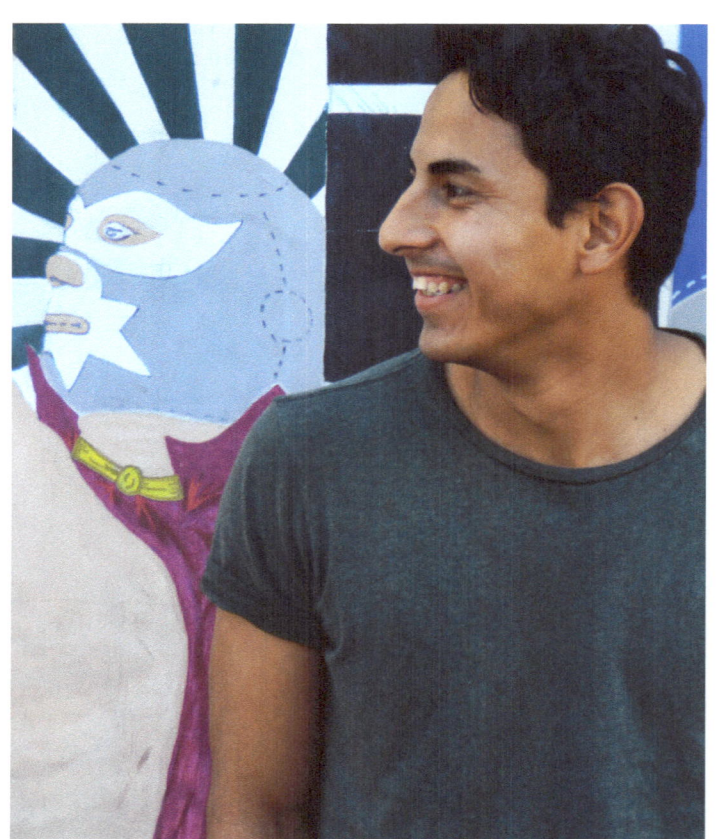

Leo Contreras smiles alongside the painted "luchador".

Photo by: David Oh

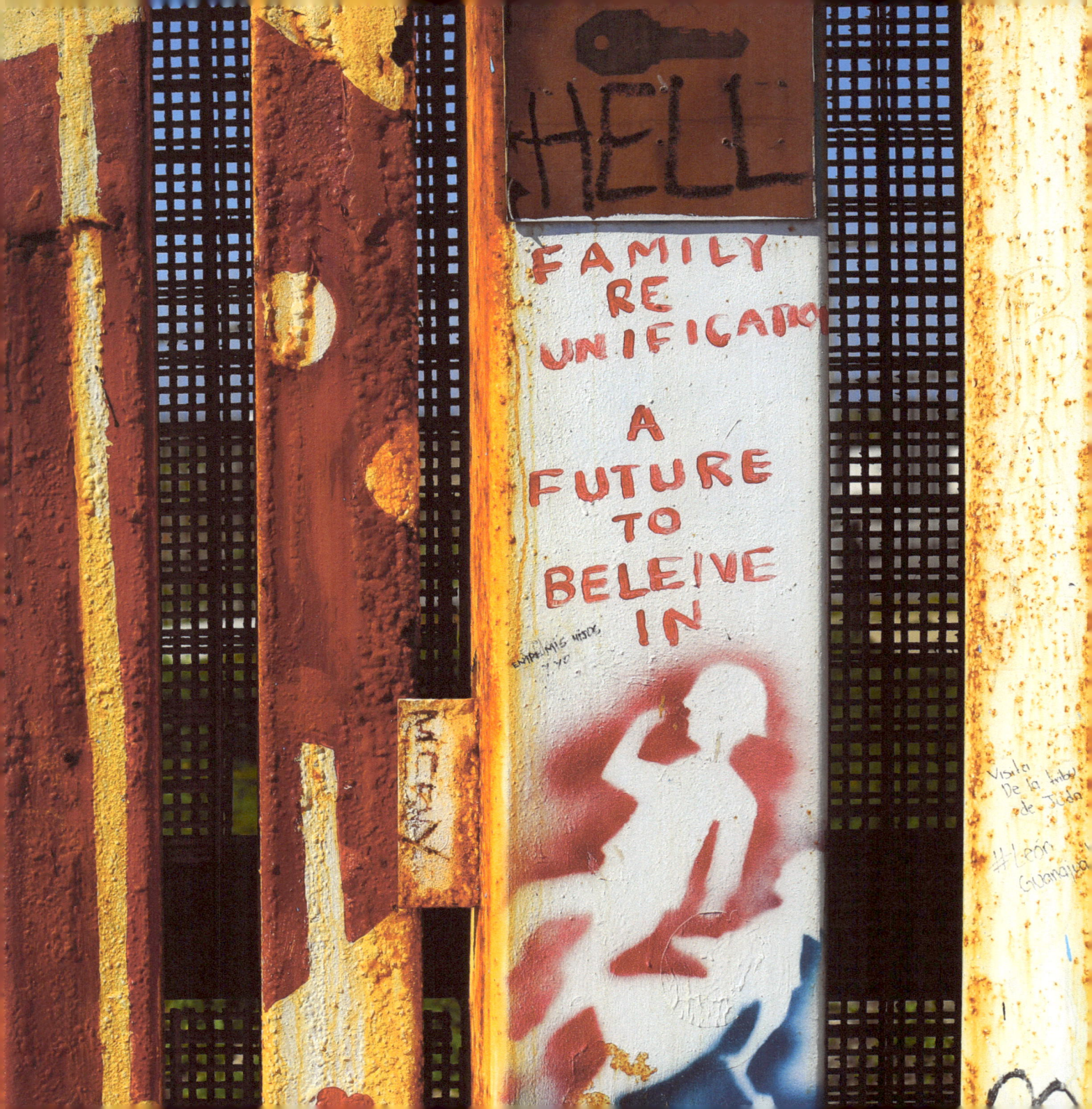

14 Family and Immigration

By Dempsey Floria

Photos by Anastasia Waltschew

" Where thou art, that is home. "

Emily Dickinson

Saul Mendoza is not the same man he was 11 years ago when he was first picked up on the side of the road by a man named Eric Perucca. Perucca recollects the day, "I have never heard God speak so clearly to me in my life than when he said, "pick him up.'" Saul shares that he wouldn't be alive today if not for Eric's decision to obey God. Since that first year, Saul has become a real part of the Perucca family, staying with them for months, even years at a time before returning to his family in Mexico.

Immigration is inseparably tied to family. It is easy to get caught in the global proportions of this issue, but if we lose sight of the individual people who live this story, we lose sight of reality. This chapter will attempt to wrestle with this issue from the perspective of immigrant families and the families they touch, to better understand the complex struggle that is illegal immigration.

When he first came to the United States, Saul was looking for a better life for himself, but after returning to Mexico, marrying and starting his own family, his trips across the border have become all about them. When he is in Mexico, he cannot even make the $100 a week it takes to feed his family of five. It's not just his wife and kids who rely on him. His brother, Lenel, was born with cerebral palsy. Because of the work Saul is able to get in the United States, he can pay for Lenel's care. Saul admits that he didn't always care for his family in this way. In the Perucca family, he was exposed to the kind of day-to-day faith in God that changes the way you live. He experienced God drawing him into his family. "There's a difference in my life after God changed my heart. I felt like I had to provide for them."

It's not just the money that draws Saul to the United States. It's also his 'Gringo family,' the Peruccas. He's torn between his family here and his family there. This is a different kind of family separation than immigrants usually face, but shows how complex this issue really is.

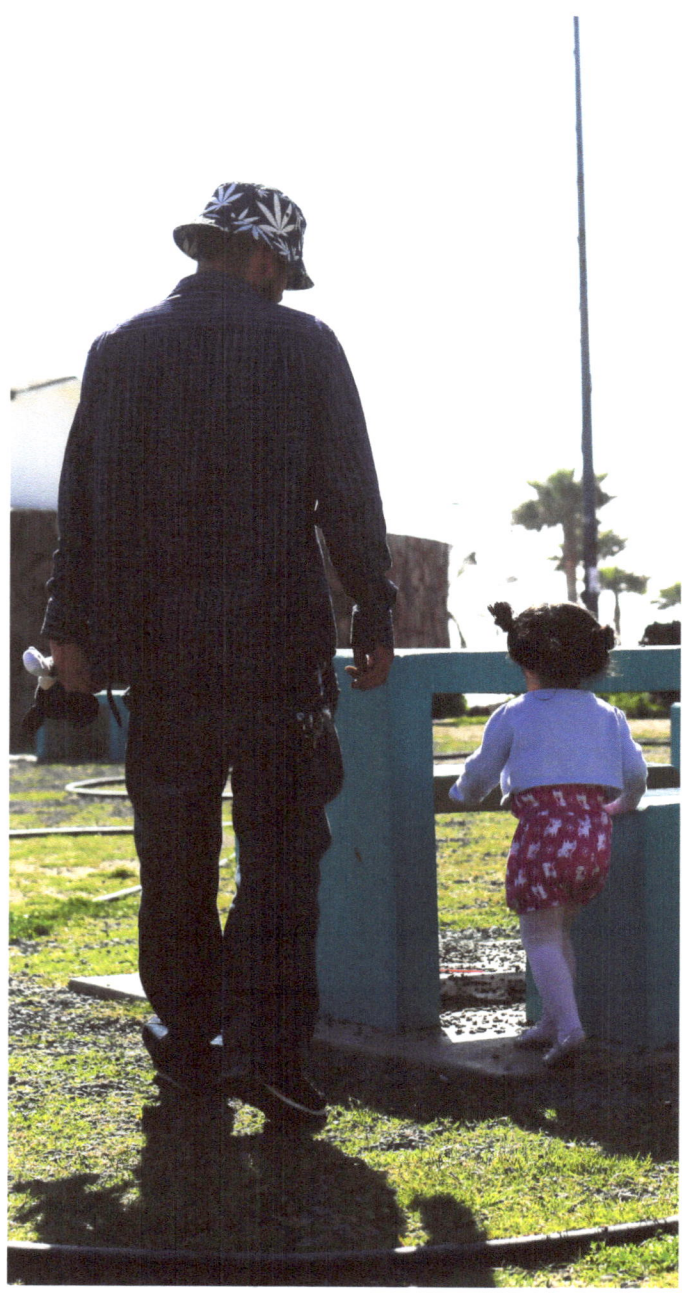

A Father and daughter spend the day among the murals and gardens of Friendship Park in Tijuana.

Eric Perucca says that he and his family have been changed by the experience of welcoming Saul into their home and lives. "It changed me. I used to not like them—illegal aliens. It brought me to a place to realize the majority of them just want to come to work to take care of their families." Perucca chokes up a little when he talks about the times that Saul has left on the dangerous journey back to his family in Mexico. "That's the hardest part. You know, my kids think of him as a brother. He's been here longer than some of them have been alive."

The current immigration system in the United States does not make it easy for families to stay together. It's nearly impossible financially and strategically for a family to stay intact while crossing the border. This may account for the fact that the number of people moving north from Mexico has declined in recent years. However, the number of Mexican-Americans is actually growing. The people who have come are here to stay, and their children are being born as United States citizens. According to a study released by the Pew Research Center in 2016, "The group's population growth has slowed in recent years and is now driven more by births in the U.S. than the arrival of new immigrants, driving down the group's foreign-born share in recent years."

The challenges of getting to the United States by border crossing include the possibility of abduction by drug cartels and death from heat stroke. Many make the dangerous journey because they have no other choice. When they do make it, the challenges are far from over.

Family is a word that American culture is constantly re-defining. With the statistical decline of traditional marriage, the idea of a family unit has become creative and fluid. A study done ten years ago by The National Academy of Sciences talks about this as the "erosion of traditional family patterns," but makes the case that Hispanic populations stand in contrast to this trend. "The Mexican-origin population stands out for its high levels of ethnic endogamy in marriage, cohabitation, and parenthood." This is still the case today, with immigrant communities claiming the highest percentages of intact traditional family units of any demographic group within the United States. Among these, Hispanic-Americans claim the second lowest percentage of divorce. Anna Sutherland, of the Institute for Family Studies, cites these marital statistics to support the claim that, "their relatively high marriage rates have propped up the national marriage rate and mitigated the decline in marriage." Sociologist Zhenchao Qian attributes this both to cultural norms from their home countries and to the fact that in a new country, immigrants need the support of the family unit. They don't have anything to fall back on, other than those who came with them.

Those who are crossing illegally with their families in tow are rolling the dice on deportation and family separation. Children raised in the United States, many whom cannot even remember setting eyes on the land of their birth, live under the threat of being deported to a place that isn't home.

Leo sits down across the table and nervously twirls his keys in his hands. He'd been open about his and his family's undocumented status, even in a time and place that does not feel safe. ICE raids have swept Orange and Los Angeles counties in the wake of the presidential inauguration in early 2017. When asked about the ICE raids, Leo laughs a little. He describes the scene as if it were something out of a movie, with people honking, little kids running through the streets with posters, and women yelling from balconies. "They're like, 'Oh, ICE is up front, so don't go down that street.' It gets pretty crazy." He doesn't have to watch this on the nightly news. He sees it on the street in front of his family home in southern California. He still somehow smiles telling the story. "Once somebody sends out that first text, it goes out to everybody. So, it's really cool in a way." He likens his community to a big family, always watching each other's backs.

Sometimes, outside pressures do bring out the best in a community, but they also bring fear to the surface in ways that can put huge amounts of stress on a family. Leo shares that his Mom has called him almost every day this week to check on him. "My mom freaks out a lot. She's always like, 'Oh, be careful of that street. Don't do this. Don't do that.'"

Leo's father has crossed the border four times. He used to go back and forth from Mexico to the United States regularly, working for months at a time and sending money back to his family. Eventually, it became too difficult to keep up this routine. That was when, at the age of three, along with his mother and younger brother, Leo followed his father to a new country, and began his life as an undocumented immigrant.

With two younger siblings who were born in the United States, the possibility of Leo's family being split up by deportation is very real. But he doesn't let the current panic surrounding the ICE raids change the way he lives. He admits that it does cross his mind regularly, but he chooses not to live in that fear. Leo compares this to living in constant fear of death. If you're always thinking about death, you're not really living. His serenity in the face of this potential chaos comes from his faith in God. "If you know that God's in control, that's it. If it happens, it's not like you caught God by surprise, like, 'shoot God, weren't you watching? They just took my brother.'"

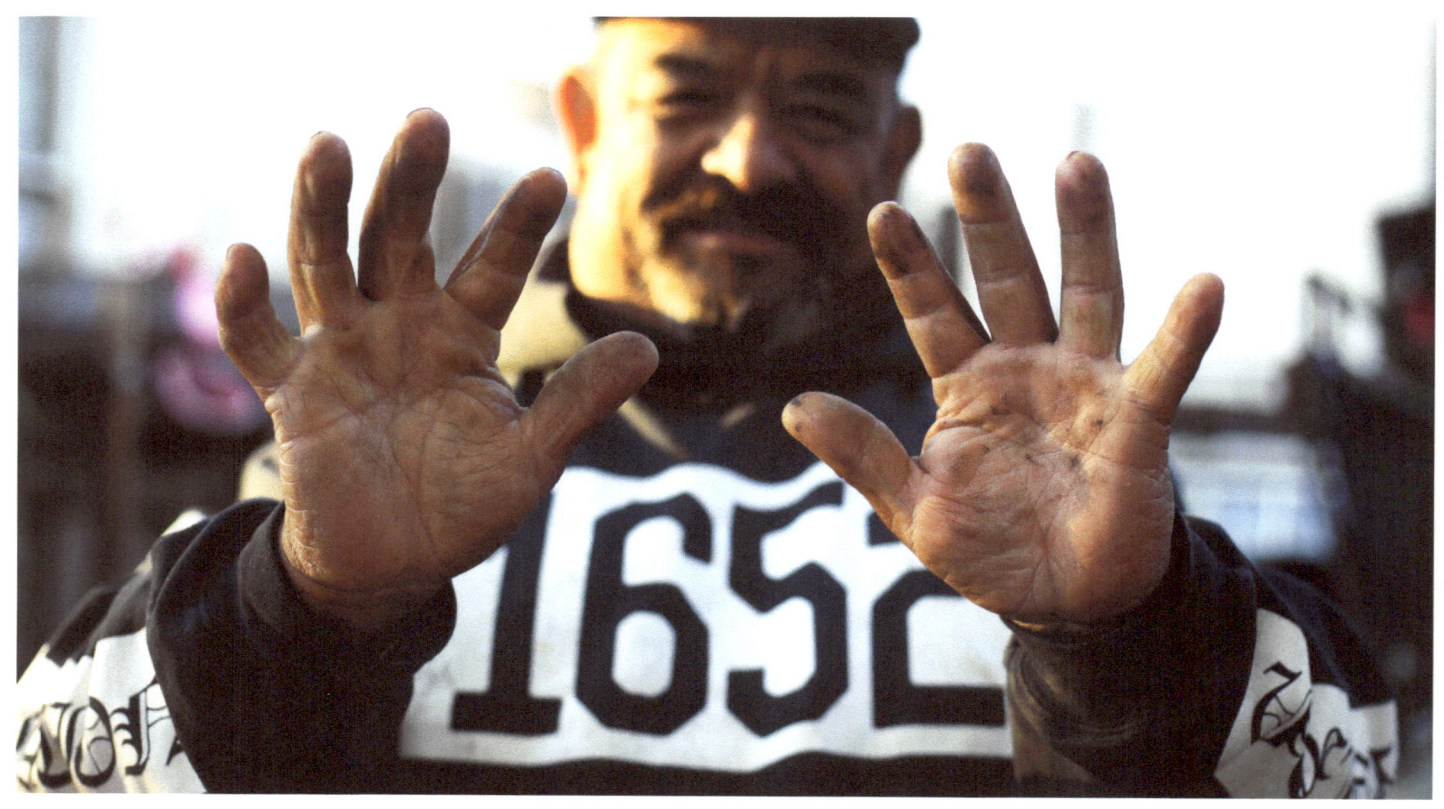

"Sometimes, people look at us as lazy or dirty Mexicans," says Leonardo Contreras. His father's hardworking hands tell a different story.

Leo's situation isn't all that uncommon. According to Craig Penny, a former board member of San Diego based non-profit, Border Angels, there are a huge number of families who live just miles from each other, separated in every practical way by the border. Craig's vivid description of the separation puts this into perspective. "Families who are separated, they go down to Border Field State Park. That's where they can meet and say hi to each other and talk to each other through a fence. You can barely get your pinky through the fence. It's so dense." The fear of family separation by deportation is not ungrounded.

When we see people in the context of their families, it is difficult to assign stereotypes. The general American public wants to assign the label "criminal" to each person who crosses the border without documents, but the reality is much more complicated than that.

Maria Sheahan, a resident of San Diego, California, works with her husband Sean to educate and equip people to better understand this issue and set about building bridges rather than walls. "Everybody wants to fight crime. But in these cases, it seems like everybody is thrown into that category, "Crime." When a person crosses the border without documents, that is a misdemeanor. But we don't call a person that runs a stop sign a criminal. And yet we call a person who crosses the border a criminal. It seems like that word is used for everybody." According to Maria and Sean, there is only a small percentage of people crossing the border to do some other kind of crime. With emotion in his voice, Sean explains the most common reasons people have for crossing the border. "The most profound one is that they would give a better future to their family. They're leaving something very violent or life-threatening."

Leo wants to change the common American public's opinion that all immigrants are criminals. His story sheds light on the lives of the people who are often objectified when the issue of illegal immigration is discussed. "Sometimes people look at us as lazy or dirty Mexicans. I honestly feel like that's the way they look at us sometimes. But I love the Hispanic community so much. My dad is a hard-working man." Leo isn't ashamed of the work his dad does as a landscaper, and even works with him on a regular basis. Most immigrant families function in this way. "I come to this school and then I go with my dad and cut grass. I do that and I feel like such a man! Like, yes, I'm using my hands. I'm getting dirty. I love this! I'm sweating and working to get money for my family. There is no shame in that."

Perhaps the view of the Hispanic immigrant community held by many Americans is based on the kinds of jobs they do. Leo challenges this view by asking whether dignity is found in legal status and type of employment or in the character of the people themselves. "There are people out there who are working hard for their families every day. They work to give their kids a better future. Some people don't see that, they just see that 'she's a maid,' or 'he cuts grass.'"

Leo wishes people would look deeper. "I find so much beauty in the work that people do. They might be the dirtiest

Friendship Park in San Diego and Tijuana acts as a meeting place for family members separated by the Mexican-American border. The wire mesh is so fine, however, that loved ones are restrained to only the touching of fingertips through the divide.

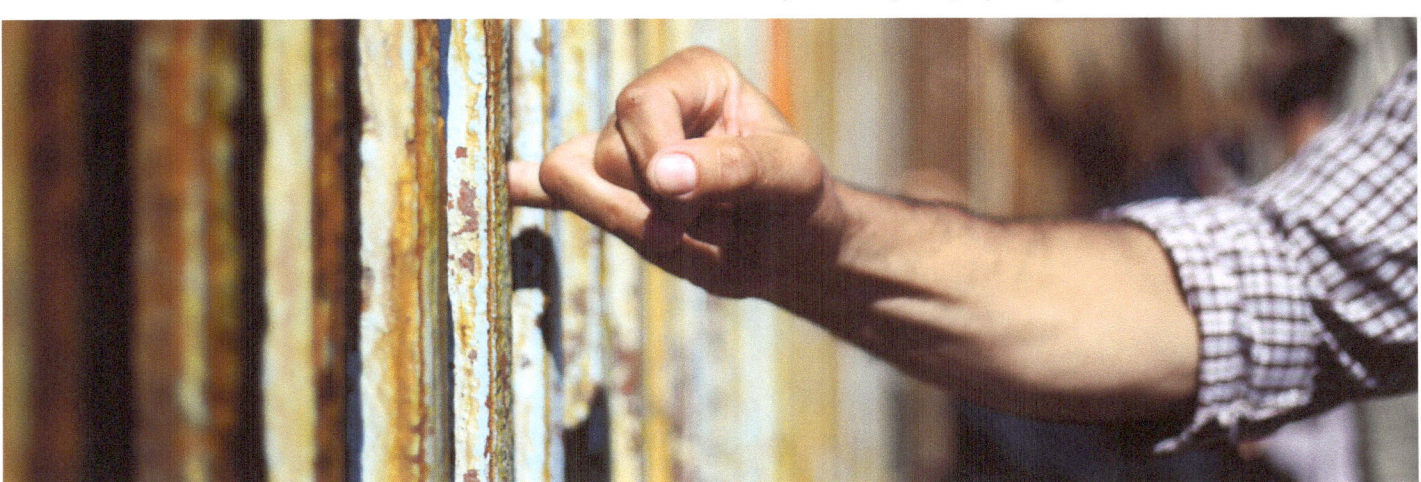

jobs ever, but I find so much beauty in that. I wish they could see that side of the Hispanic community—the hard-working, humble people." He is an example of the profound impact of being part of a tight knit, immigrant family.

His parents' choice to enter this country has given Leo the opportunity to create a future for himself, but far from selfishly taking advantage of this country's resources for his own gain, his goal is to give back to those who have given the most. "I love my parents for what they do," he says, "and I would do anything to give them a better future."

Leo and his father outside their home in Southern California.

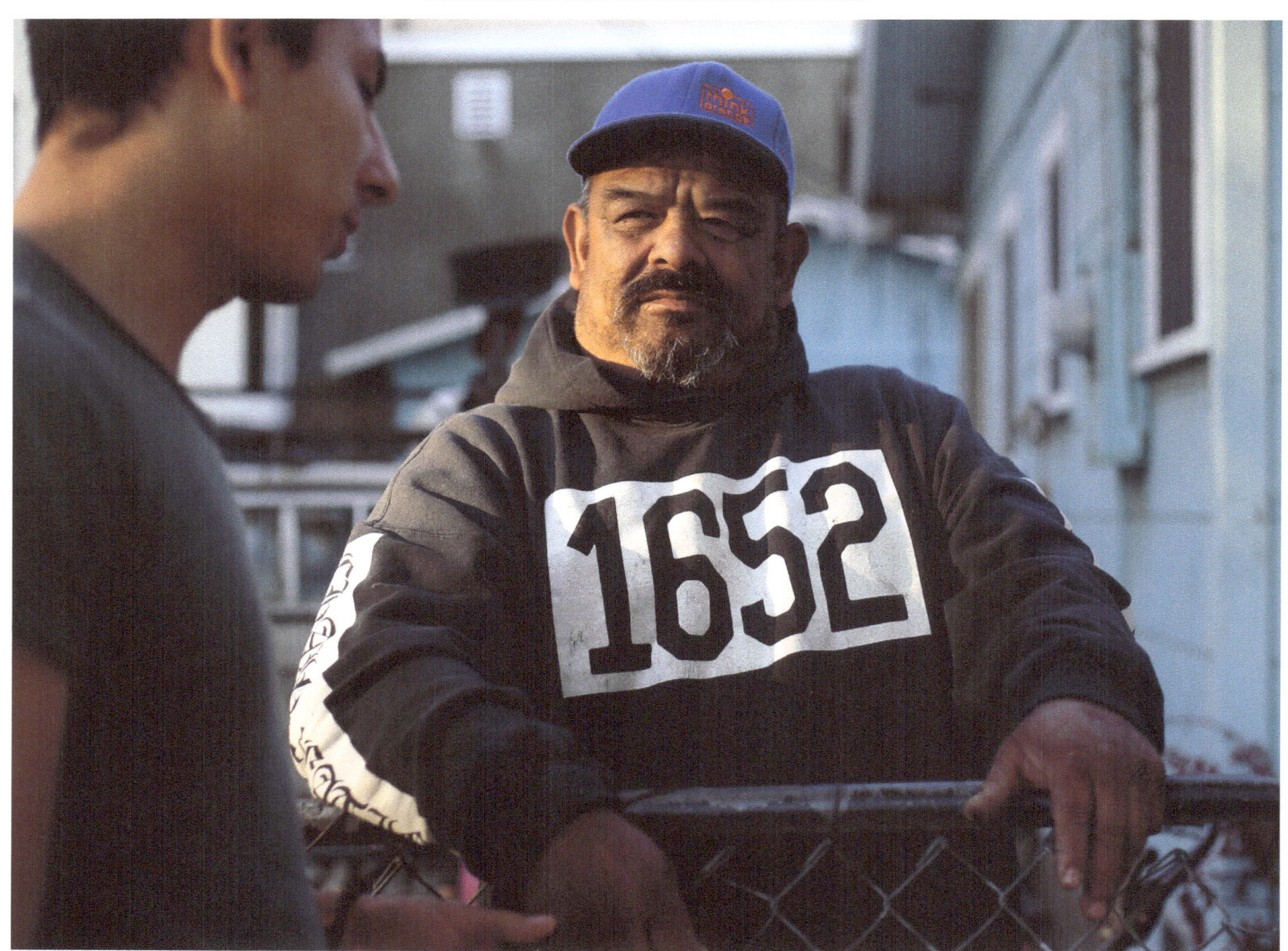

Epilogue

His tired, worn, aged hands extended toward the sky with what little strength he had left. Although his body was giving out on him, his raised hands and words of prayer were an expression of thanksgiving to his creator for a life well-lived. He was slowly breathing his last breaths, yet as he struggled to speak, his words were that of praise, gratitude, and submission to the God that had blessed him with life and family, and who had brought him this far in his journey. After battling a long illness, that evening, at the age of 79, my father breathed his last breath and was gone—peacefully.

Since that night, over the past eight years, I have often reflected on the life my father lived and I have continued to gain insights, lessons, important principles, that inform my own values even today. Generosity, compassion, sacrifice, humility, patience, love, caring, laughter, joy, resilience, servanthood—these are all values I saw modeled by my father, ones that I am continuously trying to learn and apply in my own life.

He was a man with a fifth grade education who began working at the age of twelve. As the oldest of six siblings in his family, it was his duty to enter the workforce to help his own father make ends meet to provide for the family. As a young adult he ended up working in a silver mine. After seeing co-workers around him become ill or lose their lives due to the dangerous work conditions, he knew there was no long-term future for him in this type of work. After much consideration, he decided to take a risk and relocate to a place that he had heard had an abundance of jobs and opportunity; in fact, it was often termed the "Land of Opportunity." My dad made the decision to leave his family in a small town in Mexico and venture north to the United States. He arrived and quickly landed a job working in a Downtown Los Angeles restaurant. There was only one 'small' detail that would make his stay in his new home a challenging one. He was an undocumented resident of the United States—an 'illegal alien' as some would call him.

The issue of immigration is one that has risen and fallen in controversy in this country for many decades. Over the past year, particularly as a result of the 2016 presidential election, the topic of immigration has moved to the forefront of political discussions and has become an extremely polarizing topic. For some it might be just that, a political discussion. Yet for others, those not in this country legally, the topic of immigration and the possibility of deportation is a personal, heart-wrenching matter where the future of life itself lies on the balance.

Thanks to the efforts and sacrifice of my parents, I was privileged, by no choice of my own, to be born in this country and be a U.S. citizenship from birth. But the issue of immigration has been a real part of my life from day one. The son of Mexican immigrant parents, I was born and raised in East Los Angeles, a predominantly Mexican immigrant town.

It was not until I went to college, the first in my family to do so, that I experienced the harsh reality of being a minority. I went from being a part of the majority ethnic group in East Los Angeles, an experience that I took for granted, to suddenly being a member of a clearly very small ethnic minority group. My first semester in college happened to be the fall of 1994. On the California ballot that November was an anti-immigrant piece of legislation, proposition 187. I remember visiting an online chat room at my new college where a student posed the hypothetical question, "what do you think will happen if proposition 187 passes?" I read one of the responses: "if proposition 187 passes, all Mexicans will riot, because they have nothing better to do anyway." I was crushed. Here I was, the first in my family to be attending the university, something that was a source of pride for all of us. And this is the way my family and I were perceived, as potential violent rioters who have nothing better to do

After attending the university for a couple of years, I decided it was time to give back. I participated in an internship program with a ministry called KidWorks that took me to spend the summer to live in an underserved neighborhood of a nearby city I had never been to: Santa Ana. This is a city where nearly 80% of its residents are Latino and about 50% of its population has been born in another country. It is a city of immigrants. I worked with youth there during the summer of 1996. The youth and their families received me with open arms. They were hospitable, warm, generous, welcoming. I soon realized I had found a new home in Santa Ana.

Over the past 20 years I have continued to be a part of KidWorks, a non-profit ministry that goes into some of the most challenging neighborhoods in town impacted by substandard housing conditions, gangs, drugs, and poverty. We work with community youth and families to develop local leaders that become change agents that are positively transforming their neighborhoods. KidWorks provides a pre-school, afterschool tutoring, leadership development training, and general support and mentoring to youth and their parents, most of them immigrants.

In 2006, after serving in grass roots neighborhood ministry for 10 years I was encouraged to run for Santa Ana's city council—elected public office. I figured that if things were going to change for those neighborhoods experiencing many challenges in town, it would be helpful to have someone in a position of political leadership to help raise awareness and advocate for change. I ran for office and was elected.

For the past 10 years I have had the privilege of serving as a councilman in Santa Ana. I have been able to meet many people and hear the stories of those in our community—people, who like my father, found themselves in dire situations with very few options. Many chose to risk it all, in many cases even their lives, in order to venture up to the United States to find work and simply survive. These are some of the same people that have contributed much to the fabric of our city and broader community. Some of these individuals happen to be undocumented immigrants; many of them are youth who were brought to this country by no fault of their own. So they are caught in limbo between two worlds.

My whole life I have been faced with the impacts of immigration. Whether it be growing up as a child of immigrant parents, living in a predominantly immigrant community, facing the culture shock of attending a university as a minority student, serving as a community leader in a predominantly immigrant city, or serving in a non-profit that serves immigrant families.

There is a saying:

"Privilege is when you think something is not a problem because it's not a problem to you personally."

Everything changes when things become personal. It is easy to draw conclusions and critique issues of immigration and undocumented immigrants from a safe distance. This book helps take the issue of immigration from a matter that is distant and abstract to something that is more personalized. You learned about individuals, their stories, saw images of real people, you caught a glimpse of the turmoil some people are living. You learned about our broken immigration system. You were able to catch a glimpse into the lives of the millions that risked everything to enter into this country without 'permission', all to work hard and earn an honest living. You were able to see their story of survival. You learned about the gardeners, factory workers, hospitality and restaurant workers, farm workers, housekeepers and child care providers that work long hours at low wages to allow for the rest of us to perhaps live a bit more comfortably.

In our American culture, we tend to prioritize our individual life experience and personal comfort over that of the collective community. In all honestly, it is not easy to live counter culturally. For many, the Bible is a road map to life, one of its foundational lessons is to 'love your neighbor as yourself'. In essence, don't be self-absorbed and focused on yourself. Look outward and care for the life experience of those around you. Compassion is defined as a 'concern for the sufferings or misfortunes of others'. For our society to thrive we need to be people of compassion.

By the example he set in his life, my father was a teacher of compassion. An undocumented immigrant when he first arrived to this country, by the time he passed away he was proud of having become a naturalized U.S. citizen. On his last day on earth, although his health was deteriorating and his body was experiencing physical turmoil, my father raised his hands in surrender and trust in God in whom he found all hope, peace and refuge his whole life. Today there are many in this country that are in a place of turmoil and uncertainty due to their immigration status. They similarly call out to God seeking help. The beautiful thing about God is that he uses people to be the compassionate expression of Himself here on earth. For those that feel vulnerable, uncertain and without a voice, will you choose to stand in the gap, step into the discomfort to be that expression hope, peace, and refuge?

David Benavides

DAVID BENAVIDES, a 1999 graduate of Biola University, is executive director of KidWorks in Santa Ana. He serves Ward 4 as a city council member for the city of Santa Ana, the second largest city in Orange County, California. He oversees a KidWorks staff of 36 operating in Santa Ana and investing in some 800 parents and children. He is a frequent spokesperson for community issues in Santa Ana in news media serving Southern California.

Afterword

My most vivid memory of 2016 was sitting in a circle with my students in a public library in Mecca, Calif. It was two days after the presidential election and we were holding space for a healing circle.

There, in our small group, my students and I talked about the future. Our community, the Eastern Coachella Valley (ECV), is a largely immigrant, farmworker community located about two hours east of Los Angeles and about two hours north of the Mexican border.

Post-election, our community was covered by a cloud of uncertainty, frustration and fear.

Even now, months into 2017, I cannot say for certain what the future will look like for my community or for immigrant communities across the nation.

Politics and policy change.

What I do know with all certainty is that my community is strong and resilient.

I see this strength and resilience in the mother who waits three hours to catch a bus to the grocery store, in the father who wakes up hours before sunrise to work in the 'campos' (fields) and in the elder who organizes her neighbors for better living conditions.

Like the purplish gray mountains that surrounds them, these people are strong and unshakable. Like the rich, lush crops that grow in the middle of our dry and arid desert, these people endure.

Life in our immigrant community, like many immigrant communities, is centered around stories and storytelling. As the program manager and editor of a youth media training program, I have the honor of working with fifteen Latino youth reporters in the Eastern Coachella Valley who are leading the charge to reclaim their community's narrative and who are working for a better future for all.

Far too often, the stories told about immigrant communities do not come from the communities themselves. Traditional media tends to depict Mexican immigrants as field workers, bent over and picking crops in a large green field.

It is important to note that Mexican and indigenous immigrants do put food on the tables of millions of Americans and do contribute to a multimillion dollar agricultural industry. And while working in the fields is dignified work, it is not the only story of our community.

Our youth reporters, and young people like them, are influencing the future now by telling the stories of their immigrant community. These young people take on the responsibility of telling the stories of their families, neighbors and friends because they know that if they do not tell their own stories, someone else will speak for them.

I was thrilled when Dr. Longinow and his class came out to the ECV to visit our youth reporters and other young organizers in the area because this is what journalists should be doing to accurately report on immigrant communities.

Building relationships in communities that are not your own can be difficult work but it is so necessary. Journalists need to know that the real experts are the community members themselves. These people know their community best and they know what they need to thrive.

Despite the uncertain future, we live in an exciting time when immigrants across the state and nation are stepping into their power and reclaiming their narratives. And I believe it is work like this book project that will help to further amplify the voices of our long-silenced communities.

Amber Amaya

AMBER AMAYA, a 2014 graduate of Biola University with a degree in Journalism & Integrated Media, is the program manager and editor for Coachella Unincorporated, a youth media training program located in the Eastern Coachella Valley (ECV). Coachella Uninc. is a project of New America Media, the largest coalition of ethnic media organizations in the nation, and is funded by The California Endowment. Amber trains youth reporters, ages 15-24, in the ECV to report on hyperlocal news from their rural immigrant community. Coachella Uninc. youth reporters share stories from their community online and through print publications. Their work can be viewed at coachellaunincorporated.org.

www.ingramcontent.com/pod-product-compliance
Lightning Source LLC
Chambersburg PA
CBHW060831290526
45792CB00006BB/1881